Circling the Bases

D1605928

Circling
the Bases

*Essays on the
Challenges and Prospects
of the Sports Industry*

Andrew Zimbalist

TEMPLE UNIVERSITY PRESS
Philadelphia

ANDREW ZIMBALIST is Robert A. Woods Professor of Economics at Smith College. He is the author or editor of nineteen previous books, including *The Bottom Line: Observations and Arguments on the Sports Business* (Temple) and *In the Best Interests of Baseball? The Revolutionary Reign of Bud Selig.* He is a member of the Editorial Board of *The Journal of Sports Economics,* and has consulted extensively in the sports industry for players associations, leagues, cities, and owners.

TEMPLE UNIVERSITY PRESS
Philadelphia, Pennsylvania 19122
www.temple.edu/tempress

Library of Congress Cataloging-in-Publication Data

Zimbalist, Andrew S.
  Circling the bases : essays on the challenges and prospects of the sports industry / Andrew Zimbalist.
    p. cm.
  Includes index.
  ISBN 978-1-4399-0282-0 (cloth : alk. paper)
  ISBN 978-1-4399-0283-7 (pbk. : alk. paper)
  ISBN 978-1-4399-0284-4 (e-book)
  1. Professional sports—Economic aspects. 2. Sports—Economic aspects. 3. Sports—Finance. 4. Sports administration. I. Title.

GV716.Z57 2011
338.4'77960973—dc22   2010019346

♾ The paper used in this publication meets the requirements of the American National Standard for Information Sciences—Permanence of Paper for Printed Library Materials, ANSI Z39.48-1992

Printed in the United States of America

2 4 6 8 9 7 5 3 1

I dedicate this book to the memories of baseball player Mike Coolbaugh and Colombian soccer star Andrés Escobar, two sports heroes who exemplified the best of the human spirit and whose lives were tragically shortened by their sport.

Contents

Preface ▪ ix

1 Introduction: Perspectives on the
Sports Industry Toward the Second Decade
of the Twenty-First Century ▪ 1

2 Dollar Dilemmas during the Downturn:
A Financial Crossroads for College Sports ▪ 30

3 The BCS, Antitrust, and Public Policy ▪ 47

4 Gender Equity in Intercollegiate Athletics:
Economic Considerations and Possible Fixes ▪ 75

5 Reflections on Salary Shares and Salary Caps ▪ 86

6 Facility Finance: Measurement, Trends, and Analysis ▪ 100

7 Going for Gold: The Financing and Economic Impact
of the Olympic Games ▪ 117

8 Performance-Enhancing Drugs and Antidoping Policy
in Major League Baseball: Experience, Incentives,
and Challenges ▪ 146

Notes ▪ 171

Index ▪ 215

Preface

L ANCE ARMSTRONG, Tiger Woods, LeBron James, or Roger Clemens—take your pick. Our demigods have let us down, but professional sports continue to flourish, intermittent sputtering notwithstanding. After all, Shakespeare's heroes had tragic flaws and that only heightened our interest. And, besides, as a society we love sports. We love the competition, we love the community sports engender, we love to watch mortals stretch the boundaries of human physical achievement, and we love the distraction. These elements yield the strong, abiding demand to consume sports.

The supply side of sports is equally complex, encompassing salary battles between millionaire players and owners, compromises among feuding owners, intimations of team flight absent public subsidies to assist in the construction of a new stadium or arena, the emergence of team-owned sports channels and league owned video streaming, flexible ticketing strategies, a robust secondary ticket market, and much more.

As the sports industry navigates the changing landscape of supply and demand, along with the opportunities and challenges presented by the ongoing revolution in communications technology, it does so in its own special way. Sports leagues face the unique circumstance that while their teams compete on the field, the leagues must cooperate (and compete) off the field. They cooperate to set the basic elements of competition (rules of the game, length of season, postseason structure, etc.) and also to attempt to maintain a financial and playing balance among dozens of teams from vastly different cities. That is, teams in a sports league must collude among themselves in order to produce a successful product. This simple characteristic yields an economic dynamic very different from what occurs in other industries. Understanding this dynamic is the task of sports economists.

In my view, much of the work of sports economists has suffered from a professional deformation. Its theories have grown separate from the reality they purport to explain. Mathematical models are elaborated, based on simplifying assumptions, to identify tendencies in the industry's functioning. These models can be useful in the right circumstances, but only if they are based on a realistic sense of how the industry operates.

I have consulted in the sports industry (for public bodies, for leagues, for players, for teams) for some twenty years. It is remarkable and sad how little the hard work of sports economists finds its way into the front offices of teams and leagues. The tools and insights of economics are important and potentially can make significant contributions to the efficiency and effectiveness of the sports industry. But economists must be willing to get their hands dirty, and they must concern themselves with communicating not just with each other but also with the industry itself.

I have tried over the years to make my academic work reflect my experience in the sports industry. The essays in this collection are my most recent efforts to understand what the industry's biggest challenges are as it enters the second decade of the twenty-first century and where it is headed. The first chapter serves as an introduction, sketching out the landscape of the industry in 2010, delineating choices it confronts, and projecting some likely turns the industry will take. The following seven chapters are updates and elaborations upon articles I have published in the last few years. They cover a broad terrain, ranging from the financial crisis in college sports and its reform, to antitrust policy, labor relations in professional leagues, the economic impact of the Olympics and other sport mega-events, trends in facility financing, and performance-enhancing drugs.

In researching these subjects, I have benefited enormously from superlative research assistance by Leigha Miyata and Jim Logue, as well as from ongoing dialogue with academic colleagues and individuals in the sports industry too numerous to mention. Thanks also go to Brad Humphreys and Judith Grant Long, each of whom co-authored with me an original piece upon which two of the chapters in this book are based. I am grateful to my editor at Temple University Press, Micah Kleit, for his experienced and confident guidance. My thanks also to Lynne Frost, who shepherded my book through the production process. As always, none of my efforts would be possible without the loving support from my family—Shelley, Jeff, Mike, Alex, and Ella—and to them go my eternal love and gratitude.

1 Introduction

Perspectives on the Sports Industry
Toward the Second Decade of
the Twenty-First Century

A S THE SECOND DECADE of the twenty-first century begins, the sports industry finds itself facing a shifting landscape. The world economy is attempting to emerge from its deepest downturn in eighty years. The technology and structure of the broadcasting industry is being transformed. The prospect of work stoppages, regarded by many as an immaturity that sports leagues had outgrown, is again rearing its ugly head. Legal cases seek to redefine what a sports league can and cannot do. Men's and women's soccer leagues are asserting themselves, seeking more dominant roles in the sporting universe, perhaps supplanting the National Hockey League (NHL) as the fourth major U.S. league. Intercollegiate athletics is confronting a series of financial and legal challenges that demand serious reform. All this is happening and more, yet the popularity of spectator sports has never been greater and shows no signs of abating.

Weathering the Economic Downturn

As the country became increasingly aware of the impending 2007–2009 financial crisis, many sports finance pundits declared that the industry had nothing to worry about. The common refrain is captured well in an earlier report by Moag & Company, which proclaims that Americans need their sports for distraction during recessions, and sports spending is typically the last area to be cut.[1] Such sanguine salves overlooked two salient factors. First, the sports industry had changed structurally in significant ways that would make it more vulnerable to the business cycle. Second, the 2007–2009 recession was far from typical.

The new wave of stadium construction that was heralded by the construction of Baltimore's Camden Yards in 1992 linked the fate of the sports industry more intimately to the health of the corporate sector. The Camden Yards model was to bring stadiums back downtown to take advantage of the growing corporate dollar via luxury suites, club seating, catering, and sponsorships. As higher-income clientele began to frequent the ballparks and arenas in increasing numbers, the value of signage rose, too. A sinking economy now led directly to sinking facility revenues.

We now know that the 2007–2009 recession was the most severe since the 1930s. Compared to the average of all previous recessions since 1950, GDP dropped over 3 percent versus 1.7 percent, nonfarm employment dipped more than 5 percent versus 2.1 percent, and the unemployment rate jumped 5.1 percentage points versus 2.5 points. The decrease in exports and investment was more than double the average of previous recessions. The major stock market indices all plummeted by over 50 percent. All this translated into (1) vastly reduced sponsorship revenue for the sports industry; (2) corporations not renewing premium seating contracts or removing their names from suite entrances to avoid the appearance of conspicuous consumption; (3) attendance drops of 1 to 7 percent, despite substantial discounting of ticket prices; and (4) disappearing naming-rights deals, inter alia.

Some sports, of course, were hit harder than others. NASCAR, which is more dependent on sponsorship revenue than other sports, took a body blow. Similarly, golf and tennis lost corporate sponsors and had to scramble to maintain the same level of tournaments; the women's golf tour lost several tournaments. Women's Professional Soccer (WPS), the new women's soccer league, struggled mightily, as did the new United Football League and many of the franchises in the NHL.

Still, many executives expected the recession to take a still larger toll on the sports industry. The largest attendance drop among the major sports leagues occurred in Major League Baseball (MLB). Although MLB's overall drop was 6.8 percent in 2009, baseball's revenue remained flat, thanks to the ongoing growth of Major League Baseball Advanced Media (MLBAM; MLB's Internet company, started in 2001) and the introduction of the new baseball television network. Attendance drops in the National Football League (NFL), National Basketball Association (NBA), and NHL were all contained below 2 percent through the 2009–2010 seasons. Thus, the sports industry suffered some significant cuts and bruises, but it appears to have stabilized and to be poised to continue its ascent, albeit more moderately, in the decade ahead.

The Shifting Broadcasting Industry

Broadcasting has been in flux since WWII. Here is no place to review this interesting history, but a few prominent, more recent changes need to be underscored. First, since the 1980s, there has been a steady trend away from over-the-air broadcasts toward cable for local and national telecasting. At the local level, there has been a supplementary trend toward team ownership of regional sports networks (RSNs), which has enabled teams to shift revenue away from the team toward the RSN and to diminish sharing obligations with the players and other teams. The latter tendency has been particularly strong in the larger, more lucrative DMAs (Designated Market Areas, a measure of the number of households in local television markets). To assure distribution to cable households, teams have often partnered with cable companies in launching their RSNs. Among other things, the insertion of teams into RSN ownership has sharpened the already existing revenue inequality across teams within leagues and created more tensions among ownership, complicating the tasks of league governance.

At the national level, despite some questions about the legality of league cartelization of pay television rights, ESPN has grown increasingly dominant, and, as we shall see, in late 2009, the top executives for the broadcast networks began to question the viability of their over-the-air model. The reason is that ESPN benefits from two revenue streams, advertising and subscription, while the broadcast networks benefit only from advertising. Subscription fees for the ESPN channels run in the neighborhood of $5 to $6 per month per household, yielding over $4 billion of revenue annually. The outcome is that ESPN increasingly has the wherewithal and the incentive to outbid the broadcast networks for rights fees to sports league and sporting events.

In 1992, in an effort to protect local broadcasters against the growing power of cable companies, the U.S. Congress passed a bill mandating retransmission consent, inter alia. Local broadcasters can either require the local cable companies to add their stations to the basic packages (must carry), or they can require the cable company to obtain their consent to carry the channels. The network companies (e.g., GE/NBC, Disney/ABC, Viacom/CBS, News Corp./FOX, and AOL/Time Warner/WB) own several of their local affiliate stations, covering between 35 and 45 percent of U.S. households.[2] Since the 1992 retransmission consent law, the rule relaxation allowing cross ownership of broadcast and cable channels, and the elimination of the FCC's Financial-Syndication rules in 1995, the national network companies have bought and created dozens of leading cable channels. Roughly 80 percent of the top-thirty-rated national cable channels are owned by national network companies. Overall, the national network companies control more than fifty cable channels.[3]

Through retransmission consent, the networks have derived significant economic power. It is common for the networks to require the cable companies to carry their cable channels at above-market value in exchange for the right to carry their network signals for free. According to James Gleason, chair of the American Cable Association, the network companies include nondisclosure clauses in their retransmission consent contracts, prohibiting the cable companies from revealing either the channels or their prices stipulated in the retransmission agreements. Gleason asks, "Is it really in the public interest for all of my customers to pay for recycled soap operas?"

Thus, despite facing little competitive pressure, independent cable companies are often compelled to include certain channels in their bundles, thereby adding to the costs of providing their packages. In a sense, through retransmission consent, the network companies indirectly are forcing the public to pay for the "free" television they provide. Although independent cable companies experience some unwanted price pressure, the cable industry as a whole continues to thrive from a dearth of competition.

The broadcast networks, however, still face the problem that they are not directly paid subscription fees for their major programming. It seems inevitable that something will have to give in the current model that will allow the networks to continue to be viable bidders for sports rights. FOX's late-2009 showdown with Time Warner promises to wedge open the door for the networks to receive subscription fees. FOX had been seeking a fee of $1 per subscriber per month. On January 1, 2010, FOX and Time Warner announced that they reached a compromise but refused to make public the agreed-upon fee. It is likely that the other networks will follow suit.[4] Whether the fee is $1 or something less, consumers will find themselves once again paying higher cable bills.

The formerly over-the-air networks will be financially fortified to compete with ESPN and Versus over the television rights to sports. As increasingly strong bidders enter the competition for sports-rights fees, much as occurred when the FOX network entered the fray in the 1990s, contracts for leagues and events are likely to resume their upward ascent. This tendency will be reinforced by another: The widespread use of TiVo or DVR devices for taping shows puts a greater premium on sports telecasting. Unlike evening serials and other television programming, sports fans have an intense preference to watch their games or events live. This preference makes advertising for sports events relatively more attractive compared to other forms of programming and will help sustain or augment spot prices going forward.

A final trend is the growing convergence in the quality of television and computer streaming of sporting events. Leagues have generally taken control over Internet streaming rights, and, in some cases, these rights appear to be encroaching on teams' local television markets. Large-city teams are the most threatened by this development, especially because league governance rules generally permit policies to be set by a supermajority vote of teams, and most teams would benefit from the centralization of the local revenue streams. Large-city teams may feel that their only defense is through the courts, setting the stage for possible new legal tussles. In the meantime, the leagues have discovered a new revenue source that they are beginning to aggressively exploit.

A larger technological development may challenge the basic team/ RSN model. The full convergence of television and computer streaming is being thwarted by the inadequate investment in the broadband backbone in the United States. In Japan, the average download speed on the Internet is over ninety megabytes per second; in the United States, it is below ten megabytes per second. The slower speed results from inadequate broadband space and leads to the frustrating viewer experience of intermittent frozen screens during streamed games. Cable distribution companies, such as Comcast, Time Warner, and Cablevision, have not invested in expanding their fiber-optic networks as rapidly as cable companies and governments have in many other countries. The U.S. cable companies fear the loss of control over the distribution/sale of programming once the Internet replaces the television as the principal source of accessing video content. President Barack Obama and FCC Chairman Julius Genachowski, however, have committed to aggressively developing the broadband infrastructure, and it seems that, although political delays will continue, this development will move forward during this decade. As it develops, expanded basic and extended digital packages will be replaced by another distribution protocol. The new protocol is unlikely to include the ability of teams and RSNs, via cable distribution packages, to require households within a region to pay a dollar (or two, or three) per month throughout the year to receive their programming; instead, à la carte sales by the team or RSN to households may emerge as the standard marketing model.[5] To the extent that this occurs, both subscription fees and advertising rates are bound to fall. Such an outcome would compress revenue inequality across teams in different sized markets in MLB, the NBA, and the NHL. It may also lead to a stronger tendency toward leaguewide packaging of such rights, similarly promoting a more equal revenue distribution.

Labor Relations

As I write in mid-2010, the U.S. sports industry has not experienced a work stoppage since 2004–2005, when the NHL lost an entire season. Prior to that, the previous work stoppage was in the NBA in 1998. Many had come to believe that league prosperity was too great and salaries too high for either side to risk the damage of another strike or lockout. Indeed, between 1996 and 2008, average franchise values increased at an annual rate of roughly 9.5 percent in the NHL, 9.6 percent in the NBA, 12.7 percent in MLB, and 16.1 percent in the NFL.[6] Meanwhile, average wages grew annually at roughly 6.5 percent in the NHL (to $1.9 million in 2008), 9.7 percent in the NBA (to $5.0 million), 8.5 percent in MLB (to $3.0 million), and 8.1 percent in the NFL (to $2.0 million).

To be sure, the 2004–2005 stoppage in the NHL and that of 1998–1999 in the NBA were brought about by owner lockouts. The last player strike was during 1994–1995 in MLB. Although player salaries are high and move upward in a ratchet pattern, owner returns are certainly not guaranteed to move upward, nor are they guaranteed to be positive. Further, as franchise values rise, new ownership must shell out more and more capital to buy teams. Other things equal, this situation will produce lower rates of return. On reflection, then, it is perhaps not surprising that ownership still seems willing to employ the lockout weapon. Indeed, many anticipate that the NFL owners have a strategy in place to lockout the players for the 2011 playing season if a new collective bargaining agreement is not reached. The NFL owners appear to be calling for a double-digit reduction in the salary base, and early reports suggest that the NBA owners will be demanding concessions of a similar magnitude and may also be contemplating a lockout for the 2011 season. Meanwhile, a clash between MLB and its Players Association may be on course over a potential slotting system for the amateur draft and possibly over provisions to compel or to incentivize low-revenue teams to spend their transfers on player salaries.

Given that tumultuous labor relations may no longer be a thing of the past, it is prudent to consider what is special about the business of team sports that inspires the owners to seek restraints of trade in the labor market that do not exist in other industries. A long and contentious discussion has developed over the years about why team sports need artificial controls on the players' salaries. Players' associations have argued that the team-sports industry should be able to live with the free, competitive markets that characterize other industries in a capitalist economy. It is commonly asserted that no owner has a gun pointed at his or her head, compelling him or her to offer star players $20 million or more per year. Owners have responded that artificial constraints on salaries (e.g., reserve systems, team and individual salary caps, luxury taxes on high payrolls, revenue sharing among teams, single entity structure, and debt limits) are needed to promote competitive balance across teams operating in vastly different local markets and to ensure financial viability for all teams.

Economists, as students of free markets and how they promote efficiency, have generally sided with the players in this debate. Yet, cogent economic explanations exist for why artificial constraints are needed to help level the playing field among small-city and big-city teams and to moderate out-of-control spending on players. In what follows, I present several explanations of why owners might be expected to pursue bids for players beyond the players' expected marginal revenue products.

First, team-sports markets provide disproportionately large rewards to star players and winners. The outcomes in these markets are often described well by winner-take-all markets. A sense for how winner-take-all markets differ from ordinary markets is afforded by experiments involving a simple auction called the entrapment game or the dollar auction. First described by the economist Martin Shubik, the entrapment game is a non–zero sum sequential game to illustrate a paradox brought about by traditional rational choice theory in which players with perfect information in the game are compelled to make an ultimately irrational decision based completely on a sequence of rational choices made throughout the game.[7]

The game is like a standard auction except for one feature. The auctioneer announces to an assembled group of subjects that he is going to auction off some money—say, a $10 bill—to the highest bidder. Once the bidding opens, each successive bid must exceed the previous one by some specified amount—say, 50 cents. The special feature of the entrapment game is that once the bidding stops, not only must the highest bidder remit the amount of his bid to the auctioneer; so must the second-highest bidder. The highest bidder then gets the $10 bill, and the second-highest bidder gets nothing. For example, if the highest bid were $4, and the second-highest bid were $3.50, the auctioneer would collect a total of $7.50. The highest bidder would get the $10, for a net gain of $6; the second-highest bidder would lose $3.50.

Players in this game face incentives similar to the ones that are confronted by participants in winner-take-all markets or by owners in team-sports markets as they consider whether to undertake expenditures in search of improving team performance. In either case, by investing a little more than one's rivals, one can potentially tip the outcome of a contest decisively in one's favor.

The pattern of bidding is generally predictable. Following the opening bid, offers proceed quickly to $5—that is, half the amount being auctioned in this example. A hesitation then emerges as the subjects appear to assess the fact that, with the next bid, the two highest bids will sum to more than $10, thus making the auctioneer whole.

At this juncture, the second-highest bidder, whose bid stands at $4.50, invariably offers $5.50, apparently thinking that it would be better to have a shot at winning $4.50 than to take a sure loss of $4.50.

Commonly, all but the top two bidders drop out at this point, and the top two rapidly escalate their bids. As the bids approach $10, there is another pause, this time as the top bidders assess the likelihood that even the top bidder will come out behind. The second bidder, at $9.50, is understandably reluctant to offer $10.50, but consider her alternative. If she drops out, she will lose $9.50 for sure. But if she offers $10.50 and wins, she will lose only 50 cents. So as long as she thinks even a small chance exists that the other bidder will drop out, it makes sense to continue. Once the $10 threshold has been crossed, the pace of the bidding accelerates again, and from then on it is a war of nerves between the two remaining bidders. It is not uncommon for the bidding to reach $30 before one of the bidders finally surrenders.

One might think that any intelligent, well-informed person would know better than to become involved in an auction whose incentives so strongly favor price escalation and loss. But many of the participants in these auction experiments have been highly educated business professionals; many others have had formal training in the theory of games and strategic interaction. For example, psychologist Max Bazerman reports that he earned more than $17,000 by auctioning $20 bills to his MBA students while he was a professor at Northwestern University's Kellogg Graduate School of Management. In the course of almost two hundred of his auctions, the top two bids never totaled less than $39 and in one instance totaled $407.

Shubik's entrapment game doesn't fully capture the complex dynamic of team-sports markets, but it does bear a fundamental resemblance. The second and losing bidder for a star player does not have to pay the player, or anyone else, the amount of the losing offer. Yet the losing team may suffer the experience of losing nonetheless, because the player may go to a competitor—thereby not only increasing the competitor's performance and win percentage but, because the losing team must play against the now-enhanced competitor, also lowering the losing team's performance and win percentage. Thus, this similar dynamic in team-sport labor markets may propel a similar bidding strategy to the entrapment game.

Second, abundant evidence shows that potential participants in a contest are notoriously optimistic in their estimates of how well they are likely to perform relative to others. Studies have found, for example, that most people think they are more intelligent and better drivers than the average person. Workers asked to rate their productivity on a percentile scale relative to their co-workers responded with an average self-assessment of seventy-seven, and more than 90 percent felt they were more productive than the median worker. More than 70 percent of high school seniors reported in a survey that they had above-average leadership ability; only 2 percent saw themselves as below average. When asked about their ability to get along with others, virtually all those same students said they were above average; 60 percent thought they were in the top 10 percent, and 25 percent thought they were in the top 1 percent. Another survey revealed that 94 percent of university professors thought they were better at their jobs than their average colleagues. People also see themselves as more likely than their peers to earn large salaries and less likely to get divorced or to suffer from lung cancer. Another survey found that although only a quarter of the population thought the economy would do better in the coming year, more than half thought they personally would do better.

Some psychologists have termed this widespread tendency toward sanguine self-evaluation the "Lake Wobegon Effect," after Garrison Keillor's mythical Minnesota town "where the women are strong, the men are good-looking, and all the children are above average." This tendency can also be recognized among sports-team owners who invariably believe that they can improve upon the competitive performance of the team under their predecessors.[8] Combine this deception with the strong competitive spirit of most team owners and the intense social pressure on owners to build a successful club, and, absent artificial restraints, it renders consistently exuberant behavior in the players' market.

Third, there is the hypothesis of the winner's curse. Suppose five owners in similar economic circumstances bid against each other for a player. Four of the owners bid $6 million a year for the player, while the fifth owner bids $7 million. Conceptually, each owner will bid up to the player's expected marginal revenue product. None of the owners know what the player's output will be, but each forms an expectation. There is reason to believe that if four of the owners all agree on the player's expected MRP, they are likely to be more accurate than the owner who stands alone in his higher expectation. Under such assumptions, the owner who signs the player has won the bidding contest, but he has the curse of paying the player more than his value. If such a dynamic obtains with regularity, then overpaying players will be generalized, and the financial health of the league would be jeopardized without some artificial restraint on its labor market.

Fourth, team owners in a given league are likely to possess different objective functions. Some may profit maximize, some win maximize, some win maximize subject to a constraint of not losing money on an operating basis, and so on. The potential problem here is that some owners will not treat their teams as profit centers but rather treat them as advertising vehicles for other companies they own or as consumption goods. Such an owner may be willing to more aggressively bid for a player and, in consequence, push up player costs for all owners in the league.[9]

Fifth, some owners may own businesses that are related to the sports team. For instance, the Boston Red Sox own 80 percent of NESN, the RSN that carries the Red Sox games. When the Red Sox or another similarly situated team assesses the value of a player, the team will consider the value that the player can potentially contribute to the team and to the RSN. Team owners, then, who also own related businesses will tend to overvalue the players' contribution on the field and will be in a stronger position in the players' market to attract the better players.

Given that any league will seek competitive and financial balance, these distinct tendencies lead owners to fight for restraints on the labor market for players. Players, naturally, will resist most of these restraints, because they are likely to curb salary growth. Although some of these patterns affect industries other than sports, the need for a degree of competitive balance and the public pressure to win sharpen the tensions engendered by these dynamics in team-sports leagues.

Of course, the typical restraints that are imposed can cause owners to struggle among themselves as much as against the players. Thus, the apparent origin of the current (2010) labor conflict in the NFL is really a problem among the owners. Prior to the 2006 collective bargaining agreement (CBA), the players' share of league revenue, as defined by the salary cap, was set as a proportion of all media and gate revenues plus a growing share of nonticket stadium revenues.[10] The 2006 CBA set the players' share on the basis of all league revenues. Those owners in smaller markets complained that their nonticket stadium revenues (e.g., premium seating, sponsorships, signage, catering) were much smaller than those of the large-city teams. Yet now, small-market owners were required to raise their player payrolls based on the nonticket stadium revenues earned by the large-market teams. The league dealt with this issue, in part, by introducing more revenue sharing. As the new revenue-sharing program grew to an additional $100 million with the potential to reach $200 million by the end of the 2006 CBA, however, the large-market owners began to resist.

In recent years, many writers have pointed to the exceptional political harmony and economic success of the NFL. The league, by any standards, is the most popular and financially successful sports business in the United States. The hallmarks of its success are usually described as financial vitality and superior competitive balance, which results from strong owner unity, extensive revenue sharing, and a salary cap.

The NFL's ability to pursue its "socialist" model results in large measure from the fact that, since its inception in 1920, the league has had gate revenue sharing. When sharing was extended to include national television revenue in 1962, it was done at a time when the television contract was diminutive by today's standards and in a league business culture where the prevailing philosophy was that a rising tide lifts all boats. Thus, the NFL's owners bought their teams with a sharing model already in place. Team values were adjusted to this economic reality. Undoubtedly, this simplified the problem of league governance, but it certainly did not make it go away, as Pete Rozelle's battles with Carroll Rosenbloom and others, the labor wars of the 1980s, and the current feuding within the ownership ranks make clear.

Mike Brown, owner of the Cincinnati Bengals, Ralph Wilson, owner of the Buffalo Bills, and Jim Irsay, owner of the Indianapolis Colts, along with several of their "small-market" colleagues, began to make a stink after the NFL and the NFL Players Association signed their new collective bargaining agreement in 2006. They think the NFL needs more socialism.

The NFL already does far more than any other team sport to level the playing field:

- Each team receives around $125 million yearly from the league's central fund (money from national and international media, licensing, sponsorships, and so forth).
- Teams share local gate and club-seat revenue on a 66/34 basis.
- The NFL has a (long-run) hard salary cap that sets team payrolls at a maximum of 59.5 percent of average team revenues.
- The league employs a reverse-order draft that rewards low-win-percentage teams with earlier draft picks.
- The NFL sets each team's schedule in a way to disadvantage strong teams and to favor weak teams.
- Teams can actually reduce their cash flows by going deep into the play-offs.
- The short playing season of only sixteen games creates greater randomness in divisional outcomes, and the system of one game per play-off round elevates the role of good fortune.
- Since March 2006, the league has had in place a new revenue-sharing program that transfers roughly an additional $100

million a year to the "low-revenue" teams; these amounts are over and above the supplementary revenue-sharing program that was put in place in the late 1990s that transfers approximately $30 million a year from the top to the bottom teams.

Further, most small-market teams already benefit from extensive public subsidization for their facilities. For instance, Mike Brown's Cincinnati Bengals play in a new stadium built with $481 million of public money (in 2006 dollars). Ralph Wilson's Bills play in a stadium that was renovated in 1999 with 100 percent public dollars, and the team receives an annual cash subsidy from the state. Jim Irsay's Colts are in a new home built in 2008, thanks to a public investment of around $535 million.

What, then, are Brown, Wilson, Irsay, and others upset about? It is hard to get a straight answer, but they seem to indicate that their small-city franchises do not have a fair chance of competing on the field.

The evidence is to the contrary. First, most NFL teams maintain payrolls very close to the team cap, regardless of their market size. Second, the consistent evidence over the years in the NFL is that no (statistically significant) relationship exists between team payroll and team performance.

Third, it is simply not true that lower-revenue teams do not perform well. Consider the following:

During 2004–2006

- Only five repeat teams made the play-offs in 2006—one higher-revenue club (Patriots), two mid-revenue clubs (Bears and Giants), and two lower-revenue clubs (Seahawks and Colts).
- Only three teams made the play-offs every year—one higher-revenue club (Patriots) and two lower-revenue clubs (Seahawks and Colts).
- Only four division winners repeated in 2006—one higher-revenue club (Patriots), one mid-revenue club (Bears), and two lower-revenue clubs (Seahawks and Colts).

- Only three teams won their division every year—one higher-revenue club (Patriots) and two lower-revenue clubs (Seahawks and Colts).

During 2006–2008

- Twenty-five of the NFL's thirty-two teams made the play-offs.
- Of the NFL's eight divisions, only four division leaders were repeats—the Patriots (a higher-revenue team) won two division titles; the Steelers (a lower-revenue team) won two; the Colts (a lower-revenue team) won two; and the Chargers (a lower-revenue team) won three.

The 2009–2010 season drives home the point, as two small-market teams—the Indianapolis Colts and the New Orleans Saints—dominated the regular season. Also consider the fact that over the last nine years, a different team has represented the National Football Conference (NFC) in the Super Bowl each year.

Hence, it is understandable that the medium- and large-city owners do not feel the NFL has a competitive balance problem. What the small-market owners are really after is money. They would like to make more profit and to boost their franchise values. But who would not? Is it not enough that all teams in the NFL, even poorly managed ones, have a positive cash flow?

Small-market owners want such teams as the New England Patriots to write them checks. The Krafts bought the Patriots back in 1994 for $158 million and privately funded the $400-million Gillette Stadium. When they bought the team, it had the lowest revenues and worst stadium in the league.

Meanwhile, for reasons of apparent vanity, Wilson has refused to sell naming rights to the Bills' stadium, which continues to be called Ralph Wilson Stadium. He is probably leaving $5 million annually on the table.

Similarly, Mike Brown in Cincinnati insists on the Bengals' stadium being called Paul Brown Stadium.[11] With such companies as Proctor & Gamble, Kroger, and Cintas in town, he is likely leaving even more money on the table.

It is unlikely that a team in the NFL today would sell for under $700 million. Ralph Wilson paid $25,000 for the Bills in 1959. Paul Brown bought the Bengals for $7.5 million in 1966. The Colts were purchased in pieces between 1952 and 1964 for less than $3 million total.

So, the battle lines are drawn. One side wants more socialism. The other wants more capitalism. The NFL owners' conflict simmers not far beneath the surface, despite the league's tremendous success and the fact that the league has had extensive revenue sharing from its inception. When owners exhaust the potential for compromise among themselves, they often turn to the players. This ploy is what the NFL owners have done in their 2009–2010 labor strategy. Rather than sign an extension to the existing agreement, which, by virtue of the owners' opting for an earlier out of the 2006 CBA, expires after the 2010 season, they are playing a game of brinkmanship with the union. Because a new CBA was not reached before March 2010, the 2010 season will be played without a salary cap, and players will have to wait an additional year before gaining unrestricted free agency, among other restrictions.[12] The essay on salary caps and salary shares in this volume shows that the players' salary share can be controlled without a salary cap. Extensive revenue sharing, by diminishing a team's return to performance success, is one way to do that. Indeed, the NFL's cap emerged in part because the union wanted a guaranteed share of team revenues in a league where revenue sharing had gutted the financial incentive to win and, hence, to aggressively bid for players in the free-agent market.

In U.S. leagues that commenced without a philosophy of sharing in place, the struggle to set coordinated league policy has been even more intense than in the NFL. In those leagues, the big-city owners paid considerably more for their franchises than the small-city owners. They view revenue sharing as a form of asset expropriation. So, the merry-go-round among millionaire owners, millionaire players, and millionaire agents continues. Unfortunately, the labor struggles in professional team sports appear to be as eternal as the touchdown.

What Is Going On in Miami?

Just as struggles among owners and between owners and players can produce wacky outcomes in the NFL, so, too, can they in the NBA. Three of the game's top superstars decided they wanted to play together. The players themselves, not the general managers (GMs) and the owners, decided how to allocate player talent. Although it is true that the megatalent company Creative Artists Agency represents LeBron James, Chris Bosh, and Dwayne Wade, the real story about how this happened lies in the league's convoluted salary cap system. The NBA's salary cap, in addition to controlling player costs, is supposed to promote competitive balance among the teams. Part of the league's cap system is a maximum player salary, which is defined at between 25 and 35 percent of the team cap. For James, Bosh, and Wade, the maximum for 2010–2011 is approximately $17 million (a variety of additional rules discuss length of contract and yearly increases that come into play, but they are unnecessary to elucidate the main point here).

Think about it: None of these top superstars can be paid more than roughly $17 million in his first year in Miami. Jerry Reinsdorf, owner of the Chicago Bulls, paid Michael Jordan $34 million to play for his team in 1998. Would these superstars not be worth nearly that much a dozen years later? Sure they would. So, many of the thirty-two NBA owners lined up for the mouthwatering opportunity to sign players worth over $30 million to their teams for only $17 million each.

Rather than being paid their market value, or close to it, the players took their compensation in "psychic" income by deciding that they would play together. As I write in mid-2010, no one knows whether the Miami Heat will dominate the NBA in 2010–2011. Most pundits, however, believe that there is a good chance that they will and will continue to do so for many years that follow. The outcome may well be that the rigged imbalance on the court will turn off fans and that attendance throughout most of the league will begin to suffer. The irony is that the salary cap system is supposed to produce parity across the teams, but it may be doing exactly the opposite. Fixing prices in any market usually produces perverse results, and the NBA owners may soon learn this rudimentary truth of microeconomics.

Legal Cases

As of early 2010, several lawsuits are pending that could potentially alter the shape of professional sports leagues as well as the nature of amateurism in college sports. Foremost among them is *American Needle v. NFL*, which the U.S. Supreme Court decided in May 2010 and remanded back to trial court. Back in 1957, in *Radovich v. NFL*, the Supreme Court declared that the NFL was subject to both Section 1 (conspiracy to restrain trade) and Section 2 (attempted monopolization) of the Sherman Antitrust Act, rejecting the NFL's claim that the antitrust laws were not suitable to the special characteristics of sports leagues. Since that time, the NFL has tried in at least seven different court cases to gain an exemption from Section 1 by arguing that it was a single entity; that is, NFL rules and regulations should be treated for antitrust purposes as coming from a single company (such as ExxonMobil), rather than from an agreement among the thirty-two independent business entities (football clubs). Each time, the NFL has lost. In *American Needle*, the NFL was trying to reverse this precedent that goes back over fifty years.

Until 2000, American Needle had been for over twenty years a nonexclusive licensee of the NFL, authorized to design and to manufacture knit caps and baseball hats with NFL team names and logos. In 2000, the NFL called for bidding among companies to obtain an exclusive license to produce this headgear. Reebok got the contract, and American Needle sued, claiming that the contract was anticompetitive due to its exclusivity provision and the fact that the NFL's thirty-two teams were not free to strike separate deals on their own. That is, the NFL's thirty-two separately owned teams were joining together to form a cartel for the purpose of gaining market power. The absence of competition, American Needle alleged, would reduce output and raise prices. ESPN's lawyer-reporter Lester Munson reported that, as a result of the new exclusive contract with Reebok, retail prices for NFL caps and hats rose from $19.99 in 2000 to $30 in 2001.[13]

American Needle lost its case in district court and in the Seventh Circuit Court of Appeals. Each ruled that for the purpose of licensing, the NFL was, in essence, a single entity. In particular, these judges reasoned that through centralized licensing contracts, the NFL was most efficiently able to promote its brand, and, because individual teams cannot produce football games on their own, the NFL brand could not be effectively promoted via separate team licensing contracts.

In earlier nonsports cases, the Supreme Court had defined a single entity as an economic unit where a parent company had a wholly owned subsidiary or where two or more companies had complete unity of purpose. On the belief that NFL teams do not have complete unity of purpose, because they compete against each other for players, coaches, advertising, corporate sponsorships, inter alia, American Needle appealed the appeals court decision to the Supreme Court. In an unusual move, the NFL endorsed the appeal, seeking a Supreme Court ruling that the NFL and other team-sports leagues constituted single entities for all purposes, not just licensing. The NFL's gambit was premised on the hope that the summary judgment of single-entity status to Major League Soccer (MLS), given by the district court judge in *Fraser v. MLS*,[14] and the conservative balance on the Supreme Court would enable it to gain a long-sought exemption.

Should the Supreme Court have granted the NFL its single-entity status and an exemption from Section 1, implications could have been far reaching. First, it would mean that antitrust challenges to a wide variety of sports league decisions concerning, for example, franchise relocations, expansion policies, labor-market restraints, player age limits, television contracts, and centralized Internet policies would all be dead on arrival. Second, it would mean that the players' union option to decertify itself as a collective bargaining unit and then sue the league over the imposition of labor-market restraints would no longer be available. The union arsenal would be reduced to going on strike.

Interestingly, MLB, which has enjoyed a presumed blanket exemption from the nation's antitrust laws since 1922, may also have been affected by the decision in *American Needle*. In 1998, MLB owners and the union both supported the passage of the so-called Curt Flood Act. The act, which was signed into law, stipulates that labor relations in baseball are no longer covered by the sport's antitrust exemption.[15] One principle motivation behind the act was to enable the union to defend its rights via antitrust litigation and without going on strike. However, if in *American Needle* the Supreme Court ruled that teams in sports leagues are incapable of conspiring to restrain trade, then the essence of the Curt Flood Act would have been nullified. One potential impact, then, of a single entity ruling in *American Needle* could have been to introduce a new element of turbulence in MLB's labor relations. In its May 2010 ruling, the Supreme Court unanimously held that sports leagues should not be treated as single entities for all purposes and that the American Needle complaint should be retried in district court based upon the facts in evidence.

Challenges Confronting College Sports

Elsewhere in this volume, three essays discuss in considerable detail (1) the serious financial difficulties today of intercollegiate athletics, (2) money issues behind the implementation of Title IX, and (3) the antitrust and economic implications of the prevailing Bowl Championship Series (BCS) system for organizing the putative national football championship. These essays also consider how these three subjects are intricately related to each other. For present purposes, suffice it to note that the gravity of these issues has raised the interest level among college administrators in pursuing new and more substantial reform measures.

The urgency of reform is further highlighted by a series of litigations that the National Collegiate Athletic Association (NCAA) currently confronts. These legal challenges, as those in the NCAA's recent past, are centered on the association's treatment of amateurism.

The NCAA has insisted from its inception in 1905 that the athletes in intercollegiate sports are amateurs. Direct and indirect payments to athletes, however, have been an integral part of college sports since the end of the nineteenth century. In the NCAA's first constitution in 1906, Article VI states: It is a violation "offering of inducements to players to enter colleges or universities because of their athletic abilities or supporting or maintaining players while students on account of their athletic abilities, either by athletic organizations, individual alumni, or otherwise, directly or indirectly." But the NCAA had no mechanism to enforce this rule, at least until 1948, and its hortatory stipulations seemed to have little effect. The 1929 Carnegie Report on intercollegiate athletics found that 81 of the 112 schools included in its three-year study made some kind of payment to athletes. The report recommends ending all subsidies to athletes and all pay for coaches, letting students control their games, as they did until the 1890s.

During the 1920s, 1930s, and 1940s, each conference was allowed to set its own rules regarding student aid. With the perception of a growing need for the NCAA to assert some central controls on the aid practices of schools, Article III of the new 1941 constitution declares that "an athlete shall neither be favored nor discriminated against" regarding financial aid, and no athlete shall lose aid for failure to play a sport.

In 1948, the NCAA passed its "Sanity Code," so called because it endeavored to bring some order to the chaotic situation that had evolved. The Sanity Code was a compromise between Southern schools wanting full aid and the Ivies wanting athletes to be treated no differently. The Ivies were adhering to the long-standing concept that if a student-athlete gets an inducement, such as aid, it blurs or erases the line between amateur and pro. As a compromise, the Sanity Code allowed an athlete with financial need and satisfactory academic merit to receive tuition and incidental expenses. The code still stipulated that aid could not be withdrawn if the student ceased to play. Many conferences, however, refused to enforce the code. They wanted full athletic scholarships and claimed their students needed room and board and that study and sport did not allow time for another job. The code, they believed, favored rich, private schools with their upper-class student bodies. Unable to effectively enforce it, the NCAA revoked the Sanity Code in 1950. During the ensuing six years, schools were again left up to their own devices, and scholarships for athletes were permitted to rise up to the cost of attendance (COA).

New NCAA legislation in 1956 allowed that financial aid could include "commonly accepted educational expenses" and eliminated need as a requirement. In 1957, the rules were fleshed out some more, as commonly accepted educational expenses were defined to include tuition, fees, room and board, books, and $15 laundry money per month. It was still stipulated that aid could not be taken away if a student ceased to play.

At the 1973 convention, a decisive step was taken—athletic scholarships could only be awarded for one year at a time. If it was not clear before, now it was[16]—a student's scholarship was dependent on the student's athletic services on the field. Thus, a direct quid pro quo linked the athletic scholarship to a typical employment relationship. In any event, the NCAA had now made a clean break from its original notion of amateurism, which had made it a violation for any inducement to be paid to a student for participating in intercollegiate athletics.

Throughout the following thirty-five-plus years, the NCAA has continued to tweak its morphing and seemingly arbitrary definition of amateurism. Perhaps most curiously, the NCAA now allows gifts to be given to the student-athletes, but only on occasions when the NCAA sees fit. For instance, the University of Connecticut handed out 298 championship rings in commemoration of its 1999 NCAA men's basketball championship. The nicest rings, which were ten-karat gold inset with diamonds and cost $495.50 apiece, went to the team's coaches, the athletic director, the associate athletic director, and the university president. The rings for the players were only gold tone and cost $199. Today, the NCAA allows players in bowl games to receive up to $500 in gifts.[17]

In any event, the NCAA's elusive definition and arbitrary treatment of amateurism has provoked a spate of litigations over the past decade. Since its 1998 loss in the restricted earnings case (*Law v. NCAA*, which cost the association $54.5 million), the NCAA has been eager to settle claims outside court before a legal precedent can be rendered. Thus, in the *Jason White et al.* suit, which asked that the limit of athletic scholarships be raised to the full cost of college attendance (some $2,500 above the official limit), the NCAA settled the matter in 2008. Although the nominal settlement was for $228 million, in reality the NCAA was only required to pay less than $20 million in new funds, with no additional money committed to athletic scholarships beyond 2012–2013.

In October 2009, Andy Oliver, a former pitcher for the Oklahoma State baseball team, received a $750,000 settlement from the NCAA. Oliver had challenged the NCAA's regulation that prohibits amateur athletes from employing legal counsel in contract negotiations with professional teams. Just prior to his pitching in the 2008 NCAA tournament, the association declared Oliver ineligible, because it had determined that his adviser was in contact with MLB's Minnesota Twins after Oliver had been drafted by the team out of high school in 2006. This meeting was to obtain information for Oliver, and Oliver had never signed a professional contract, much less been paid by a pro team for playing baseball. Oliver's suit was the first one challenging this NCAA legal counsel rule. In February 2009, the district court judge ordered the NCAA to reinstate Oliver and voided the adviser rule, branding it "arbitrary and capricious," exploitative, and impossible to enforce. The $750,000 settlement may have been good for Oliver, but it left the NCAA restriction intact.

As I write in mid-2010, the NCAA faces some new challenges over its publicity rights regulations that have been brought by current and former athletes. The contradictions here are deep and serious, and the law firms involved for the plaintiffs have strong track records.

Sam Keller is a former starting quarterback for Arizona State University and the University of Nebraska. He filed a class-action complaint against the NCAA, the video-game manufacturer Electronic Arts (EA), and the Collegiate Licensing Company (CLC) on May 9, 2009, in U.S. District Court for the Northern District of California. EA is producing video games with near-photographic likeness to actual college football and basketball players. The "fictional" EA players also come with personal stats and characteristics that mimic those of the actual student-athletes. Through CLC, the NCAA receives licensing revenue for its cooperation with EA. Keller's complaint states:

> [The] suit arises out of the blatant and unlawful use of NCAA student likenesses in videogames produced by EA. . . . Despite clear prohibitions on the use of student names and likenesses in NCAA bylaws, contracts, and licensing agreements, EA utilizes the likenesses of individual student-athletes in its NCAA basketball and football video games to increase sales and profits. EA also intentionally circumvents the prohibitions on utilizing student-athletes' names in commercial ventures by allowing gamers to upload entire rosters, which include players' names and other information, directly into the game in a matter of seconds. Rather than enforcing its own rules, the NCAA and its licensing arm, the CLC, have sanctioned EA's violations.[18]

Significantly, NCAA Bylaw 12.5 "specifically prohibits the commercial licensing of an NCAA athlete's name, picture, or likeness."

O'Bannon et al. v. NCAA, a second publicity-rights litigation from 2009, is broader in scope.[19] In addition to video games, the *O'Bannon* suit enumerates several other areas where, it alleges, student-athletes' publicity rights are being usurped, including the selling of rights to rebroadcast classic games; DVDs of games and highlights; stock footage for use by corporate advertisers; photographs (Replay Photo has contracted with at least sixty-two schools to offer thousands of photos for sale of athletes—framed versions can cost up to several hundred dollars); jerseys and other apparel items, figures, trading cards, and posters. McFarlane Toys goes through CLC to enter into contracts with current pros to get rights to images of them in college uniforms. Schools also sell actual jerseys worn by players.[20]

The NCAA requires all students to sign release forms each year (which are purportedly in effect until new forms are signed, so they exist in perpetuity for former athletes). Form 08-3a supposedly allows commercial use of their images. This form is an eligibility document regarding no drug use and amateur status but includes under Part IV the following: "You authorize the NCAA [or a third party acting on behalf of the NCAA (e.g., host institution, conference, local organizing committee)] to use your name or picture to generally promote NCAA championships or other NCAA events, activities, or programs." Because all student-athletes must sign whether or not they receive scholarships, these forms are executed under duress and are unlikely to survive a legal challenge.

It is noteworthy that the *O'Bannon* case applies to current and former student-athletes. Former student-athletes are no longer amateur athletes, and no philosophical precept should preclude their being compensated when their images are still being used. Indeed, side deals exist between EA and MacFarlane, on the one hand, and current NBA and NFL players, on the other, that provide for payment for use of their images in these games. If preserving amateurism were truly the central concern, current college athletes need not be remunerated while they are in college; escrow accounts could be established in their names for later use, either as deferred income, for educational expense accounts, or for a variety of other possible plans. The NCAA has been able to hold on to its quixotic ways largely because plaintiffs have been willing to settle. This time, settlement might not come so easily.

Perennial Problems

At least going back to *Raiders v. NFL*, the location of sports teams in the United States has been subject to heated legal contestation. Even in MLB, where the league is presumed to benefit from a blanket anti-trust exemption (save labor relations since the 1998 Curt Flood Act), battles have erupted, and one is currently raging over the potential move of the Oakland A's into San Jose, which has been part of the San Francisco Giants exclusive territory since 1989. Meanwhile, the NFL's Minnesota Vikings have been seeking new digs in the Twin Cities, and MLB's Tampa Bay Rays are doing the same in the greater Tampa area. Both teams have made utterances about relocation. In 2008, Seattle struggled to keep its NBA SuperSonics in town but eventually allowed the team owner to buy his way out of the remaining two years on the lease, and the team moved to Oklahoma City.

More dramatically, perhaps, several teams in the NHL—particularly those below the Mason-Dixon line—have been struggling financially for some time. Commissioner Gary Bettman has been steadfast in defending his Southern strategy and has not allowed teams, even ones in bankruptcy or near bankruptcy, to relocate.

An ever-present part of the discussion regarding team location has been the debate about whether sports teams and facilities benefit their local economies. The scholarly literature on this question has been clear: A city should not anticipate that a team or a facility by itself will boost employment or per-capita income. Of course, this conclusion is based on large panel regressions involving dozens of teams and cities over several decades. It is a statement about the typical case. Each city can hope to plan better and to strike a more favorable financing and lease deal, thereby hoping to end up on the positive side of economic impact. Significantly, many deals during this century have included, along with the sport facility, a private funding commitment to build adjacent retail, commercial, or residential developments. In these cases, it is more likely that the economic outcome would be salutary.

But, in all cases, it is crucial for the city to plan its use of space and public funds carefully. This planning includes negotiating the best possible deal for arena or stadium financing and for the facility lease. An essay in this collection addresses the evidence and the trends regarding facility finance.

Closely related is the question of whether sports megaevents, such as the World Cup or the Olympics, bring positive economic development impulses to cities or regions. This topical issue is analyzed in "Going for Gold" in this volume.

Another issue that appears to be here to stay is the use of performance-enhancing drugs (PEDs) in sports. Leagues and sporting bodies can certainly make forward strides by establishing tougher testing and sanctioning policies, but the chemists and their collaborators seem to be able to stay a step ahead. Down the road a few years, gene doping will occur.

Baseball's infamous list of 103 players who were supposed to be tested anonymously for PEDs in 2003 and showed positive results appears doomed to have a few names leaked out each year. Fans and sportswriters appear ready to debate endlessly how to assess the statistics of these players and, indeed, all those of the entire steroid era. The PED conundrum is discussed at some length in another essay in the volume.

Conclusion

Like everything around us, the business of sports is evolving. Professional soccer is ascendant, and women's sports continue to knock on the door of commercial success. Labor relations shift from tumultuous to quiescent and possibly back again. The sports industry has become more closely linked with the corporate sector and, hence, more vulnerable to the vicissitudes of the U.S. and world economies. The telecommunications revolution has changed the way we consume sports and provided the industry with new sources of revenue.[21] At the same time, the Internet has engendered new alliances and combinations that have inspired the wrath of some fans and invited the possibility of additional governmental oversight. It has also spawned a battle over the designation of local-market rights and, in some cases, heightened existing tensions among owners.

Meanwhile, big-time college sports have increasingly come to reflect the hallmarks of professional sports. The contradictions of the hybrid model, combining market pricing with amateurism and a putative commitment to education, are becoming more prominent by the day. Sharpening inequality across university athletic programs is leading to a caste system in which the overwhelming majority of schools is discovering that the status quo is not sustainable financially. All the while, the demands of gender equity assert themselves.

So, the sports industry in the second decade of the twenty-first century faces many challenges and much uncertainty. The essays herein attempt to shed some light on the choices that lie ahead and their implications for sports fans, players, owners, and leagues.

Dollar Dilemmas during the Downturn

A Financial Crossroads for College Sports

THIS ESSAY undertakes three challenging tasks. First, I attempt to lay out the dimensions of the current financial crisis that confronts intercollegiate athletics. Second, I propose three reforms that I believe, if enacted, would go a long way toward ameliorating the financial situation and also bring the practice of college sports more in line ethically with its purported mission. Third, I assess the prospects of these reforms being carried out, given the history of failed reform efforts in the past.

Although a group of economists argues that big-time college athletic departments run a surplus in reality, I am not in that group. Based on figures I have seen from the NCAA, from the Equity in Athletics Disclosure Act (EADA) filings with the U.S. Department of Education from individual conferences, and from individual schools (from 1099 forms and open public record documents), I believe that all but a handful of schools' athletic departments run a deficit when

This essay is based on an article by the same name that appears in *Journal of Intercollegiate Sport* 3, no. 1 (2010): 111–124.

properly accounted. Indeed, late NCAA President Myles Brand stated on a number of occasions that only a half dozen schools run a true surplus on a consistent basis. Similar appraisals were made by his predecessors Ced Dempsey and Dick Schultz.

Consider the NCAA figures. According to its 2009 report for the 2007–2008 year, out of 119 schools in the Football Bowl Subdivision (FBS) of Division I (formerly DIA), only 25 athletic departments generated a net operating surplus.[1] These schools had an average reported operating surplus of $3.87 million. The remaining ninety-four schools generated an athletic operating deficit, which, among them, averaged $9.87 million. For the entire 119 schools, the median operating deficit was $8.1 million.[2]

The NCAA does not release financial figures for individual colleges, and, other than incomplete and irregular data reported to the U.S. Department of Education in the annual EADA reports and the release of program financials in public-record documents, the public rarely gets a candid look at the bottom line for particular athletic departments. One recent and striking exception is the budgetary information of the athletic department at the University of California, Berkeley, which the school's faculty senate made public in early November 2009. According to the information sheet, the school's athletic department was a net loser of between $7.4 million and $13.5 million every year between the 2003–2004 and 2009–2010 school years, costing the university a total of $78.1 million over this seven-year period. Furthermore, these losses do not include the annual debt service on two new capital projects (the $321-million renovation of Memorial Stadium and the $136-million Student Athlete High Performance Center; access to the latter will restricted to the school's 450 student-athletes).[3]

It is important to point out that the summary NCAA figures can be misleading. Although Jim Isch, Dan Fulks, and others have made heroic efforts to standardize and to rationalize intercollegiate athletic accounting and reporting practices, a great deal remains to be done.[4] I will not go into all the gory details, but a few salient issues should be mentioned. First, schools do not regularly report capital expenses, and those that do do so unevenly and incompletely. As Jonathan and Peter Orszag have demonstrated in their 2005 study for the NCAA, capital costs, properly reckoned, can be appreciable. Based on facility replacement cost, the Orszags estimated an annual capital cost in DIA athletic departments of $24 million, just a few million dollars below the average annual operating costs of DIA intercollegiate athletic departments at the time.[5] Alternatively, NCAA data reveal that the top decile of FBS programs paid out a median of $6.56 million of debt service on a debt of $98.1 million in 2007–2008. This debt service is generally paid outside the athletic department (e.g., by the university or the state) and does not appear as an expense item in the athletic department budget. Thus, if capital costs were fully and properly accounted, it is safe to assume that these reported deficits would balloon significantly.

Second, it is not clear to what extent indirect costs are included in the financial reports of athletic departments. Although NCAA reporting forms have been modified to call for the inclusion of many indirect costs, the instructions are often not explicit or detailed. Some schools may include, for instance, estimates of the costs for the time university administrators spend on athletics, while others may not. The same is true for a pro rata share of the administrative building capital and operating costs, and so on.

Third, schools follow varying practices regarding accounting for athletic grants-in-aid (GIAs). The basic conundrum here is that some schools count the value of the GIA at full tuition and room and board, when the marginal tuition cost may be negligible. If a school has empty beds in its dormitories, the marginal cost of filling such a bed with an athlete is trivial. If that athlete attends classes, no additional instructional cost is incurred, and the athlete is sleeping in a bed that would otherwise be empty. The athletic department might record the operating cost associated with this athlete's GIA at its full nominal value—say $35,000—while the actual incremental cost to the school might be closer to $5,000 or $10,000.[6] To the extent that this experience applies at certain state universities, athletic costs and operating deficits are overstated.

Fourth, where generated revenue is used, the exclusion of student fees may understate the market value created from student attendance at games. Practices at different schools vary widely, regarding the size and use of the student fees and whether students are given free tickets or sold subsidized tickets to sporting contests.

To be sure, when all adjustments are made, it seems that true athletic deficits would be considerably larger than reported deficits; that is, the omitted costs appear to significantly exceed the overstated costs.

The reasons why athletic departments virtually all run in significant deficit are manifold. Foremost among them is that athletic departments are large, not-for-profit bureaucracies. Rather than following a bottom-line imperative to boost quarterly profits and stock prices, they tend to follow the bureaucratic imperative to grow at any cost and to do anything they can to win. Actual FBS budgets, then, run in the red, and the gap between expenses and revenues is growing at the vast majority of schools.

What about the often-heard responses that the value of big-time college athletics lies in its ability (a) to increase student applications and (b) to generate increases in donations to the university general fund?

One hears frequent claims that a successful football or basketball team increases student applications[7] and that this, in turn, enables a school to be more selective and to increase the quality of its student body. Although it appears to generally be the case that big-time athletic success may modestly increase applications, it is less clear that that this increase leads to better students. The reason is that the large majority of new applications tend to be from students at the bottom of the academic performance ladder. The econometric scholarship on the effect on student quality is somewhat contradictory. Nonetheless, the bulk of the extant econometric research suggests that any such effect is either nonexistent or small and short-lived.[8]

An important related point is that many large state universities do not fill all their beds. If athletic success increases applications, even if the school is not able to be more selective, it may be able to increase enrollment and, hence, revenue. In this way, athletic success may provide a financial benefit.

The literature is also somewhat uneven and inconclusive on the question of athletic success promoting donations to a school's general fund. Undoubtedly, for some schools, particularly those experiencing a meteoric rise from athletic oblivion to national prominence, success does lead boosters, alumni, and state legislators to open their wallets. In general, however, to the extent that some studies find positive and significant effects in panel data research, it is very modest in magnitude. Many studies find no significant effect.[9] Although it is likely that athletic success will lead to increased giving to the athletic department or its foundation, giving to the general fund is more uncertain. Indeed, some evidence shows that increased donations to athletics have cannibalized donations to the general fund. For instance, between 1998 and 2003, a period when overall giving to universities was flat, athletic departments received an increased share of total gifts—from 14.7 percent to 26 percent.[10]

In the cases of increased applications and increased donations, it is necessary to remember that a positive and significant coefficient implies that the relationship goes in both directions. That is, if improved athletic performance generates increased applications or donations, then deteriorated performance engenders decreases in applications and donations. In the end, the average win percentage is .500, and one college's gain will be another's loss. A particular college will also find its gain one year may be its loss the next if it cannot sustain its athletic success. Moreover, the quest for victory often leads schools to transgress NCAA rules. Investigations and scandals may ensue, and their negative impact may last for years.[11]

From the perspective of an individual university, even if a clear link could be established between athletic success and increased applications or donations, there is an opportunity cost in investing in improved athletic performance. If a university's goal is increased applications or donations, then investing in athletics must be compared to investing in the best alternative. Only if athletic investment yields higher returns than, say, investing in excellent faculty and science laboratories or growing the development office does it make economic sense to increase spending on athletics. Further, competition among schools to capture the expected gains from athletic success would eventually eliminate those gains as schools spent more and more money on recruitment, facilities, coaches' salaries, and the like, while the fact remained that only ten schools can be ranked in the top ten.[12]

The final pattern to observe is that the situation appears to be growing worse in the aggregate and also distributionally. A 2009 Knight Commission study has reported that in the FBS, athletic spending has been growing at four times the rate of the general educational budget.[13] The 2009 *Revenues and Expenses Report* of the NCAA found that the median net operating deficit for FBS athletic programs grew from $5.57 million in fiscal year 2005 to $8.09 million in fiscal 2008, a 45.2 percent increase over the three years.[14]

As the aggregate situation deteriorates, the top schools in the leading conferences continue to be able to generate operating surpluses. Meanwhile, the condition for all the other programs grows worse and worse. The 119 FBS schools constitute the upper echelon of athletic programs among the over 1,200 colleges belonging to the NCAA. In 2005–2006, the nineteen programs that reported operating surpluses (based on generated revenue) had a median surplus of $4.3 million, while the one hundred programs with operating deficits reported a median deficit of $8.9; that is, the gap between these two groups of have and have-nots was $13.2 million. This gap had grown by $2 million since 2003–2004.[15]

If the 119 FBS athletic programs are divided into deciles, the following pattern emerges for the 2006–2007 academic year. As depicted in Table 2.1, the median revenue of programs in the lowest decile (ranked by revenue) was $13.1 million, while that of the highest decile was $89.1 million, almost seven times higher than the lowest 10 percent of programs. It is important to emphasize that these figures are for total revenue; that is, they include revenues generated by the athletic department and allocated revenues (transfers from the

TABLE 2.1 FBS revenue and expenditure distribution, median by decile, 2006–2007

Decile	Grand total expenditures ($)	Grand total revenue ($)	Grand total generated revenue ($)
1	14,143,000	13,135,000	5,351,000
2	19,705,000	19,954,000	7,925,000
3	23,417,000	23,390,000	11,609,000
4	27,955,000	27,098,000	15,062,000
5	33,783,000	33,783,000	24,652,000
6	42,967,000	44,944,000	35,283,000
7	52,255,000	53,719,000	47,756,000
8	57,987,000	60,967,000	58,167,000
9	68,377,000	72,256,000	70,358,000
10	83,135,000	89,080,000	89,028,000

Source: Jay Weiner, College Sports 101 (Miami, FL: Knight Foundation Commission on Intercollegiate Athletics, 2009), available at www.knightcommission.org (accessed January 6, 2010).

university and the public sector). If only generated revenues were considered, the bottom decile would have a median of $5.4 million, while the top decile would have a median of $89.0 million—for a top-to-bottom ratio of over 16–1.[16] Only the top decile reports a surplus without institutional subsidies, and, again, these figures exclude capital expenses.

Despite the clear superiority in the performance of the top decile, when capital and indirect expenses are included in the balance, it is probable that not even all the top 10 percent of revenue programs generates surpluses in a typical year.

The economic challenges are greater still if one acknowledges that (a) the NCAA's rules restrict an athlete's GIA in most cases to being $2,500 or more below the full cost of attending college, (b) the NCAA and its member schools in Division I face a serious antitrust and unjust enrichment challenge over their appropriation of athletes' publicity rights,[17] and (c) despite impressive progress, women still lag well behind men in athletic participation and resource allocation. Across the NCAA in 2007–2008, women were 42.6 percent of all athletes (this share was basically stagnant during the two terms of the Bush administration) but approximately 55 percent of all undergraduate students.

The financial landscape, then, is marked by widespread and growing deficits as well as a deepening divide between the have and have-not schools. The 2007–2010 global financial crisis and economic downtown have only exacerbated the already untenable situation. Further, the concomitant crisis in the financing of higher education and increasing questions about the future viability of the basic economic model of U.S. universities shine yet a brighter light on the growing deficits in intercollegiate athletics.

A saying of growing currency states that no good recession should go to waste. Recessions are times to curb excesses and waste, and many athletic programs have been shaken out of their long-standing complacencies and growing extravagances into cost-cutting modes. So some positive steps have been taken by certain schools and conferences,[18] but they are all incremental and insufficient given the magnitude of the problem.

Even the athletic directors (ADs) of Division I have recognized that business as usual is not sustainable, and they have called for a series of reforms, such as cutting back on glossy media guides, shortening the playing season in nonrevenue sports (this is likely to be in violation of Title IX), reducing traveling squads, restricting off-season practices, eliminating some sports, and ending the common practice of lodging teams at local hotels before home games. The danger also exists, however, that, as in the past, some reforms will spring loopholes. For instance, several years ago, the NCAA passed a regulation that prevented student-athletes from being segregated in separate housing. Schools began to put student-athletes in special married-graduate-student housing complexes, which, in effect, had the same impact as segregated housing. If student-athletes are prohibited from staying in local hotels, the response may be to build more luxurious "graduate-student" housing. Notably, the Division I ADs stayed away from recommending more substantial reforms; thus, while the ADs' plan may slow the pace of ballooning deficits, it is unlikely to reverse the tide.[19]

In the next section, I suggest some deeper measures that could make more significant contributions to achieving fiscal sanity and greater financial balance in big-time intercollegiate athletics.

Policy Reforms for Fiscal Solvency

Unless they decide to opt out of competition, schools cannot solve the budgetary crisis on their own. Competitive forces compel ADs to spend on coaches, facilities, and amenities. The only reasonable path to reform is through collective action. The problem is that certain types of collective action by the NCAA can be construed to be in violation of Section 1 of the Sherman Antitrust Act.

Seek a Partial Antitrust Exemption to Regulate Coaches' Salaries

Examples of waste abound in Division I athletics, but perhaps the most egregious is the salaries paid to head football and men's basketball coaches, which often exceed the salaries of the universities' presidents by a factor of five to ten.[20] Today, over one hundred college football coaches receive compensation packages exceeding $1 million; more than a dozen exceed $3 million, and several exceed $4 or $5 million in monetary compensation alone.[21]

Men's basketball coaches are not far behind: In 2005–2006, the coaches of the sixty-five Division I teams in the NCAA tournament had an average maximum compensation of $959,486, with the top-paid coach earning a guaranteed salary of $2.1 million and a maximum salary of $3.4 million.[22] The salaries have continued to grow. For instance, in 2009, the University of Kentucky agreed to pay John Calipari a guaranteed $31.65 million (plus incentives) over eight years. Rick Pitino's compensation at the University of Louisville exceeded $7 million during the 2009–2010 academic year. These figures exclude bonuses as well as extensive perquisites, including free use of cars, housing subsidies, country-club memberships, private jet service, exceptionally generous severance packages, and more.[23] The coaches also have handsome opportunities to earn outside income via apparel or sneaker endorsements, the lecture circuit, and book contracts.

Not surprisingly, assistant coaches have also experienced an explosion in their pay packages in recent years. For instance, the University of Tennessee lured Monte Kiffin, its new defensive coordinator in

2009, with a $1.2 million salary, a $300,000 bonus for staying through the end of the regular season,[24] up to another $100,000 in incentives, and the use of two cars. The average salary for the nine assistant football coaches at Tennessee was $369,000 in 2009. *USA Today* identified over one hundred assistant coaches in the FBS who receive over $250,000 in base compensation. Bob Stoops, the University of Oklahoma's head football coach, is guaranteed $4.3 million in 2009, and his nine assistants will total nearly $2.5 million before bonuses. The University of Alabama and Louisiana State University also boast $6-million-plus staffs.[25]

Back in 1924, Centenary College in Shreveport, Louisiana, the nation's first liberal-arts college west of the Mississippi, was denied accreditation by the Southern Association of Colleges and Schools, because the school placed an "undue emphasis on athletics." The primary evidence of Centenary's misplaced priorities by the Southern Association was that the college paid its football coach more than it paid its college president. The next year, the football coach was gone, and the college gained accreditation.[26]

More recently, Bear Bryant, the legendary head football coach at the University of Alabama (1958–1982), adhered to a firm policy of always keeping his salary $1 below that of the school president. Bryant believed that it was symbolically important for the university president to be paid more than the head football coach.[27]

Defenders of multimillion-dollar head coaches' salaries are wont to repeat the mantra: "Coaches' compensation packages are driven by market forces." Fair enough, but what drives the market forces? It is clear that the market for coaches is sustained by several artificial factors: (a) no compensation is paid to the athletes, (b) intercollegiate sports benefit from substantial tax privileges, (c) no shareholders demand dividend distributions or higher profits to bolster stock prices, (d) athletic departments are nourished by university and statewide financial support, and (e) coaches' salaries are negotiated by ADs whose own worth rises with the salaries of their employees.

In a normal competitive market, college football coaches would not be getting compensated almost at the same level as NFL coaches. The top thirty-two college football programs generate revenues in the

$40- to $80-million range; the average NFL team generates around $230 million.

The central point is that if the NCAA placed, say, a $400,000 limit on coaches' compensation packages, it would not affect the quality of coaching or the level of intercollegiate competition one iota. This is because the next best alternative for top college coaches (the reservation wage) is likely to be well below this level. Anything above the reservation wage is what economists call "economic rent."

It is clear that coaches are being paid in part for the value produced by the athletes they recruit, who do not get paid. That is, the marginal revenue product of the star players accrues largely to the head coach rather than to the players. This is reason enough to cap coaches' salaries. It is more of a reason, because much of the work of recruiting is done by assistant coaches, and much of the attraction a school has to a player has to do with the school's conference, reputation, and facilities, all factors independent of the head coach.

Finally, coaches' compensation does not appear to be significantly correlated with team performance. Although one could make the argument that certain coaches have turned around the fortunes of teams, taking them from oblivion to prominence over the course of a few years, and, therefore, they have added sufficiently to the schools' revenues to justify their high salaries, such coaches are few and far between. Even in these cases, the athletes are producing the winning teams, and their compensation is being suppressed. In the end, only ten schools can be in the top-ten rankings, and the average win percentage of all schools will always be .500. Nonetheless, virtually every head football coach in the FBS earns over $1 million. This obviously includes coaches of perennially losing teams.

I collected data on compensation levels of head coaches in Division I men's basketball and Division IA football and compared these levels to different measurements of team performance. I ran multiple regressions and panel regressions to explore the extent of correlation between coaches' salaries and team performance with different lag structures. The regression results do not suggest that the more highly paid coaches are associated with more successful teams in current years; rather, they suggest that higher salaries are positively correlated with a school's historical success. That is, team success appears to be correlated with long-standing institutional factors rather than the performance of the current coach.[28]

Thus, strong economic and ethical reasons justify attempting to cap coaches' salaries.[29] Doing so would save millions of dollars for the typical FBS program.

Reduce the Number of Football Scholarships

Another example of extravagance is the size of FBS football teams. DIA football teams do not need eighty-five scholarships: Sixty (or fewer) would do fine.[30] NFL teams have a maximum active roster of forty-five, plus a maximum inactive roster of eight additional players.[31] The average FBS team has thirty-two walk-ons plus eighty-five scholarship players.[32] If football scholarships were cut to sixty, the average college would probably save over $1 million annually[33]—easily enough to finance an average FBS soccer team plus an average FBS golf team, or an FBS tennis team plus gymnastics team, and have several hundred thousand dollars left over.[34] Even assuming the number of walk-ons would not increase with the lower scholarship limit, the average squad size would still be ninety-two.

Introduce an FBS Playoff System

In eighty-eight other varsity sports and divisions, the NCAA has organized play-off competitions for national championships. In the Football Championship Subdivision (FCS) of Division I (formerly Division IAA), Division II, and Division III football, there are play-offs, some with sixteen teams. Only in FBS football does the NCAA not organize a national championship play-off. Instead, the NCAA has allowed its six equity conferences to organize their own putative national championship that involves no play-off but instead substitutes its own highly flawed, unfair, and anticompetitive Bowl Championship Series (BCS) five-game bowl system.

First, the BCS system is flawed, because the method it uses to select its ten participating teams, including its top two teams for the national championship, includes an inadequately and improperly specified set of criteria in its computer algorithms and coaches' and media surveys that involve a conflict of interest and unbalanced information.[35] Ultimately, disputes about the selected teams and doubts about whether the true national champion has been crowned always ensue. The fact of the matter is that no system is perfect, but U.S. sporting culture embraces a play-off system. In a play-off, the teams compete against each other on the field to see who is better. Play-offs prevail in all other NCAA championships and throughout professional sports. The championship is not left up to a largely arbitrary numerical and subjective system.

Second, the BCS system is unfair, because it distributes its slots for BCS games as well as the revenue from these games prejudicially. The six equity conferences that created and control the BCS system each have their conference champions receive automatic berths to one of the five BCS bowls. In 2008–2009, each of the six automatic qualifying (AQ) conferences received a guaranteed $18.6 million. The five non-AQ conferences in the FBS can earn an automatic berth if (a) the team ranks in the top twelve of the final BCS standings, or (b) the team ranks in the top sixteen of the final BCS standings and its ranking is higher than that of the champion of one of the BCS conferences. However, no more than one team from a non-AQ conference can earn an automatic berth in any given year; thus, no automatic berth is available for a second non-AQ team.[36] If a non-AQ team did compete in a BCS bowl, its conference received only $9.8 million in 2008–2009, or just over half of what an AQ conference received.

Overall, during the first twelve years of the BCS system, there have been ninety-eight appearances by BCS conference teams and only six appearances by non-BCS conference teams, five of which occurred during the last four years. A non-AQ team has never been selected to participate in the national championship game, and, given the parameters in the selection process, it is unlikely in the extreme that one ever will be selected. During the three-year period 2007–2009, total payouts from the BCS bowls amounted to $410.1 million, of which $355.1 million (or 86.6 percent) went to BCS conferences.[37]

The effect of this lopsided selection and distribution process is to calcify the FBS into a caste system.

Third, the BCS system is anticompetitive, because it restricts output (quantitatively and qualitatively) and reduces consumer welfare. Currently, only *five* BCS bowl games are played, and, of these, only *one* is relevant to deciding the putative national champion. In an eight-team play-off, *seven* games would be played, and *all seven* would be relevant to deciding the national champion. All 120 schools in the FBS would be equally eligible for selection, and a broader cross-section of the country would be interested in the results. It is not imaginable that the television contracts would grow by anything less than 100 percent under the circumstance of an eight-team play-off.[38]

Over the years, the BCS has offered a series of justifications for its system. I discuss these at length in the next essay. In my view, these rationales are patently self-serving and unconvincing.

In addition to creating a fairer and more revenue-enhancing system, an FBS play-off would have one other significant salutary impact. The revenue from an NCAA-organized FBS play-off would be distributed more equally across the 120 schools in the FBS, and it would share more of the revenue with the other schools in the rest of Division I, as well as share 4.37 percent with Division II and 3.18 percent with Division III. Not only would this help narrow the growing divide between rich and poor athletic programs; it would blunt the incentives to chase football success. With a smaller payoff, schools would have less incentive to spend for coaches, for recruiting, for facilities, and so forth, and the arms' race should slow down.

The Prospects for Implementing Structural Reform

I have no illusions that deep reform will come easily. People have been trying to thwart the juggernaut of commercialization in college sports since the 1890s. What is different now is that the financial stakes have multiplied, the athletic bottom line has become acutely more problematic, and the traditional university model is suffering. The necessity for incremental change has already been recognized by the Division I ADs. These sensibilities are only heightened by the difficult and uncertain macroeconomic environment in the country.

College presidents are expressing more interest in serious reform measures, and a 2009 survey of FBS presidents sponsored by the Knight Commission has identified astronomical coaches' salaries as college sports' most urgent financial problem.[39] Members of the U.S. Congress and President Barack Obama have manifested concern over the absence of a play-off system in the FBS.

Whether this energy can be harnessed and mobilized into an effective reform movement remains to be seen. The same college presidents who identified high coaches' salaries as financial enemy number one evinced pessimism about being able to do anything about the problem. Most appear to be skeptical about seeking an antitrust exemption from the U.S. Congress. There is an unspecified fear that if colleges invite government into their business, then Congress will seek greater control and regulation over it.

But why would some intervention by the government be so bad? Since 1995, the NCAA has faced many major legal challenges, beginning with the restrictive earnings coaches suit and continuing with the National Invitational Tournament antitrust case against the NCAA's March Madness, the preseason tournament limitation rule case, the cost of attendance versus scholarship limit litigation brought by Jason White, Ohio baseball player Andrew Oliver's suit against the NCAA that prohibits the use of lawyers by players to discuss professional contracts, and the *Keller* and *O'Bannon* cases over current and former college players' publicity rights. The NCAA has not fared well in most of these cases, and, in my view, its prospects are not good in the last two. Most of these matters, even though some have reached costly settlement, have not been put to rest. The NCAA's hybrid model, combining elements of amateurism and professionalism, seems to engender legal ambiguity and to invite litigation. The NCAA could use some help, it seems, and a bit of congressional intervention may prove constructive.

That said, the U.S. Congress is already well aware of issues in college sports and has called numerous hearings to explore them. The U.S. government is deeply involved in matters concerning higher education and even in intercollegiate sports via such programs as Title IX and Pell Grants. The IRS has reevaluated its taxing policies regarding donations for seating priorities and Unrelated Business Income Taxation, as has the Congressional Budget Office. In short, the government does not need a discussion around a partial antitrust exemption for the NCAA to tempt it to become more intrusive. As renowned journalist and former U.S. State Department official Hodding Carter III stated recently, "If college sports wants government out of its business, then college sports should remove its snout from the government trough."

Another obstacle to reform is the NCAA itself. The association, in essence, functions as a trade association for coaches, ADs, and conference commissioners. The few college presidents who have become involved in NCAA committees often tend to be passionate sports fans and have little instinct to rock the boat. All presidents who serve on NCAA committees are expected to represent the interests of their conferences. President Bernie Machen at the University of Florida was quoted in the *Sports Business Journal* as saying that the Southeastern Conference would not allow him to be the conference representative, because he believes there should be a more equitable distribution of BCS monies.[40]

The vast majority of presidents who do not serve on NCAA committees generally have abdicated responsibility for their sports programs to the ADs and, secondarily, to the provosts and faculty athletic representatives whom they appoint. The ADs and coaches have little motivation to reduce the number of football scholarships or to seek an antitrust exemption that might lead to the decimation of their salaries.

The representation on NCAA committees is heavily weighted toward Division I, and within Division I toward the FBS, and within the FBS toward the BCS or equity conferences. Given this power structure, it is understandable why the NCAA has not pushed for a football play-off in the FBS. What all this means is that momentum and pressure for reform will likely have to come from outside the association.

The history of Title IX instructs us that this is possible. Further, it is becoming increasingly apparent that current patterns are not sustainable. Schools are cutting back some sports and eliminating others. A few rich programs at the top are thriving, and some are just surviving, but the overwhelming majority of programs realizes that business as usual is over.

The reforms outlined above are possible politically. Their intent is to preserve and to strengthen intercollegiate athletics by putting them on a sounder and more equitable financial footing. Whether they come to fruition will depend upon the organizational effort and skill that are put behind them. One thing is certain: If reform-minded university presidents and others give up before they begin, as many appear to have done in their answers to the Knight Commission survey, then no productive change will result.

3 The BCS, Antitrust, and Public Policy

I T SEEMS that every year, the Bowl Championship Series (BCS) comes under fire. In 2008–2009, Florida (13–1) beat Oklahoma (12–2) to win the putative national championship. No one disputes that Florida and Oklahoma were among the nation's best teams, but Utah (13–0), USC (12–1), and Texas (12–1) all felt they deserved a shot at the title. Indeed, Texas even beat Oklahoma in a regular-season game.

In place since 1998, the BCS purports to determine the national champion in college football, while preserving the century-old system of postseason bowl games.[1] To make its determination of which teams go to the championship game, the BCS employs the *USA Today* Coaches Poll, the Harris Interactive College Football Poll, and an average of six computer rankings. Without fail, the annual selection invites strident criticism. Invariably, many fans and colleges feel cheated.

Now, the president of the United States is also weighing in. Referring to 2008–2009, President Barack Obama stated, "If I'm Utah, or

This essay is based on "The BCS, Antitrust, and Public Policy," *Antitrust Bulletin* (Winter 2010).

if I'm USC, or if I'm Texas, I might still have some quibbles. That's why we need a play-off."[2] As in the past, many politicians are ready to take up the cause. Congressional Representative Joe Barton (R-Texas) introduced a bill that would prohibit the BCS from marketing its title game as the national championship unless it was the culmination of an equitable play-off system. The bill was approved in a House Energy and Commerce Subcommittee vote on December 8, 2009. The Utah attorney general is investigating the BCS for possible antitrust violations, and on February 9, 2009, the Utah State Senate unanimously passed a resolution (SJR11) calling for a national football play-off. Representative Neil Abercrombie (D-Hawaii) and other House members have asked the Justice Department to investigate the BCS and possible antitrust violations.

The Senate Judiciary Committee held hearings on the possibility that the bowl system violated the country's antitrust laws back in May 1997, in October 2003, and again in July 2009.[3] The House Subcommittee on Commerce, Trade, and Consumer Protection held similar hearings in December 2005 and in May 2009. And on January 29, 2010, the assistant attorney general of the U.S. Department of Justice (DOJ) sent Senator Orrin Hatch a letter indicating the DOJ was considering opening an investigation into the BCS to determine if it violated the country's antitrust laws. Among the options also mentioned in the letter were "encouraging the NCAA to take control of the college football postseason at the FBS level; asking a governmental or nongovernmental entity or a commission to study the benefits, costs, and feasibility of a play-off system; asking the Federal Trade Commission to examine the legality of the current system under consumer protection laws; exploring whether other agencies may be able to play a role; and legislative efforts aimed a encouraging adoption of a play-off system."

In fact, out of eighty-eight collegiate varsity championships, Division IA (or FBS) football[4] is the only one in which a winner is not determined through some kind of play-off-bracket system.

The BCS is attempting to fight back. In November 2009, it hired Ari Fleischer to do its promotional work. Fleischer jumped out of the gate proclaiming, "Opposing the BCS is easy—organizing a real play-off is really hard" and "Once people see both sides of the issue, they will see why the [BCS] system has its great support."[5] As we shall see, organizing a play-off system is straightforward, and, as someone should inform Fleischer, a 2009 *Sports Illustrated* poll found that 90 percent of college football fans do not support the BCS system.[6]

Historical Background

The Rose Bowl became the first college bowl game in 1902. It became a regular annual event in 1916. Most major bowl games have been in place since the 1930s.

College bowl games generally are organized and controlled by local chambers of commerce, convention and tourist bureaus, and assorted businesses. The bowl games' understood purpose is to generate business for the local economy, which they usually do to some extent, because the majority of attendees come from out of town.[7] The bowls have contracts with individual conferences that provide for conference champions, runners-up, or other designated teams to participate in the bowls each year. On behalf of the conferences, the participating schools get shares of the bowl revenue and, in turn, are obligated to purchase substantial blocks of tickets for the game, which they attempt to resell to their alumni, students, boosters, and others.

Under this system, historically each bowl did not know the quality of the teams it would be getting until the end of the season. The conference champion associated with a particular bowl may have had a relatively low national ranking, and the opposing team may have been no better. TV networks found themselves in the uncomfortable position of reserving a prime spot for a bowl and paying top rights fees yet facing the possible prospect of two teams ranked below the top ten going against each other. David Downs, senior vice president of ABC Sports, explained, "All of the networks were souring on the bowl business. We couldn't go one more cycle where we wake up on the 1st of December and find out that we have a bad matchup and that we were going to get hammered in the ratings."[8] Under the circumstance, selling ad spots for top dollar was next to impossible.

The other significant consequence of these arrangements was that it was next to impossible to structure a national championship. Between 1935 and 1991, the top two ranked teams met each other in a bowl game only eight times.[9] It would have had to have been a coincidence that the top two teams were in the two conferences playing in a given bowl game.

The first step to rectifying this commercially threatening situation was taken in 1991, when the Atlantic Coast (ACC), Big East, Big Eight, Southeastern (SEC), and Southwest conferences, along with Notre Dame, formed a bowl coalition with the prestigious college bowl committees of the IBM Fiesta Bowl, the Mobil Cotton Bowl, the USF&G Sugar Bowl, and the Federal Express Orange Bowl. Under the agreement, the Orange, Sugar, and Cotton bowls continued to be hosted by their affiliated conference champions, while the Fiesta Bowl had two open slots.

Although this coalition improved the chances of top, competitive matchups, it precluded contests between the number-one and number-two ranked teams if they came from the Big East (champion obligated to play in the Orange Bowl), the SEC (obligated to play in the Sugar Bowl), or the Southwest (obligated to play in the Cotton Bowl). Nonetheless, this arrangement did manage to produce "national championships" between the number-one and number-two ranked teams in 1992 and 1993. The other problem from the networks' point of view was that there was no guarantee that any of the individual bowls would be host to the top matchup. Selling advertising under these conditions remained problematic.

The next step was taken in 1994 with the formation of the Bowl Alliance. The Big East, the ACC, the Big 12 (a merger of the Big 8 with four teams from the Southwest), the SEC, and Notre Dame agreed to the following terms with the Orange, Sugar, and Fiesta bowls: The champions of the four conferences plus Notre Dame (unless the team had a losing season) and one other top-ranked school either from within or without the alliance would play in these three bowls; the traditional conference/bowl ties would be severed in the interest of maximizing the possibility of having a national championship;[10] and, the highest ranked game each year would rotate among the Orange, Sugar, and Fiesta bowls. Because the bowls would share the championship game, advertisers were assured of the top matchup at least one out of every three years.

From the perspective of the Bowl Alliance conferences, there was still one missing piece. The champions of the Big Ten and Pac-10 conferences had been matched in the Rose Bowl for over fifty years. Moreover, teams from these conferences were often ranked either first or second in the nation. Without the Big Ten and Pac-10, the alliance goal to offer a national championship game every year was elusive.

In June 1996, the alliance struck a deal with the Big Ten, the Pac-10, the Rose Bowl, and ABC (which had broadcasting rights to the Rose Bowl). Beginning with the 1998–1999 season, the national championship game would rotate among the four bowls, and ABC would have broadcast rights for all four games over a seven-year period (for which the network paid an estimated $700 million, or $25 million per game, which was roughly 2.5 times the average 1996 rights fees for the four games).[11] The teams for the national championship initially were picked on the basis of the *USA Today*/ESPN coaches' poll and the AP media poll, the average of three computer rankings (*Seattle Times, New York Times,* and Jeff Sagarin), team records, and a strength-of-schedule index. The new scheme was initially known as the Super Alliance but eventually came to be called the Bowl Championship Series.

What was good news for the BCS was bad news for virtually all the other bowl games and the non-BCS conferences in Division IA. As the four BCS bowl games came increasingly to be associated with a national championship, interest in the other bowls waned. Accordingly, TV ratings and attendance for the other bowl games have suffered.

Although many fans welcomed the heightened prospect of a national championship game in college football, the Super Alliance came under sharp attack and close scrutiny from many observers. Senator Mitch McConnell (R-Kentucky), for instance, was concerned that his home state school, the University of Louisville, was being excluded from a reasonable opportunity to participate in the most prestigious and lucrative bowl games. The University of Louisville belonged to the Conference USA (C-USA), which, along with three other Division IA conferences[12] and eleven independents at the time, was not invited to join the Bowl Alliance. Senator McConnell first raised the issue in 1993, when Louisville had a 7–1 record and a top ranking but was automatically excluded from the leading bowls. The DOJ commenced an inquiry, and the alliance agreed to open up for consideration two of the six alliance bowl slots "to any team in the country with a minimum of eight wins *or* ranked higher than the lowest-ranked conference champion from among the champions of the ACC, Big East, Big 12, and SEC."

This new, "more open" policy was put to the test in 1996–1997. Brigham Young University's (BYU's) football team, from the Western Athletic Conference (WAC), met *both* the alliance criteria, compiling a 13–1 record and earning a no. 5 ranking nationally, yet it was not invited to any of the alliance bowls. BYU's record and ranking were superior to that of nearly every alliance team that went to an alliance bowl that year, including Penn State (11–2 record and number-seven ranking), Texas (8–5 and number-twenty ranking), Virginia Tech (10–2 and number-thirteen ranking), and Nebraska (11–2 and number-six ranking).[13]

The BCS, instead of promoting the highest level of postseason competition, seemed to be promoting the economic fortunes of its members and the college bowls, to the exclusion and detriment of other Division IA schools. The bowl committees continued to prefer to host universities with large, spendthrift student bodies and alumni. BYU is from the sparsely populated state of Utah (bad for TV ratings), and its students and alumni have the reputation of frugality and sobriety. Senator Bob Bennett (R-Utah) stated before the May 1997 U.S. Senate hearing on the Bowl Alliance: "BYU does not travel well. I'll be very blunt. There is a perception out there, and it may be true, that [BYU fans] do not drink and party the way the host city would prefer. Our football coach has been quoted as saying that BYU fans travel with a $50 bill and the Ten Commandments in their pocket, and they leave without breaking either one."[14] Bowl host committees preferred teams from larger, wealthier, and wilder states.[15]

As the ongoing inequities in the system were revealed and challenged politically, the BCS administrators modified the plan. Between 1998 and 2008, the BCS selection process became incrementally more open and the revenue distribution marginally less unequal. Thus, the system to date has avoided legal challenges or congressional action. Nevertheless, the BCS system remains fundamentally closed and acutely unequal, as the ensuing discussion details.

The Functioning of the Bowl System

Beyond the BCS, of course, there is a plethora of postseason bowl games. Indeed, there has been a steady proliferation of bowl games since the 1930s, as Table 3.1 shows.

Thirty-four games mean that 68 of the 119 Division IA (FBS) teams, or 57.1 percent, play in a postseason bowl game. It is not a very selective club.

Outside the BCS bowls, schools usually lose money by playing in bowl games. Participating teams receive as little as $180,000 before

TABLE 3.1 Number of post-season bowl games

Year	Number
1930	1
1940	4
1950	8
1960	8
1970	11
1980	15
1990	19
2000	25
2009	34

expenses for some lesser bowls.[16] Including travel and per diem for the team, marching band, cheerleaders, administrators, boosters, guaranteed seat purchases (which can vary from ten thousand to fifteen thousand tickets), a school can quickly drop a million dollars to play in a bowl game.

The experience of Rutgers University in the 2008–2009 Papa Johns.com Bowl is illustrative. Rutgers received $1.188 million for its participation. It incurred the following costs: $282,610 for transportation for 205 players and staff (average cost $1,379); $165,799 for transportation for 187 marching band members and cheerleaders (average cost $887); $28,950 for transportation for 21 executives and administrators (average cost $1,379); $168,424 for six days' meals and lodging for team and staff ($137 per person per day); $34,724 for three days' meals and lodging for band members and cheerleaders ($62 per person per day); $60,186 for six days for executives and administrators ($478 per person per day!); $217,651 for entertainment, promotion, and miscellaneous; $214,000 outlay for ticket guarantees (the school had to guarantee 10,000 ticket sales, of which 5,350 the school had to pay for); and $268,365 for bonuses for football coaches and staff for making a bowl game. Thus, the net cost to Rutgers from playing in this bowl game was $252,709. And Rutgers scaled back in 2008–2009, because a public scandal erupted about athletic department excesses the previous year.

With this kind of potential financial loss, it is sensible to ask: Why do colleges accept invitations to the lesser bowls? The explanation may lie along the following lines. First, the perception exists that bowl participation and national television coverage will help the football coach recruit future players. Whether this is true for top-rated talent is an empirical question, but it seems unlikely to be true for any but the BCS games. It may, though, aid in the recruitment of the second tier of high school players. Given the low television ratings of the non-BCS bowls, any such advantage derived may be due more to avoiding the dishonor of not going to a postseason bowl game than the purported glory of going. Second, a perception may exist that the exposure of a bowl game helps recruit prospective students. Some evidence shows that football success can increase applications to a school, but any such increase does not lead to an increase in the SAT scores or class rank of the entering class. This is because students who apply to a school because it has a good football team do not tend to score highly on entrance exams or rank highly in their high school class. Further, it is not clear that being in a non-BCS bowl game qualifies as perceived success. Third, for some bowl games, the college may have a historical relationship with the local bowl organizing committee that is important to the college. Participating in the bowl game may be seen as helping preserve this relationship. This is particularly true at the conference level. Fourth, when a conference team goes to a bowl game, it produces revenue for the conference, which is then distributed to the conference schools. These schools experience no direct cost from the bowl, so they experience a (modest) net revenue gain. Many conferences, therefore, require their schools to accept bowl invitations. Fifth, going to a bowl game is a reward to the players on the team. Sixth, NCAA rules limit practice time for teams. Participating in a bowl game gives the coach extra practice time to work with his players, most of whom will return the next year. Finally, the top administrators and governors of the school may enjoy the weather, the parties, the ambience, and the competition of the bowl games, and the hope always persists that the wining and dining will induce some boosters or state legislators to reach deeper into their pockets or the state's coffers.

The Skewed Economics of the BCS

Although the BCS has edged toward more inclusiveness since 1998, the selection criteria of the elite bowl system today remain significantly skewed. Beginning with the 2006–2007 season, a fifth BCS bowl was added—the self-proclaimed national championship, which would be played between the number-one and number-two ranked teams, according to a BCS-established formula. The venue for this game would be rotated among the existing four BCS bowls. The existing BCS bowls would continue on the same basis; that is, the champions of the six BCS conferences (ACC, Big East, Big Ten, Big 12, Pac-10, and SEC) would have automatic berths.[17] The teams from the five non-BCS conferences in the FBS (C-USA, the Mid-American Conference, the Mountain West Conference (MWC), the Sun Belt Conference, and the WAC) can earn an automatic berth if (a) the team ranks in the top twelve of the final BCS standings, or (b) the team ranks in the top sixteen of the final BCS standings and its ranking is higher than that of the champion of one of the BCS conferences. However, no more than one team from a non-BCS conference can earn an automatic berth in any given year. That is, no automatic berth is available for a second non-BCS team.[18]

The BCS bowls are not only the most prestigious; they are the most lucrative. BCS conference teams that appeared in one of the five BCS games in 2008–2009 took home $18.6 million to their conferences. A non-BCS conference with a school in a BCS bowl received only $9.8 million in 2008–2009.[19] Because the six BCS conferences are guaranteed at least one participant in the series, they were guaranteed at least $18.6 million (on average this comes to $1.62 million per school guaranteed).[20] If one of the six BCS conferences had a second team in a BCS game, then it received $4.5 million for the second team.[21] Overall, during the first eleven years of the BCS system, bowls have included ninety appearances by BCS conference teams and only four appearances by non-BCS conference teams, three of which occurred during 2007–2009. During 2007–2009, total payouts from the BCS bowls have amounted to $410.1 million, of which $355.1 million (or 86.6 percent) has gone to BCS conferences.[22]

In addition to the BCS payouts, the BCS conferences have numerous tie-ins (guaranteed appearances) with other bowls: The SEC has a total of nine bowl ties, as do the ACC and Big 12, while the Big Ten and Pac-10 each have seven tie-ins. Overall, in 2008–2009, forty-four BCS teams (including Notre Dame) and twenty-four non-BCS teams played in postseason bowl games.[23] Significantly, the total payout from the twenty-nine non-BCS bowls in 2008–2009 was $82.6 million (an average of $2.8 million per game, or $1.4 million per participating team), while the total payout from the five BCS bowls was

$142 million (an average of $28.4 million per game, or $14.2 million per team). The total payout from all bowl games in 2008–2009 was $224.6 million, of which $187.7 million (or 83.6 percent) went to the BCS schools.[24]

Although the incremental reforms to the BCS selection process have allowed the BCS conferences to allege that their system is open to all, the outcomes in participation and in revenue bear no resemblance to an open system. Given that the BCS conferences with 54.6 percent of the FBS teams receive approximately 87 percent of the BCS revenues, it is hardly surprising that the BCS teams are able to maintain their competitive superiority. The revenues are used to build the biggest and best facilities, to provide the best academic support networks, to hire the most renowned coaches, and to conduct the most extensive and expensive recruitment drives.

The postseason revenue advantage for the BCS schools is thereby extended to a regular-season revenue advantage. Among other things, the BCS schools play in larger stadiums; this, together with their greater prestige, enables them to make the case that when they play non-BCS schools during the regular season, they should not play home-and-home schedules. Rather, they play disproportionately at the BCS teams' home fields. The non-BCS teams receive modest guarantee fees, and the BCS teams retain the lion's share of the gate, concessions, catering, signage, and parking revenue from the games. In fact, between the 2002–2003 and 2008–2009 seasons, 80.7 percent of the 751 games between BCS and non-BCS teams were played on the BCS fields.[25]

The inequality is further aggravated by the presence of a clear home-field advantage. In the 570 regular-season matchups between BCS and non-BCS teams from 2002–2003 to 2008–2009 that were played at the BCS home fields, the BCS won 493 for a .865 winning percentage. In the 181 matchups played at the non-BCS home fields during this period, the BCS won 113 for a .624 winning percentage.[26] Thus, despite the occasional superlative performance of a standout team (e.g., the regular-season records of Tulane [11–0 in 1998], Boise State [12–0 in 2006], Hawaii [12–0 in 2007], Utah [12–0 in 2008], plus a decisive BCS bowl victory against Alabama),[27] the prejudicial selection and revenue rules of the BCS appear to be bifurcating the FBS subdivision of Division I and engendering a caste system.

The BCS Defense of Its System

SEC Commissioner Mike Slive was asked about the possibility of a play-off system replacing the BCS. As published on FOX's BCS Web site, Slive's response was: "There really is no interest exhibited presently by our presidents or chancellors or many others in having a play-off. I try to think about it in terms of, 'What is in the best interest of college football?' I think three principles need to be applied. One is that college football is part of higher education, part of the academic mission of our institutions, and that's an important piece of the puzzle that's always going to be there. Two, football has a wonderful regular season, an exciting regular season that's maybe the best regular season of all sports. Three, we've had a wonderful 100-year relationship with the bowl system. So the postseason has to meld those three systems into something that is good for college football."[28]

Slive's three-part explanation is the standard defense. The first point is that if the FBS went to a play-off system, it would interfere with the integrity of the educational process. Presumably, the substance behind this point is that if there were an eight-team play-off, then some schools would have to play two additional games in January beyond what they play in the current arrangement, or three additional games if there were a sixteen-game play-off. Adding more games to the season would require more time away from classes for the football student-athletes.

The second point is that introducing a play-off system would undermine the integrity of the regular season. Here the substance is less apparent, but the reasoning goes something like this: In a play-off system, a school might qualify for a berth before it completed its season; in the present bowl system, qualification for the national championship game depends on a school's performance in all its games, via the BCS rating system. In the case of qualification for the play-offs occurring before the season's end, the qualifying team may not make an all-out effort to win in its last game. It is asserted that this would be less likely to happen under the BCS arrangement.

The third point is that the bowl system offers unique tradition and historical value. A bowl culture has emerged around this system that works commercially as well as emotionally, and it would be risky to tinker with it.

Response to the BCS Rationale

The first point is frequently met with derision by BCS detractors. If the BCS conferences are concerned with the length of the playing season, why have they steadily added games over the past two decades? Most recently, a twelfth regular season game was added by the NCAA in 2005, and many conferences have introduced conference championship games. Further, any additional games likely would be played during the Christmas and interterm break. If the BCS conferences are willing to let their basketball teams top off the hoops season with a sixty-five-team play-off in March, during the academic semester, how can they credibly argue that they are holding back the further commercialization of football to preserve academic integrity? Finally, the Football Championship Subdivision (FCS; formerly Division IAA), Division II, and Division III football all have postseason play-offs, some with sixteen teams, as do all other NCAA championship sports. It is nonsensical to pretend that the FBS (Division IA) should be any different, particularly when the national championship is at stake.

The integrity of the regular-season argument may contain a grain of truth; that is, over time it may turn out that there will be a few more games at the end of the season during which one of the teams is not making a full effort under a play-off system. It may also not be true. Among other things, it would depend on the play-off selection process. For instance, if the winners of the eleven FBS conferences with the eight best records (against FBS schools) were chosen, then there would be no reason for such an effect. Additionally, if the play-off seeding system depended on the entire regular season, the probability of any slacking off during the last game would be minimized. The larger point, however, is that opening the championship game and the other BCS bowls equally to all FBS schools or, a fortiori, developing an eight-team play-off would vastly increase the number of regular season games that are meaningful.[29]

A corollary to this argument is that the BCS would never produce significant postseason anomalies, such as that occurring in the NFL in 2008–2009 when the Arizona Cardinals, with nine wins and seven losses, made it all the way to the Super Bowl. Doubtless, this is true. No 9–7 team would ever make it to a BCS bowl. Yet one must recall that the philosophy of postseason competition in the NFL is cast differently. The NFL wants to maintain as much excitement in the regular season as long as possible, so it takes both division winners and wild cards into the play-offs. In all, the NFL admits twelve of its thirty-two teams (37.5 percent) in the postseason chase to the championship. NFL fans do not complain that the regular season loses integrity. In fact, as we shall see, a different kind of integrity emerges. The BCS currently accepts 10 of the 119 FBS teams (8.4 percent). Further, the NFL postseason deliberately seeks a geographical spread in its team selection, something that is not an explicit concern or necessary outcome of the BCS process.

Either way, the response to this concern is clear and compelling: The same problem inheres to all U.S. professional and college team sports, and in all other cases the leagues and the fans have shown clear preferences for the play-off system. One does not hear NFL fans calling for a one-game championship, with team selection based on a numerical ranking system, to replace the current multitiered play-off system, thus avoiding the possibility that a first-place team would not make a full effort during its last game.

The argument about the tradition of bowl games is rarely fleshed out. The most persuasive explanation I have heard goes something like this: The current bowl system includes a one-week, one-venue postseason. This enables students, boosters, and other fans to make one trip to one Southern city during the Christmas and interterm break. They usually make a several-day or week-long vacation out of the trip and hang out with their fellow students and fans. It is a bonding and fun experience. The host city of the bowl game, in turn, fills its hotel rooms, bars, and restaurants, and it is thought to provide a significant economic benefit to local businesses. The business community returns the favor by providing perquisites and comforts to conference and college administrators.[30] College presidents, trustees, and their families all have a grand time in the warm climate. Such is the unique tradition of college bowl games. Why would any beneficiary school or conference want to share this privilege?

The explanation continues that, in a play-off system, if your team is successful in round one, then it plays a second game in a new venue the next week. One cannot reasonably expect the entourage of students, boosters, fans, and administrators to repeat their spending sprees from the first week. And the logic extends with greater force to the third and possible fourth (in a sixteen-team play-off) week. The host cities do not reap the same bonanza, and the special quality of week one is diluted.

The reasoning here appears sound—the culture of the bowl games probably would change somewhat. BCS detractors, though, see little reason to hold a play-off system hostage to this peculiar cultural tradition. Under a play-off system, students, boosters, fans, and administrators could choose how many and which games to attend. They could still plan a festive vacation at the site of the first-round game. Bowl cities could remain the hosts of the first-round games[31] and possibly subsequent-round games as well.

A variant on the bowl-culture argument is that the twenty-nine non-BCS bowl games would suffer if the FBS adopted a play-off system. It is claimed that the number of such games may diminish substantially. The consequent output reduction, then, is held up as an antitrust defense of the BCS system.

The problem with this argument is twofold. First, the proper output metric is not the number of games but the number of fans consuming these games and the quantity of money spent in this consumption. There are very good reasons to believe (discussed below) that total bowl consumption and spending will increase under a play-off system. Second, it is not clear that there would be a substantial reduction in the number of non-BCS bowls. These bowls today are universally regarded as secondary or tertiary in importance. On a per-game basis, the non-BCS bowls have an average payout that is less than one-tenth the payout of BCS bowls. The same forces that cause these lower-tier bowl games to be produced today would continue to exist under a play-off system.[32]

If the three proffered defenses are unavailing, then the question remains: Why do the BCS conferences cling to the system? The answer is simple: money. The BCS functions largely as a de facto College Football Association (CFA),[33] the short-lived organization of the equity conferences in the late 1970s and early 1980s that threatened to withdraw from the NCAA and strike its own national television deal. The CFA did not want to share its revenue-generating potential with the other Division IA conferences, much less the rest of the NCAA. The BCS provides a structure that guarantees top bowl appearances, guarantees $18 million per BCS conference, and guarantees the privileged relationship with host cities. The BCS conferences share roughly 13 percent of BCS revenue with non-BCS schools.[34] The rest is theirs. If the NCAA organized a play-off for the national championship, as it does with its other championship sports, the generated revenue, in all likelihood, would be shared equally within Division IA (FBS), more fully within the rest of Division I, and with a standard share going to Division II (4.37 percent) and Division III (3.18 percent). More on this below.

Critique of the BCS Ranking System

When the BCS ranking system was first introduced in 1997, it contained four distinct elements that were then averaged to produce the overall rankings. Since that time, the system has been changed in one way or another at least seven times.[35] The BCS likes the public to believe that these tweaks are part of perfecting the system. The reality appears to be rather different. The changes seem to respond to political pressure, mostly from BCS coaches, and to have done nothing to make the rankings more statistically robust.

The use of computer rankings gives the appearance of a scientific selection process. The truth is that the computer rankings are only as good as the human instructions that are inputted into the computer. In this sense, computers are like transportation vehicles: If I am driving from New York to Boston, and I end up in Middlebury, Vermont, I could not persuasively blame my car.

The BCS computer rankings lack conceptual clarity. The BCS has never made it clear what it is that they want the computer rankings to do. Do they want them to (a) measure each team's accomplishments (e.g., whom they played and whom they beat), (b) predict the probability of each team winning going forward, (c) weigh equally early-season and late-season victories, (d) give greater weight to recent performance of the teams, (e) award teams for their consistency, (f) give greater recognition to a team's dominance, and so forth? The BCS has never publicly discussed nor identified these possible desiderata. In economists' jargon, if an objective function is not specified, then maximization makes no sense.

The lack of conceptual clarity is then aggravated by the periodic shifts in the formula. Notably, in 2000, as in many years, the first choice for the national championship game was obvious; the second choice was ambiguous and hotly disputed. Oklahoma got the first nod. The BCS system selected once-beaten Florida State, even though Florida State had lost to once-beaten Miami during the season. Miami, in turn, had lost to once-beaten Washington. Had the quality-win bonus been in effect in 2000, then Miami, which won out in the coaches' poll, would have been selected over Florida State. Not surprisingly, the quality-win bonus was introduced in 2001—and has since been dropped. A similar conundrum presented itself in 2001, this time between selecting Nebraska or Oregon to play the manifest choice, Miami. Once-beaten Nebraska was chosen over once-beaten Oregon, even though Nebraska was solidly defeated in its last regular season game and was not even the Big 12 champion. The popular perception was that the computer rankings gave too much weight to Nebraska's large margin of victory in its early-season games. The BCS commissioners decided to expunge margin of victory as an element in the formula from 2002 forward.[36]

We have here an arbitrary decision and a statistical curiosity. To be sure, there is an issue of good sportsmanship, and no one wants to encourage teams to run up the score when facing weak opponents. However, the BCS has mandated that margin of victory cannot enter the equation at all, so a 20–17 win has to be treated as identical to a 30–10 win. This is throwing away valuable information. It would make more sense to truncate the margin of victory at, say, twenty points, so a 49–10 win was treated the same as a 30–10 win, than to not consider it a matter of irrelevance whether a team wins by twenty or three points.

Interestingly, the suppression of the margin of victory interacts with another feature of FBS scheduling to further tilt the scales against teams in non-BCS conferences. Each year, teams self-schedule their out-of-conference contests. Non-BCS schools attempt to set up games with the strongest possible BCS teams to improve their chances to move up in the BCS rankings. BCS schools generally refuse to schedule home-and-home games with non-BCS schools. Thus, non-BCS schools first face the competitive disadvantage of having to play more away games against BCS opponents. They then face a second disadvantage, because the top BCS schools have little incentive to play the top non-BCS schools and risk a defeat against a lower-ranked non-BCS team. Thus, for instance, the athletic director at Boise State, Gene Bleymaier, reported having a next-to-impossible time attempting to schedule a contest against a BCS opponent for 2011. Bleymaier said he was turned away repeatedly by schools that had open dates on their schedule.[37]

One outcome of this pattern is that the top non-BCS schools end up with a weak strength-of-schedule score. They would be able to (at least partially) compensate for their weaker schedules by running up larger margins of victory, but this has been precluded by the BCS rule that suppresses margin of victory as a ranking criterion.

The BCS has also decided that the site of a game cannot enter into the formula. This stricture appears to be little more than intellectual stubbornness, at best, and obscurantism, at worst. Clear evidence, some of it presented above, shows that there is a decided home team advantage in college football. Statistician David Harville has estimated this advantage to be approximately four points per game.[38] If college football fans are to be stuck with the BCS system to determine the national championship, the least the BCS could do is devise a less politically driven and more statistically robust ranking system.

Finally, the coaches' poll and the AP poll themselves have been subjected to sharp criticism. The fundamental concern with the coaches' poll is that coaches have a potential conflict of interest when they cast their votes. They also see a small number of the eligible schools in action, so questions arise about the empirical basis upon which coaches form their evaluations. Many voters appear to believe that the non-BCS conferences are inherently inferior, making it less likely that they support schools outside the equity conferences regardless of their performances.[39] One study found that voters in human polls favor teams that appear more often on national television—another factor favoring BCS schools.[40] Evidence also exists of a bias toward teams that coaches have observed firsthand. Similar problems exist with the AP poll, which surveys sixty-five sportswriters and broadcasters, sixty-one of whom represent local newspapers, television stations, and radio stations. A 2010 study found significant bias favoring local teams, schools from equity (automatic qualifying) conferences, and teams appearing more frequently on national television.[41]

Antitrust Considerations

Does the BCS violate U.S. antitrust laws, and is it vulnerable to an antitrust challenge? As anyone familiar with the record of antitrust litigation in this country knows, there is always substantial uncertainty in such matters. Part of the uncertainty results from the merits of the case, but a significant part of it results from the venue of the challenge, the judge and the jury selected, and the skills of the lawyers bringing the case. It seems that these subjective elements become particularly prominent in antitrust matters.[42]

A good place to begin to assess the antitrust substance involved is with the 1984 Supreme Court decision in *Board of Trustees of the University of Oklahoma v. NCAA.* In this landmark case, the University of Oklahoma sued the NCAA over its national TV contract, in which the NCAA limited the number of appearances on national television to a maximum of three for any team and arranged for each participant to receive the same payment, whether it was a popular game, such as Oklahoma playing Michigan, or an obscure game, such as Appalachian State playing Temple. The decision in this case against the NCAA established much of the relevant jurisprudence for understanding the antitrust treatment of college sports.

First, the Supreme Court made clear that horizontal restraints on output (and price) are condemned. Second, the Court found that "the NCAA creates a price structure that is unresponsive to viewer demand."[43] The Court further stipulated that "a restraint that has the effect of reducing the importance of consumer preference in setting price and output is not consistent with this fundamental goal of antitrust law."[44] The Court concluded, "Today we hold only that the record supports the District Court's conclusion that, *by curtailing output and blunting the ability of member institutions to respond to consumer preference,* the NCAA has restricted, rather than enhanced, the place of intercollegiate athletics in the Nation's life"[45] (emphasis mine).

As it pertains to the BCS, these are the key precepts from the 1984 decision. They lead to the following fundamental question: Can it be shown that there is a horizontal combination that restricts output, distorts prices, and drives resource allocation away from maximizing consumer welfare?

That there is a horizontal combination among the sixty-five BCS schools is not in question. The only question is whether this combination is incidental and necessary to developing a national championship, and, if it is, whether it is the least restrictive form this combination can take. Let us consider these various elements in turn.

Does the BCS create a reduction in output? The answer here depends on to what the BCS is compared. If it is compared to an eight- or sixteen-team play-off system, it seems manifest that there is a reduction in output. The only issues here are (a) whether the extension of the postseason into January for a minority of teams would compel a reduction of regular-season games by one and (b) whether the total eyeballs watching and the total revenue generated by the postseason would increase. The first issue would become irrelevant either if no regular-season reduction in the number of games occurred or if the market were defined to include only competition for the national championship. The latter appears plausible, given the 1959 Supreme Court decision in *International Boxing v. United States,* which ruled that championship fights are a separate market from nonchampionship fights because of the huge payout differential.

The second issue is empirical, but a priori does not appear to be a serious concern. Many television industry mavens have estimated substantial growth in rights fees by a move to either an eight- or sixteen-game play-off from the current BCS arrangement. Depending on the play-off system, a doubling or more of television revenue is often estimated.[46] Indeed, in testimony before the House Subcommittee on Commerce, Trade, and Consumer Protection on December 7, 2005, Jim Delaney, the commissioner of the Big Ten conference, stated:

I am absolutely sure that an NFL-style football play-off would provide maybe three or four times as many dollars to the Big Ten than the present system does. In fact, a number of corporations have come forward and tried to lure us into a play-off with those kinds of dollars. There is no doubt in my mind that we are leaving hundreds of millions of dollars on the table for the reasons that have been expressed here around this table, so there is more money out there, and we have turned our back, we don't get very much credit.

If the play-off were effectively organized, it seems that the only practical question would not be whether it attracted more eyeballs and created more revenue but whether, given the diminished share of the overall take going to the BCS schools, it generated more net revenue for the BCS schools.

The BCS response to this argument would probably be that the wrong standard is being applied. The BCS should not be compared to some future hypothetical play-off system but rather to the system that prevailed prior to the organization of the BCS. Prior to 1992, there was no national championship game, and the top two ranked teams rarely played each other at season's end. The BCS precursors (the Bowl Coalition and the Bowl Alliance) improved on this situation, and the BCS added the Pac-10 and Big Ten into the mix, giving still greater legitimacy to the national championship. Since that time, the BCS has made it marginally easier for non-BCS schools to play in a BCS bowl. Hence, the BCS can argue that each step it has taken has been toward opening competition rather than shutting it down. From this perspective, the BCS is procompetitive.

This is a substantial argument. Yet the previous system was itself a network of exclusive dealing contracts that also probably violated the antitrust laws, so going from one anticompetitive system to another does not make the latter procompetitive.[47]

The question remains whether the BCS is engaging in ongoing exclusionary acts to curtail greater competition. At least five antitrust claims might be advanced against the BCS in this regard. The first is a Section 1 claim of unlawful boycott or concerted refusal to deal— that is, a collective action by a group of competitors for the purpose of excluding or otherwise interfering with a potential competitor's access to the market in which they compete. For such a claim to prevail, the plaintiff must prove harm to competition and consumer welfare, not just harm to an individual competitor. The second is a Section 2, or attempt to monopolize, claim. Given the Supreme Court's finding in *International Boxing v. United States,* the case could be made that the BCS is monopolizing or attempting to monopolize the market of college championship football. Here, the argument could be that the BCS conferences are allowing access to the market, but they are not doing it in an objective, nondiscriminatory manner. As such, they have the specific intent to exercise monopoly control over this market and are doing so by an exclusionary act rather than by superior economic management. The third claim is related and usually represents a more problematic legal path to pursue. It could be argued that the BCS is an essential facility, and without fair access to the facility, it is impossible for potential competitors to enter the market.[48]

The fourth claim might be challenging the rule that limits the non-BCS conferences to one automatic appearance in a BCS bowl as a restraint of trade. Such a rule produces inferior BCS matchups if the second non-BCS school is stronger than one of the selected BCS teams. For instance, in 2008–2009, undefeated Utah did not have a chance to compete for the national championship, while undefeated Boise State did not have a chance to compete in any BCS bowl game, despite the fact that it ranked higher nationally (ninth) than Ohio State (tenth), Cincinnati (twelfth), or Virginia Tech (nineteenth). The latter three schools, with two, two, and four regular-season losses, respectively, all appeared in BCS bowl games, because they belong to BCS conferences.

Finally, the BCS may also be vulnerable to claims of price fixing. Each of the five BCS bowl games, including the national championship, carries the same payout to the participating BCS conference teams. This is so despite the fact that the national championship game regularly has the strongest ratings by a healthy margin, and some of the remaining BCS games have considerably higher ratings than others; the payout is identical to all bowls, regardless of ratings or attendance.[49] The only exception is that non-BCS conference teams are subjected to discriminatory price fixing. For instance, as a result of Utah's BCS bowl appearance in 2008–2009, the MWC received only $9.8 million, while the Big East, the ACC, and the Pac-10, each with one team in a BCS bowl, received $18.6 million. This is not a market outcome.

One sometimes hears the claim that nothing is stopping the NCAA or the non-BCS conferences from organizing their own championships. Unlike in the *MIBA v. NCAA* case, where the National

Invitational Tournament (NIT) blamed its inability to attract top teams to its postseason tournament at Madison Square Garden on an NCAA rule that obligated member colleges to play in the association's March Madness tournament if selected, Division I teams are not required by the NCAA to play in the BCS if selected.[50] Similarly, coercion was involved in the *Board of Regents v. NCAA* case, because the NCAA threatened CFA schools with retaliation if they went ahead with their own TV contracts. The NCAA further stipulated that any retaliation would not be limited to the schools' football programs.[51]

Yet this defense of the BCS is unavailing. In fact, the BCS does require its schools to participate in the bowl games for which they are selected, making it next to impossible for a rival competition for the national championship to be established.

The question remains of whether less-restrictive alternatives are available to the current BCS system. It seems there are several compelling, less-restrictive alternatives. The most obvious is to have the NCAA run a national championship tournament, as it does in basketball and in Division IAA (FCS), Division II, and Division III football, among play-offs in all its other championship sports.[52] The Division III championship, for instance, began in 1973 as a single-elimination tournament with four teams. It became an eight-team single-elimination tournament in 1975, and the current format has sixteen teams. Division IAA also has a sixteen-team play-off. Another option would be to reform the BCS into an eight-team play-off that opened more automatic berths to today's non-BCS conferences, along the lines proposed by the MWC in early March 2009. The MWC proposal, inter alia, calls for any of the non-BCS conferences that maintain .400 or better win percentages in interconference games against schools from the current BCS conferences to receive automatic berths.[53]

The foregoing discussion makes clear that substantial antitrust concerns exist, but so does the basis for a viable legal defense by the BCS. The outcome of a rule of reason case would be far from certain.[54] It is also a valid question to ask whether it is likely that a legitimate plaintiff will emerge. The non-BCS conferences and schools have shown no inclination to jump into the fray. Any antitrust battle would be protracted, risky, and expensive. Because past damages may be difficult to establish, even a legal victory might result in an injunction rather than a payment of triple damages. Moreover, there is a high degree of mobility among coaches and administrators, so any high-level actor would be reluctant to promote a legal challenge when it might restrict his or her future career opportunities.

Certainly, state attorneys general can threaten to sue, but such efforts have not proceeded to court and are more likely public relations displays of frustration, holding out for the possibility that the BCS will throw a few more crumbs to the non-BCS conferences. To be sure, the suit threatened by the Utah attorney general (along with persistent pestering from Utah Senator Orrin Hatch) may have been one of the Pac-10's motivations when it included the University of Utah, along with the University of Colorado, in its June 2010 expansion. The Federal Trade Commission has no jurisdiction over the nonprofit sector, which leaves the Antitrust Division of the DOJ as the only hope at the national level. Although the Antitrust Division has looked into this matter in the past, it has never decided to prosecute. Gary Roberts suggested that there have been strong political pressures on the DOJ not to tinker with the elite bowl system.[55] It is possible, however, with President Obama's critical attitude toward the BCS that this dynamic might shift. However, depending on the path that the 2010 merger and acquisition movement among FBS conferences takes, the political pressure to break open the BCS and to create a play-off system may be largely dissipated.

Pursuing Legislation, Not Litigation

The evolving jurisprudence on antitrust has made the pursuit of litigation increasingly difficult and enormously costly. The problematic antitrust landscape is compounded by the schizophrenic existence of college sports. The NCAA and its members have been successful in being legal chameleons—depending on the exigencies at hand, they appear either purveyors of an extracurricular educational activity or sellers of big-time sports entertainment. With this confusion, the law has often given college sports a pass, no doubt because big-time college sports are so popular with the public, making radical change of the status quo politically unacceptable to most courts. Until now, attacking the BCS has also been too politically perilous for most legislators, but the new administration may embolden a few key members of Congress to awaken from their slumber.

It seems apparent that the NCAA will not be motivated to initiate a plan for a postseason play-off. Indeed, former NCAA President Myles Brand stated that the NCAA has no interest in a postseason FBS play-off. The BCS conferences dominate the association's governing structure. For instance, even though the sixty-five BCS schools represent less than 7 percent of the NCAA's membership, they occupy five of the eighteen seats (28 percent) of the seats on the association-wide Executive Committee, and even though the BCS schools compose less than 20 percent of the Division I membership, they hold six of the eighteen (33 percent) seats on the Division I Board of Directors.[56] Beyond this, the BCS schools represent the commercial and revenue-generating might of the NCAA. If the NCAA attempts to compete with the BCS conferences via a postseason football play-off for the national title, the expectation is that the BCS conferences would withdraw from the NCAA. This would effectively undermine the NCAA's power in intercollegiate sports. Therefore, the NCAA would need exhortation, guidance, and support from the courts or Congress before it would organize a football play-off system.

Congress could address legislation to promote a football play-off in multiple ways. Perhaps the most direct would be to introduce legislation that withdraws the tax preferences for intercollegiate athletics,[57] if the NCAA does not initiate a championship play-off.

It might be helpful if such legislation also gave the NCAA a limited antitrust exemption so that it could require member schools, if selected, to participate in its play-off structure. The BCS conferences now require their schools to participate in bowls when selected. Mandatory participation requirements may be problematic, because they restrict potential competition. If one concludes, however, that the college football championship system constitutes a natural monopoly, then such a participation requirement would not be problematic.

Alternatively, the legislation could bypass the NCAA and set up a National Sports Commission. The commission could establish its own college football championship and perhaps fulfill other oversight functions in the sports world as well, including drug testing. After all, if sports leagues are natural monopolies, economic theory teaches us that it is more efficient to regulate them than to break them up.

The legislative details would be easy enough to work out, if Congress has the will to act. The central argument in this piece is that a true national championship in college football has been held hostage by a football cartel of the six equity conferences in the BCS. The argument for breaking apart this cartel is too compelling to leave to the caprices of our legal system and antitrust practice. A national football play-off would increase output, redirect output to be more responsive to college football fans across the country, give broader opportunity to football players throughout the FBS, and assert a commitment to the basic principles of fairness that inhere to the ideals of democratic governance.

Today, all FBS teams do not start out on a level playing field. They cannot have the experience of the Rice University baseball team, from the smallest FBS school in the country, which rose to win 2003 College World Series.

Bernie Machen has been the president of the University of Florida, a SEC/BCS school, since January 2004. Prior to this, he was president at the University of Utah, so he has seen the BCS debate up close from both perspectives. In February 2009, President Machen commented, "When I was at Utah, our athletics budget was around $20–$22 million per year. Our budget here is $84.5 million ... and the major difference is the bowl revenue and TV revenue. ... I don't think most people begrudge what we got because of being in the championship game, but all SEC schools got the same amount of money that we got. And Utah could beat a lot of SEC schools. That's the unfairness. I think that's got to be fixed one way or the other. One way to fix it would have been a play-off."[58]

Scott Cowen, the president of Tulane University, put it well in this testimony before the House Judiciary Committee in September 2003: "Our country is based on the idea of equal opportunity for all, and our educational institutions are dedicated today to the principles of access, inclusiveness, fairness, and consistency. It goes against everything we hold dear to allow—even encourage—a system that showers financial and reputational rewards on one member while unnecessarily denying or limiting the opportunity for another member to earn the same rewards."

4 Gender Equity in Intercollegiate Athletics

Economic Considerations and Possible Fixes

THIS ESSAY first briefly reviews the history of Title IX. It then considers ways that women's sports can continue to be promoted without reducing men's sports and without increasing athletic budgets.

Title IX is about gender equity. It is a law that was passed in June 1972 as part of the educational amendments to the civil rights laws of the 1960s. The law simply states: "No person in the United States shall, on the basis of sex, be excluded from participation in, be denied the benefits of, or be subjected to discrimination under any education program or activity receiving federal financial assistance." As such, it applies broadly to all educational programs and activities, not just athletics. Athletics stand out for a number of reasons, one of which is that almost all sports have gender-segregated teams.

Title IX encompasses a wide range of issues, including equity in facilities, equity in marketing and promotional resources, pay equity

This essay is based on "Gender Equity in Intercollegiate Athletics: Economic Considerations and Possible Solutions," in *Sports Economics,* ed. Leo Kahane and Stephen Shamske (New York: Oxford University Press, 2010).

TABLE 4.1   Female participation numbers

	1971	2007	Increase
High school sports	294,015	3.06 million	10.4×
College sports	31,852	166,800	5.2×

Source: Nancy Hogshead-Makar and Andrew Zimbalist, *Equal Play: Title IX and Social Change* (Philadelphia: Temple University Press, 2007), 2.

for coaches, equity in financial aid, retaliation against employees or students who speak out against discrimination, sexual harassment of female students and employees, and equity in travel and accommodations, among many others. Nonetheless, most of the public discussion around Title IX concentrates on the opportunities for athletic participation by female students. Simply put, without female participation in sports, most other forms of unequal treatment cannot occur.

One fact that stands out about Title IX is its enormous success (see Table 4.1). Let us take a step back and consider the history of Title IX.

Early Years

Prior to the emergence of the women's movement in the 1960s, female participation in organized sports was minimal. The prevailing ideology asserted that playing competitive sports was incompatible with women's reproductive roles and that women who played competitive sports risked being masculinized; frequently, it was claimed that these masculinized athletes must be homosexuals. Indeed, many leagues and organizations, including the Amateur Athletic Union, the All-American Girls Professional Baseball League, and the Ladies Professional Golf Association tour, found it necessary to promote the high percentage of its players who were married or looking for husbands as a way to combat this prejudice.

Attitudes began to change with the resurgent women's movement, catalyzed by the 1963 publication of Betty Friedan's *The Femi-*

nine Mystique. In 1967, the Commission on Intercollegiate Athletics for Women (CIAW) was formed with the goal "to give college women more opportunities for high level competition in athletics." The CIAW evolved into a permanent organization in 1972, the Association for Intercollegiate Athletics for Women (AIAW). At the time, the NCAA's policy still banned women from its championships. Throughout the 1970s, the AIAW effectively promoted and organized women's college sports under its own philosophy, which was based on the social and psychological value of athletic participation to women. This philosophy was encapsulated in the first clause of the AIAW policy statement, which stipulated: "The enrichment of the life of the participant is the focus and reason for the existence of any athletic program. All decisions should be made with this fact in mind." Insistent on keeping women's athletics as amateur activities, subordinate to academics, the AIAW adopted many policies, such as one that prohibited coaches from recruiting off campus. Student-athletes would try out for teams on campus, just as student thespians tried out for school plays and student musicians tried out for the orchestra.

Meanwhile, as women began to participate increasingly in sports, the emotional, social, and physiological benefits therein became more and more apparent. Research has shown, inter alia:

- High school girls who play sports are less likely to be involved in unwanted pregnancies, less likely to watch television, less likely to be overweight, more likely to have positive body images, more likely to get better grades in school, and more likely to graduate than girls who do not play sports.
- Girls involved in organized sports are less likely to smoke cigarettes or marijuana or to use recreational drugs; and the more teams they play on, the less likely they are to indulge in these habits.
- As few as four hours of exercise a week may reduce a teenage girl's risk of breast cancer by up to 60 percent; breast cancer is a disease that afflicts one out of every eight American women.

- 40 percent of women over the age of fifty suffer from osteo-porosis (brittle bones). Proper physical exercise is believed to lower the incidence.
- Girls and women who play sports have higher levels of confidence and self-esteem.
- Sports teach team work, discipline, goal setting, the pursuit of excellence in performance, and other achievement-oriented behaviors—critical skills necessary for success in the workplace. One study found that 80 percent of the female executives at Fortune 500 companies identified themselves as former "tomboys"—having played sports.[1]

The NCAA did not know what to make of the surge in women's athletics. Initially, being a men's organization, the association saw it as a threat to its domain. The NCAA spent most of the 1970s first lobbying in Congress and then fighting in the courts to clip the wings of women's college sports. The NCAA's first plan was to lobby Congress to remove the entire realm of intercollegiate athletics from coverage by Title IX. That having failed, the association then supported Senator John Tower's amendment to exempt the "revenue-producing" sports from Title IX. When that effort foundered, the NCAA in 1976 sued the U.S. Department of Health, Education, and Welfare (HEW)[2] over its regulations to implement Title IX. Among other things, the NCAA here claimed that athletic departments that did not directly receive federal subsidies should not be covered, even if the universities did. Having also lost in the courts, and given the rapid growth in women's sports and their popularity during the 1970s, the NCAA decided its next best option was to use its financial muscle to take over the administration of women's sports from the AIAW—which it did in 1982.

In 1979, the Office of Civil Rights (OCR) of the HEW issued what were to become the most controversial regulations regarding the implementation of Title IX. These regulations related to how to identify whether women were being discriminated against with regard to the level of women's sports participation relative to men's.

The goal of Title IX and these regulations was to promote equal opportunity for women, not necessarily equal outcome. These regulations included the infamous three-prong test. This test stipulated that to be in compliance, one of the following three criteria (or prongs) must be met:

▪ Opportunities for males and females must be substantially proportionate to their respective enrollments.
▪ Where one sex has been underrepresented, the program must show a history and continuing practice of program expansion responsive to the developing interests and abilities of that sex.
▪ Where one sex is underrepresented and the school cannot show a continuing practice of program expansion, it must be demonstrated that the interests and abilities of that sex have been fully and effectively accommodated by the existing program.

This three-pronged test has been litigated heavily, but its legality has been upheld by every one of the eight federal appeals courts that have considered it.[3]

The early success during the 1970s of Title IX led to a backlash. In 1981, the incoming Reagan administration cut funding for the Department of Education and took the position that Title IX should only apply to those departments within a university that received direct federal funding. This position was tested in the courts and upheld in the 1984 Supreme Court decision in the *Grove City College* case. Four years later, it was overturned by Congress with the Civil Rights Restoration Act. The administration of George Herbert Walker Bush showed little interest, however, in supporting Title IX implementation, and, by 1992, the share of women in all intercollegiate athletes leveled off at 32 percent, just 2 percentage points higher than a decade earlier (see Table 4.2).

Gains resumed under the Clinton administration, with women's share among intercollegiate athletes rising a full 10 percentage points, to 42.3 percent. Title IX's detractors, however, regrouped and made

TABLE 4.2 Share of women in intercollegiate athletics

1971–1972	15%
1981–1982	30%
1991–1992	32%
2001–2002	42.3%
2005–2006	42.8%
2007–2008	42.6%

Sources: Hogshead-Makar and Zimbalist, *Equal Play,* 3, 302–303; NCAA, *Sports Sponsorship and Participation Rate Report: 1981–82 to 2007–08,* April 2009.

hay during the two administrations of George W. Bush. The last available figures show the proportion of women in all NCAA athletes had risen by only three-tenths of a point to 42.6 percent by 2007–2008. Indeed, the October 2008 *Gender Equity Report* of the NCAA finds that there had even been backsliding in many areas during the Bush administration. For instance, in Division I, the share of all athletic spending going to women fell from 37 percent in 2003–2004 to 34 percent in 2005–2006.[4]

Rodney Paige, Bush's secretary of Education, established a "Commission on Opportunities in Athletics" with the purported role of making a balanced assessment of Title IX. However, the commission's composition and the selection of preponderantly anti–Title IX witnesses laid bare the intention of weakening the law. After a year and a half of "investigating," the commission came out with a series of recommendations, many of which would have set back gender equity in athletics (e.g., excluding walk-on athletes in the proportionality count or allowing relative interests to be determined solely by a survey of prospective or current students). After the commission's recommendations were made public, critical reaction was strong and persistent, leading Secretary Paige to assert that only recommendations that were supported unanimously by the commission's members would be adopted. Secretary Paige's pledge notwithstanding, following Bush's reelection in November 2004, the OCR issued a new clarification in March 2005 that stated that, henceforth, it would be acceptable for a school to do an e-mail survey of its current student body as the only evidence to ascertain whether the school was meeting prong three by fully and effectively accommodating the interests and abilities of the underrepresented sex. This stood in direct contradiction to the OCR's 1996 Clarification, which stipulated that several tests, such as high school participation in the sport, the existence of club sports, and the petition of students to add a sport, among others, should be used. Now an e-mail survey could stand as the sole determinant of students' interests. Ironically, the OCR itself was about to release a study that showed that between 2002 and 2006, student response rates to these surveys varied between 1 and 78 percent, and in more than two-thirds of the surveys, the response rate was below 40 percent. Further, the March 2005 Clarification indicates that nonresponses can be counted as "no interest." The Clarification says not a word about the OCR or any other body providing oversight to ensure that the surveys are properly designed and carried out. Both the NCAA and the U.S. Congress subsequently rejected the use of e-mail surveys as the sole determinant of relative athletic interests.

In this context, it should be underscored that in 2007, the number of women participating in intercollegiate sports was 160,800, while the number of girls participating in high school sports was 3.06 million. Thus, today, for every 100 girls playing high school sports, only 5.5 are playing in college. This is prima facie evidence that the interest and ability level is there to support continued growth in intercollegiate athletic opportunities for women.[5]

Despite tremendous outcry from Title IX detractors about OCR activism, just forty-four Title IX participation cases came before the OCR during the eight-year time frame 1992–2000. Further, no college has ever lost any funds for a violation of Title IX standards, despite OCR's being responsible for overseeing the athletic programs at more than 1,200 colleges and universities. Notably, between 2002 and 2006, out of the 416 complaints filed regarding Title IX's implementation, only 1 of these was initiated by the OCR.

The Bush administration also encouraged a suit brought by the National Wrestling Coaches Association. One of wrestling coaches' main claims was that Title IX had promoted the growth of women's participation at the expense of cutting men's teams. The evidence suggests otherwise. The greatest drop in the number of men's wrestling teams occurred between 1982 and 1992, from 363 to 275. These were years, as we saw above, when Title IX was virtually unenforced. Title IX cannot fairly be blamed for this drop. Also during this time period, the number of men's gymnastics teams decreased from seventy-nine to forty; men lost thirty-nine gymnastics teams, while women lost eighty-three gymnastics teams. Again, Title IX is not responsible. What, then, explains the drops in these sports? Men's allegiances have been shifting to football and soccer; and with both gymnastics and wrestling, there have been growing college concerns with serious injury and liability.

More generally, Title IX's critics have argued that women's participation gains have come at the expense of men. But a 2007 U.S. government report found that the number of male participants in intercollegiate athletics grew by 21 percent between 1991–1992 and 2004–2005.[6]

The critics have pointed out that the reported growth in the absolute number of male student-athletes can be misleading. This is because the NCAA has experienced rapid growth in its membership, as schools have moved from the National Association of Intercollegiate Athletics to the NCAA. The number of four-year colleges in the NCAA grew from 847 colleges in 1991–1992 to 1,045 in 2004–2005.

To adjust for this factor, the General Accounting Office (GAO) considered a group of 750 colleges that were consistently members of the NCAA throughout the 1991–2005 period. Even in this fixed group, however, the report finds that the number of male athletes grew by almost fourteen thousand, or 9 percent during the fourteen-year period.

Thus, although it is true that the number of male wrestling teams has diminished, the overall level of male athletic participation continues to rise. Title IX cannot properly be blamed for reducing the number of male athletes, because, simply put, there has been no reduction.[7]

The Road Ahead

Nonetheless, there are no free goods, and devoting resources to women's sports means that fewer resources are available elsewhere. If gender equity in intercollegiate athletics is to continue to advance, it is desirable to find the new resources for women's sports without cutting men's sports and without straining university budgets. The most obvious source for such resources is the elimination of extravagant and superfluous expenditure. The reality that college athletic departments do not have shareholders who are residual claimants means that they do not face the typical pressure of private sector firms to economize on resources and to generate profit. This feature, along with some others, engenders endemic waste.

One example of extravagance is the size of Division IA football teams. DIA football does not need eighty-five scholarships. Sixty would do fine. NFL teams have a maximum active roster of forty-five, plus a maximum inactive roster of eight additional players.[8] The average Division IA team has thirty-two walk-ons plus eighty-five scholarship players.[9] If football scholarships were cut to sixty, the average college would save more than $1 million annually (including the additional savings from reductions in staff, equipment, and women's scholarships), enough to finance more than two wrestling teams.

Other examples of waste abound, but perhaps the most egregious are the salaries paid to head football and men's basketball coaches—which often exceed the salaries of the universities' presidents by a factor of five to ten. An argument that these astronomical salaries are neither justified economically nor ethically is developed at some length in the essay on financing college sports in this book. Seeking an antitrust exemption to enable schools to legally cap the salaries of coaches will potentially save several million dollars per athletic program annually. Significantly, it will do this without affecting the quality of college coaching. The illogic in supporting today's excessive compensation for college coaches is further evidenced by econometric work that shows a lack of statistical correlation between high coaches' salaries or overall spending and team performance.[10]

Conclusion

Although Title IX has helped promote enormous gains for women in intercollegiate athletics, a strong and well-organized opposition to its advance still exists. Given the demonstrated physical, emotional, academic, and career benefits associated with women participating in school sports, it is important to continue to push gender-equal opportunity in this area. In 2007, women constituted 56 percent of undergraduate students but less than 43 percent of intercollegiate athletes.

The question thus emerges: If gender equity is to move forward, whence shall the resources come? I argue that it is possible to obtain large resources from reducing the waste and inefficiency in men's programs. One area of extravagant and unnecessary expenditures is in the compensation packages of head coaches in men's basketball and football. Not only do such astronomical remuneration levels engender an ethical issue, they are also superfluous to the efficient allocation of resources. Beyond that, it is clear that the lion's share of head coach compensation constitutes economic rent.

If a modified Bear Bryant Rule were followed (not paying head coaches more than the university president), universities could save millions of dollars in their athletic budgets.[11] A typical Division I, nonrevenue intercollegiate sports team costs a couple hundred thousand dollars to support. Several such teams could be added, and there still would be savings leftover to reduce the university subsidy to athletics.

The obvious hurdle to such a policy is the inevitable confrontation with the nation's antitrust laws. The NCAA already saw its limitation on payment to the fourth basketball coach rejected by the courts in *Law v. NCAA*. Although the NCAA may be able to defend a restriction on head coaches' salaries on the grounds that it is necessary to preserve the amateur branding and financial viability of intercollegiate sports (rule of reason), the more prudent course would be for the association to go to Congress to ask for an antitrust exemption. There would be no good reason for Congress to reject such an appeal.

The problem is motivating the NCAA, which essentially functions as a trade association for coaches, athletic directors, and conference commissioners, to take this initiative. Coaches and athletic directors would be legislating lower salaries for themselves.

The good news is that many sources of waste exist in intercollegiate athletic departments and, hence, so do various opportunities to free up resources. In the end, Title IX needs to advance. As with all social progress, however, it will take the political will and organization to achieve the goal of equal athletic opportunity for men and women.

5 Reflections on Salary Shares and Salary Caps

W RITING FOR *Yahoo! Sports,* on November 12, 2007, Jeff Passan asserted that the players' salary share of Major League Baseball (MLB) revenue in 2007 was only 41.3 percent.[1] Passan's number was then picked up by Pete Toms, writing for *Baseball Digest,* and other journalists.[2] If Passan were correct, or even nearly so, then it would be big news indeed. Because the salary shares in total revenue in the National Basketball Association (NBA), the National Football League (NFL), and the National Hockey League (NHL) are all in the mid- to high fifties, and MLB is the only one of the four major professional sports leagues in the United States without a salary cap, it might suggest to some that Don Fehr and the Major League Baseball Players Association have been fighting the wrong fight all these years. Passan's assertion, then, is another reminder that, whether we are theorizing about optimal labor-market structures or doing empirical testing, it makes sense to get the numbers right before plowing ahead.

This essay is based on "Reflections on Salary Shares and Salary Caps," *Journal of Sports Economics* 11, no. 1 (2010): 17–28. Sage Publications Ltd./Sage Publications, Inc. All rights reserved. Copyright 2010, http://online.sagepub.com.

Accordingly, in this essay, I discuss many of the empirical issues involved in properly measuring the players' shares in MLB, along with the NBA, the NFL, and the NHL. I then suggest a preliminary set of conclusions on these shares and conclude with some reflections on what these shares imply about the underlying collective-bargaining institutions.

Getting the Numbers Right

Team payrolls can be measured in a variety of ways. First, they can include only the active roster; the active roster plus the disabled list players; or the active roster, disabled list, plus the reserves. The league with the largest "reserves" list is MLB, where there are fifteen players under major league contracts who are not on the twenty-five-man active roster. Second, they can include or exclude player benefits, usually amounting to between 4 and 7 percent of salaries. Third, they can include or exclude deferred salaries. If they include them, there is a question about what discount rate to use. Fourth, they can be based on opening-day, mid-season, or end-season rosters.[3]

Fifth, player contracts have varying lengths. In MLB, there is no limit on the length of a contract, and some players receive guaranteed deals for as long as ten years. In the NBA, player contracts are limited to five years for non-Bird free agents and to six years for Bird free agents. In the NFL, contract length is not limited, but, with few exceptions, players sign nonguaranteed contracts.[4] The contracts may be multiyear, but, because they are not guaranteed, the team can terminate the contract after any year. In lieu of guaranteed contracts, a large share of players' compensation is paid via substantial signing bonuses. These bonuses account for roughly 50 percent of total NFL player compensation in any given year. Normally, these bonuses are amortized over the nominal length of the contract in computing annual team payrolls. Here, too, the discount rate employed will affect valuation, and the nominal contract length is a rather artificial standard to apply, because it is rarely realized.

Sixth, in MLB, teams spend over $20 million annually on average on player development; of this, approximately 60 percent goes to minor league player compensation.[5] In the NHL, teams typically spend $1 to $2 million annually on their minor league team salaries, but they also frequently own these teams and therefore own the revenues the teams generate; this is true for only a minority of major league baseball teams. In the NBA, a very modest outlay goes for its fledgling development league, the NBDL, and here, too, revenues go to the NBA owners. In the NFL, there is no payment for minor league players.

Thus, when comparing player shares at the top level, it is relevant to consider the substantial additional expenditure on player compensation in MLB due to the structure of its extensive minor league system. To a lesser extent, this is true for the NHL. To be sure, it is important to employ a uniform accounting system across the leagues for all these issues in measuring player compensation.

Revenue data, like payroll data, come in different shapes and sizes. One only has to read the definition of revenues in the three salary-cap leagues to be convinced of this. In the NFL, the NBA, and the NHL, the salary cap is defined as a share of defined revenues. Thus, the definition of revenues is an integral part of the payroll-determination process, and, hence, it is a subject of intense negotiations during collective bargaining. The NFL and the NBA have changed the definition of revenues with each new collective bargaining agreement (CBA), because the union has sought a more inclusive definition, and because new revenue sources have become available over time.[6]

Here are some examples of the conundrums that must be sorted out. When a team owner also owns another business that trades with the team, the owner can arrange for that trade to occur at any price. This is known as a related-party transaction. In a salary-cap league or a league with revenue sharing (e.g., baseball), there is a strong incentive for the owner to price the trade in a way that minimizes team revenue or profit and maximizes the revenue or profit of the related entity. The CBA must sort out a way to treat such transactions. The NBA CBA, for instance, has a clause that states that the

Knicks' deal with MSG network (both companies are owned by Cablevision) must be valued at the price that the Los Angeles Lakers receive from the team's local TV rights holder.

The NFL introduced its G3 program in the late 1990s to help teams with the private financing component of building new stadiums. In essence, under the program, the league would make a grant[7] for between $60 million and $150 million to the team, depending on the size of the team's capital contribution to construction and on the size of the team's market. The NFL Players Association (NFLPA) agreed that because new stadiums help grow league revenues and, thus, help increase salaries, the union would support the G3 program by allowing a cap credit in proportion to the size of the private contribution to stadium renovation or construction.[8] The upshot was that this credit was the equivalent of leaguewide revenue reduction of tens of millions of dollars annually.[9] With the new CBA, which took effect in 2006, the adjustments for G3 loans and security expenditures were made still more complex.[10] There are further complications, because NFL stadiums are invariably used for other events (e.g., college football, concerts, mass rallies, and so on). Because the union does not want to contribute to raising the team owners' revenues from events that do not enter the computation of football-related revenues, involved formulas had to be devised to parse revenues from nonfootball events and to adjust the allowed deductions from cap-based revenues. By 2008, the G3 program's funding had been exhausted, and the formal program was terminated.

A similar revenue-attribution problem emerges when an arena hosts multiple types of events during the year. It could be that a city's NBA and NHL teams play in the same arena, which might also host the WNBA, the circus, the rodeo, concerts, and more. In such a case, how is the NBA or the NHL to determine which proportion of permanent signage or yearlong suite revenue is attributable to each category of event?

The leagues and unions bargain over these and other arcane issues, and the result is long, complex sections in each league's CBA to set rules for defining revenue. The 2005 NBA CBA, for instance, contains twenty-five pages dedicated to defining Basketball Related

Income (BRI), the base upon which the salary cap, the escrow threshold, and the luxury tax are defined.

Although no salary cap exists in baseball, the revenue-definition issue is still hotly contested for several reasons. Chief among them is that MLB introduced a revenue-sharing system among the teams back in 1996 that has grown considerably over the past fourteen years. In 2009, approximately $440 million was transferred from the high- to the low-revenue teams. The higher a team's revenue, the more it has to contribute. The lower the revenue, the more it receives. The principal (though not the only) terrain of disputation is related-party transactions, where team owners also own the regional sports networks (RSNs) that broadcast the teams' games. It appears that several teams underreport the market value of the RSN revenue received by tens of millions of dollars, and, in one case at least, this underreporting appears to have exceeded $100 million by a substantial margin.

As mentioned above, the NFL, the NBA, and the NHL each have concepts of sport-related revenues that are intended to be inclusive. Yet the specifics of the definitions of league revenues, as defined in each league's CBA, still vary. Regarding gate revenue, the NHL's Hockey Related Revenue (HRR) includes revenue that would be generated by complimentary tickets if they were sold, while the NBA's BRI allows for the exclusion of 1.35 million complimentary tickets. The NFL's Total Revenue (TR) excludes the value of tickets exchanged in barter transactions, while BRI and HRR include them.

Regarding media revenues, the leagues have different conventions for deducting the value of advertising spots used to promote the league. Regarding signage and sponsorship revenues, HRR includes 100 percent of facility-naming-rights revenues, while BRI includes 45 to 50 percent of such revenues. BRI includes 40 percent of fixed-signage revenue, while HRR includes 65 percent (or 32.5 percent for two-team arenas). Regarding premium seating, TR includes all luxury-suite revenues net of direct expenses, while BRI includes only 40 percent and HRR includes 65 percent (32.5 percent for two-team arenas.) Regarding related-party transactions, HRR is less inclusive than BRI.

The foregoing should serve as a caution flag about the nuances in the ways different leagues define salary and revenue. Certainly, the nature of these differences needs to be understood before meaningful salary and revenue comparisons can be made.

A Preliminary Look at the Evidence

With the above caveats in mind, we can proceed cautiously to review some of the available evidence on salary shares in the top four team sports leagues in the United States. (See Table 5.1.)

The following numbers from the NFL are based on total player compensation, measured on a cash, end-of-season basis, and including benefits. The player shares are given both in relation to Defined Gross Revenues (DGR) and TR, as defined in the collective bargaining agreements.[11] Up until 2006, the NFL salary cap was calculated as a share of DGR, but DGR came to include a larger and larger share

TABLE 5.1   NFL salary shares, 1994–2008

League year	Player compensation as % of TR	Player compensation as % of DGR	TR/DGR
1994	62.10	69.40	1.118
1995	64.70	73.10	1.13
1996	65.00	74.00	1.138
1997	57.60	66.20	1.149
1998	61.40	69.00	1.124
1999	63.00	71.30	1.132
2000	62.60	70.80	1.131
2001	56.90	64.40	1.132
2002	56.10	63.60	1.134
2003	54.50	62.00	1.138
2004	57.50	65.70	1.143
2005	54.30	62.30	1.147
2006	58.40	N/A	N/A
2007	58.00	N/A	N/A
2008	57.70	N/A	N/A
Avg 1994–2008	59.32	67.65	1.136
Avg 1994–2000	62.34	70.54	
Avg 2001–2008	56.68	63.60	

Note: TR, total revenue; DGR, defined gross revenues.

TABLE 5.2 NBA salary shares (postescrow), 1995–1996
through 2008–2009

	Salary share of BRI (%)
1995–1996	53
1996–1997	55
1997–1998	57
1998–1999	59
1999–2000	62
2000–2001	65
2001–2002	57
2002–2003	60
2003–2004	57
2004–2005	57
2005–2006	57
2006–2007	57
2007–2008	57
2008–2009	57
2003–2004 through 2008–2009	57
2000–2001 through 2008–2009	58
1995–1996 through 2008–2009	58

of football's total revenues. In the agreement that commenced in 2006, it was decided to use TR as the base for the salary-cap calculation but to lower the nominal cap percentage from 65.5 percent of DGR in 2005 to 57 percent of TR in 2006.[12] As a result, the salary and benefit share of TR jumped from 54.3 percent in 2005 to 58.4 percent in 2006.

Two interesting points about this jump need to be made. First, although the share jumped appreciably in one year, the share in 2006 was less than 1 percentage point higher than it was in 2004, and it was below the average share of 59.55 percent during the entire period from 1994 to 2006. Second, the 2006 agreement added a Cap Adjustment Mechanism (CAM) that made it more difficult for clubs to regularly use signing bonuses as a means to go over the official cap. In other words, it tightened the cap.

Table 5.2 reports the trend in player shares for the NBA since 1995. These data are reported as a share of BRI. As discussed earlier, BRI is more inclusive than DGR and roughly as inclusive as TR.

TABLE 5.3 Hypothetical illustration of hockey team profits relative to league revenues and a fixed players' share

	Year 1 (millions of dollars)	Year 2 (millions of dollars)	Year 3 (millions of dollars)	Year 4 (millions of dollars)	Growth rate (%)
Revenues	70	77	84.7	93.2	10
Payroll (54%)	37.8	41.6	45.8	50.3	10
Other costs	30	30.9	31.8	32.8	3
Profits	2.2	4.5	7.1	10.1	66.2

Salary represents cash payouts and includes benefits. As depicted, the players' share rose between 1995–1996 and 2000–2001 but then fell. With the escrow system and luxury tax to supplement the basic NBA team cap, the salary share has remained steady at 57 percent since the 2001–2002 season. Although precise calculations are not available, it appears that the players' share in total basketball revenue, as opposed to BRI, would be between 55 and 56 percent.

Reliable data for the players' share in NHL revenues are not available over a multiyear period. However, the 2005 CBA clearly stipulates a mechanism to maintain the players' share in the 54 to 57 percent (of HRR) range. The NHL has an escrow system that ensures the players' share remains within the set parameters.

Interestingly, the players' share rises as hockey revenues increase: Players are to receive 54 percent of league revenues (including benefits) when league revenues are below $2.2 billion; 55 percent when between $2.2 billion and $2.4 billion; 56 percent when between $2.4 billion and $2.7 billion; and 57 percent when over $2.7 billion.[13] The hypothetical illustration shown in Table 5.3 makes clear why it is sensible for the players' share to rise as revenues increase.

If league revenues increase at a faster rate than the economy-wide inflation rate and if player salary growth follows revenue growth, then the pattern of outcome will resemble that shown in the table above. Because overall revenues and player compensation grow at the same rate, but the remaining roughly 55 percent of costs augment only at the national inflation rate, the profitability necessarily has to grow, and it may do so very rapidly.

TABLE 5.4 MLB salary—revenue data: 1990–2007

Year	Total player compensation (thousands of dollars)	Total revenue (thousands of dollars)	Ratio (%)
1990	532,740	1,277,399	41.7
1991	681,488	1,456,217	46.8
1992	906,420	1,669,878	54.3
1993	1,007,887	1,862,682	54.1
1994*	758,536	1,209,286	62.7
1995*	864,783	1,384,990	62.4
1996	1,036,930	1,775,170	58.4
1997	1,213,741	2,067,220	58.7
1998	1,383,764	2,478,850	55.8
1999	1,618,518	2,761,060	58.6
2000	1,878,436	3,324,828	56.5
2001	2,149,660	3,536,546	60.8
2002	2,298,347	3,432,156	67.0
2003	2,355,663	3,728,096	63.2
2004	2,341,007	4,257,770	55.0
2005	2,493,938	4,743,972	52.6
2006	2,636,186	5,205,535	50.6
2007	2,882,560	5,654,511	51.0
2008	3,057,623	5,982,116	51.1
Avg 2003–2008			53.9
Avg 2000–2008			56.4
Avg 1994–2008			57.6

*Shortened seasons due to players' strike.

A similar pattern holds when comparing salary shares across leagues. Because teams in MLB, the NFL, the NBA, and the NHL all have certain basic costs, such as front office, facility rental and/or maintenance, team travel, promotion, ticketing, and so forth, the share of total revenues represented by these costs shrinks as revenues rise. Other things equal, this leaves more room for profit, at any given player compensation share, in those leagues with higher revenues.[14]

As depicted in Table 5.4, despite stability between 2006 and 2008, the player salary share of total revenues in MLB displays more volatility than with the other U.S. team sports—understandably so, because MLB is the only U.S. league without a salary cap. That said, the MLB share has stabilized at around 51 percent since 2006.

The player compensation figures in Table 5.4 include benefits and bonuses for all players on the forty-man major league roster.[15] The revenue data includes only the revenue emanating from baseball-related activities. Thus, for example, if MLBAM (MLB's Internet business) earns revenue from selling tickets to nonbaseball events, this revenue would not be included above. Overall revenues generated by MLB-connected businesses exceeded $6.5 billion in 2008; of this, approximately $6.0 billion came from major league baseball activities. The numbers were similar in 2009.

The player share reached a peak of 67 percent of revenues in 2002 but since has fallen to approximately 51 percent. This decrease is a function of new provisions in the 2002 CBA (sharply increased revenue sharing with high marginal tax rates, a higher luxury tax on the top payrolls, and debt limitation rules) as well as the rapid growth in MLB revenues over this period (causing the players to play catch up) and more stringent player disability-insurance rules with higher premiums.

Before comparing MLB's apparently low 51 percent with the 57 percent of HRR in hockey, the 57 percent of BRI in basketball, or the 58.4 percent of TR in football, it is necessary to make at least one important adjustment. MLB teams have to cover very substantial minor league player costs, while the NBA (NBDL) and the NHL (AHL and a few players in the ECHL) have modest minor league player costs, and the NFL has none. The NBDL and the AHL also generate revenues that help defray the player costs. The minor league MLB teams are mostly independently owned, and, in any case, the revenues earned do not go to the major league team, yet the major league team pays the salaries of all the players on affiliated clubs.

In 2007, for instance, the average MLB team spent more than $20 million on its player development system. Of this, over $11.5 million went to pay the salaries of the minor league players. Generally, each MLB team has six minor league affiliates. Teams also run fall and winter development camps and leagues. Together, an average of 6.2 percent of MLB revenues went toward these minor league player salaries.

If we add the 6.2 percent that goes to minor league baseball players (without generating revenue for the major league club), the total player share in MLB revenue rises to 57.2 percent, roughly the same shares as the NBA and the NHL. Other special features of the baseball labor market reinforce the downward pressure on annual player salaries. First, baseball does not have statutory limits on the length of player contracts. Alex Rodriguez has a ten-year contract worth between $275 and $300 million. If MLB had a rule, as does the NBA, limiting A-Rod's contract to six years, how much would he have been paid on an annual basis? Competitive forces would have led to something considerably higher than $28 or $29 million a year, and MLB's salary share would be higher.

Second, some of the money that teams pay out for players in MLB does not go to the players; rather, it goes to Japanese companies, thanks to the idiosyncrasies of baseball's posting system.[16] Thus, the Red Sox paid $101 million for Daisuke Matsuzaka, but only $51 million of this went to Matsuzaka, and the Yankees paid $46 million for Kei Igawa, but only $20 million went to Igawa and was part of the players' salary share.

That said, MLB has higher total revenues than hockey or basketball, and, other things equal, we would expect its players' compensation share to be higher. The MLB adjusted share of approximately 57 percent during 2006–2008 is basically at the same level as the NBA share. Because some NHL teams do not own their AHL affiliates (and do not reap revenue from the club's activities but nonetheless cover compensation for the team's players), some of their minor league costs should also be added to its players' share. After this adjustment, the NHL players' share appears also to be nearly 59 percent. Thus, the recent MLB adjusted share is very similar to the adjusted share in the NBA, but, given the higher revenues in MLB, one would expect its share to be above the NBA's and NHL's.

Discussion

The abiding question is why, given the presence of a salary-cap system in the NBA, the NHL, and the NFL and the absence of a cap in

MLB, MLB players do not command a higher share of sport revenues. The MLB Players Association (MLBPA) has made a religion of avoiding a salary-cap system at all costs and, as a result of this orthodoxy, has endured multiple work stoppages over the years. Has the fight been in vain?

Unfortunately, there are no definitive answers to that question, but the very fact that the question can be asked is of profound interest. After all, if cap and open systems are salary-share neutral, but cap systems, as economic theory instructs us under most assumptions, are more likely to promote competitive balance, then cap systems would appear to be a preferred mechanism for optimizing league performance.

The tensions experienced in the NFL since the 2006 move to using TR as the cap base, however, suggest a possible disadvantage to a cap system. Namely, in the presence of unequal club revenues, if all teams are compelled to have payrolls within a certain narrow range, and such range is determined based on leaguewide revenues, then markedly unequal rates of profit across the clubs may result. Minimally, this outcome produces tension and conflict among the team owners, and, maximally, it could challenge financial stability across the league.

In this way, the more open system of MLB may be preferable. As stated above, MLB has noncap mechanisms that appear to be very effective at controlling team payrolls. When MLB introduced its more extensive and mature system of revenue sharing in the 2002 CBA, the owners offered the MLBPA the option of setting a minimum team payroll at $40 million. The Players Association rejected this offer for three stated reasons: (1) The MLBPA has always maintained that it was in favor of free labor market, and having a payroll floor would be inconsistent with this position; (2) the MLBPA saw the floor as a prelude to a ceiling that it wanted to avoid; and (3) back in 2002, the lowest team payroll was close to $40 million anyway, and the MLBPA expected all teams to naturally rise above this threshold.

The owners' thought behind the minimum payroll was that some teams would be receiving revenue transfers upward of $40 million annually in the name of promoting competitive balance. If the transfers were indeed to level the playing field, then the recipient clubs should use their transfers on improving their rosters. The minimum payroll would support this goal.

What was perhaps not anticipated by the MLBPA is that the introduction of the revenue-sharing welfare system in baseball would create a new model for financial success of low-revenue franchises. Basically, if a team received $30 or $40 million in sharing transfers and another $30 million from the central fund (from national and international media, sponsorship, and licensing revenues), by low-balling payroll, such a team could almost guarantee itself an operating profit at season's end. Indeed, several teams apparently adopted this strategy and lowered payroll into the $14- to $30-million range over the ensuing years. The good news was that this option preserved the profitability and financial strength of low-revenue clubs, but the bad news was that it did little to provide ownership incentive to produce a winning team or to promote the desideratum of competitive balance. Indeed, some of the low-revenue teams have been among baseball's most profitable.

One of the strongest claims in favor of more open labor markets from the union's perspective is that they are the mechanism by which higher team revenues lead to higher player salaries. That is, under competitive conditions, a team will find itself pushed to offer a player a salary equal to his expected marginal revenue product (MRP).[17] Thus, as revenues rise, so will salaries. This argument is sound but requires two caveats.

First, a salary-cap mechanism can accomplish the same result, as salaries are defined explicitly as a share of revenues. Indeed, in the NHL cap system, the salary share increases as revenues grow. Nonetheless, the issue remains under a cap system: whether all the appropriate revenues are being reported accurately. If, for instance, some related-party revenues are being underreported, then a cap system potentially will not capture a fair share for the players. In contrast, an open system is more likely to capture such revenues, because teams with auxiliary revenue streams will take these into account as they bid for players in the open market. This point segues directly to the next caveat.

Second, the presence of substantial related-party revenues lends greater attractiveness to a cap system. This is because related-party revenues are another source (in addition to market size or facility characteristics) of major revenue differentials among the clubs. To the extent that some clubs may be receiving $100 million or more annually in related-party revenues, the ability of such clubs to outbid their competitors for the best free agents and to raise the price on other players beyond the means of clubs without related-party revenues is heightened, and the issues of competitive imbalance and financial fragility become more pressing. Under such circumstances, the desirability of a cap system may become greater. Of course, as indicated above, salary caps have come with salary floors, and minimum payrolls require a certain degree of revenue balance across teams to be viable.

The foregoing is a general consideration of some of the extant structural issues confronting the management of sports leagues. The purpose of these reflections has not been to resolve the issues but, rather, to point out the need for empirical rigor in defining the dimensions of the problem and for more nuanced analysis of the complex forces at play.

6 Facility Finance

Measurement, Trends, and Analysis

ONVENTIONAL WISDOM has it that the public share of stadium and arena construction costs has been falling in recent years. Many have attributed this perceived decrease in part to the emergence of the academic literature in the 1990s, finding that one cannot expect that a new team or sport facility by itself would promote economic development in an area.[1]

Measuring sports-facility costs is rarely as straightforward as the public authorities, team owners, and newspapers would have us believe. In this essay, we use both the available reported-cost data as well as adjusted-cost data and find that trends in public financing are considerably more complex than traditionally thought. We proceed first by discussing issues in the measurement of costs, then by elaborating the methodology we employ for our estimates, next by expositing our results, and lastly by offering an interpretation for our findings.

This essay is based on Judith Grant Long and Andrew Zimbalist, "Facility Finance: Measurement, Trends, and Analysis," *International Journal of Sport Finance* 1, no. 4 (2006): 201–211.

Issues of Measurement

Numerous measurement conundrums and pitfalls complicate the assessment of overall and public costs of sports facilities. First, and most obviously, publicly released figures may apply to initial, intermediate, or final cost estimates. Because bells and whistles are often added after the original design or political approval, because of mistakes in the a priori cost estimation, and because cost overruns can easily run at 30 percent or more of budgeted expenditures, it is important that final costs be measured consistently.

Second, released figures often refer to building costs alone; less often, they can also include land and infrastructure. Land cost estimated at market value can produce widely different interpretations, or its value may be erroneously recorded at the "write-down" or discounted amount. Infrastructure is easier to value if publicly provided, yet it presents attribution issues, because it often includes on- and off-site improvements, such as nonadjacent roads, utility upgrades, public transportation improvements, or environmental remediation. Released figures rarely include opportunity costs.

Third, identifying what does and what does not constitute a public subsidy can be tricky, to say the least. Consider the following: The project to build a new Yankee stadium in the Bronx is estimated to have cost approximately $1.5 billion; above this, public expenditures for infrastructure come to roughly $300 million. The latter is for park space, public sports facilities (e.g., ball fields, tennis courts), and parking. Some of the public sports facilities will replace existing facilities, but some will be incremental. Should the spending on the incremental facilities be considered a subsidy to the Yankees? A large share of the "public spending" was on new parking garages, but the government put out a request for proposal to private construction companies to build and to operate the garages. Revenue from the garages accrues to the company winning the contract, not to the Yankees. Should the garage construction spending be counted as a public investment? Further, the city made $5 million in rent credits available annually each to the Yankees and the Mets toward the planning of their new stadiums that the city could then recover under certain conditions; how should this benefit be reckoned?

The new Yankees, Mets, and Nets facilities projects reportedly will benefit from sales-tax exemption on construction materials, and none of the teams will pay property or possessory interest tax. Some commentators consider these provisions to be public subsidies. Perhaps, but in four of the five boroughs of New York City (other than Manhattan), new construction projects receive these benefits. That is, they are generally "as of right" or available to all builders; should they be considered a subsidy?

Or consider, for instance, the ballpark in Washington, D.C., opened in March 2008. It cost approximately $670 million. A bond was issued for this amount, which is being financed as follows: $5.5-million rent payments by the team; roughly $12.5 million from taxes on tickets, concessions, and merchandise at the ballpark; and roughly $24 million from new business taxes. What is the public share? It depends entirely on how one treats the taxes from stadium revenue. If one assumes conservatively that 50 percent of these taxes are passed on to the consumer, then the annual public cost is $24 million plus $6.25 million, or $30.25 million—72 percent of capital costs. If one assumes that the team passes along none of the stadium taxes, the public share would be 57 percent; or, assuming that all the taxes are passed on, the public share would be 87 percent. To say the least, some subjectivity is involved here.[2]

Adding a relatively new twist to the subsidy story, team owners are also pursuing the right to develop land adjacent to their new facilities. Sometimes the owners must buy this land, but they typically do so on preferential terms, and usually they receive tax preferences as well. Other team owners benefit from zoning variances. How should these subsidies be evaluated?

Many teams enjoy financing schemes that enable the use of tax-exempt bonds for the private contribution to facility construction. This exemption amounts to a subsidy from the federal government and is generally not counted as part of the public subsidy, but given that some of the debt issues amount to hundreds of millions of dollars, it is conceivable that they could affect a municipality's bond rating and, hence, cost of capital. Notionally, these, too, are subsidies, but they have never, to our knowledge, been included, nor do we include them.

Lastly, and importantly, it is problematic to assess the public burden in sports facility projects by only considering the construction costs. When teams and municipalities agree on a new stadium or arena, the deal includes not only construction costs but also an ongoing operating agreement (e.g., a lease in the case of a publicly owned facility). The terms of the operating agreement are likely to include annual rent payments; sharing arrangements pertaining to facility revenues from sport and nonsport events (parking, concessions, premium seating, signage, local media, and so forth); tax privileges; and contributions to operating, maintenance, and improvement costs. Thus, an entire package defines the local government's financial relationship to a sports facility, and to consider any part of that package in isolation of the other parts can yield misleading results.

For instance, the Metrodome in Minneapolis was built in 1982 for $84 million (in 1982 dollars) with 100 percent public funding; however, the domed stadium housed the Twins and the Vikings, and each team had a lease that was very favorable to the city. The outcome was that after considering the substantial revenue streams that flowed back to the city from the Metrodome, the city not only received back its initial investment but, in present-values terms, received a return of 94 percent on its initial capital outlay. This trade-off between initial public outlays and revenue/cost obligations going forward became sharper after the 1986 tax reform act, discussed below.

If the researcher gathers copious information on each facility deal, in theory each of the issues above can be resolved. The problem is that full information is not usually available, and studying trends in facility finance involves dozens of distinct projects, with over 230 major league stadiums and arenas built since 1870 for franchises still operating today, 104 facilities in use in 2010, and several more in the planning stage. Given the complexity of each individual deal, details and nuances invariably escape the grasp of even the most careful analysts.[3]

Methodology

While we do not have sufficiently detailed information to adjust for all the factors alluded to above, we have gathered enough data to allow us to begin to consider the entire financing and operating packages of in-use facilities. Because our information on the latter is incomplete, we present two sets of results: on capital costs (building, land, and infrastructure) and on total cost (capital and operating).

Populations

Data are drawn from the population of over 230 facilities that were built for "big four" (MLB, NFL, NBA, NHL) franchises and where those franchises are still in operation today. "Public capital cost," the first data set, includes capital cost data for 106 major league sports facilities opened between 1950 and 2009 for franchises still in operation at 2009, as well as 5 facilities due to open between 2010 and 2013 (Table 6.1). "Total public cost," the second data set, includes public capital and operating cost data for all ninety-one facilities opened between 1990 and 2009 (Table 6.2). The data analyzed are restricted to this time period, because these facilities are still in use, and current operating data is available; and where the public participates in revenue sharing, current agreements and leases are available. Although public operating-cost data is available for some facilities built prior to 1990, including many opened during the 1980s and a smaller number opened in earlier decades, it is only available for those with active leases. We chose not to include these data. We do include all facility renovations over $50 million (nominal) in both populations.

Public Cost and Public Share Models

Public subsidies are estimated and analyzed using three measures: "public capital cost," "total public cost," and "public share."[4] "Public capital cost" estimates the present value of all reported public expenditures for building, land, and infrastructure, adjusted to 2010 using the consumer price index (Equation 1).

$$(1) \quad PV_{2010} \text{ Public Capital Cost (\$)} = \\ PV_{2010} \text{ Public Building Cost} \\ + PV_{2010} \text{ Public Land Cost} \\ + PV_{2010} \text{ Public Infrastructure Cost}$$

"Total public cost" includes "public capital cost" as well as estimates of the present value of all ongoing annual public expenses (maintenance, capital improvements, and municipal services), minus the present value of the sum of all ongoing annual public revenues (base rent, ticket surcharges, and shares of revenues from gate, premium seating, concessions, advertising, naming rights, parking, other major league tenants, and other tenants), based on lease terms in effect in 2009, discounted to 2010 based on an average lease duration of thirty years, and foregone property taxes estimated at 1 percent of replacement value, incurred over a thirty-year lease and discounted to 2010 (Equation 2). The discount rate is set at 7 percent and is intended to reflect the public cost of capital for a term similar to the life of the project.

$$(2) \quad PV_{2010} \text{ Total Public Cost (\$)} = \\ PV_{2010} \text{ Public Capital Cost} \\ + PV_{2010} \text{ Net Annual Public Cost} \\ + PV_{2010} \text{ Foregone Property Taxes}$$

$$(3) \quad PV_{2010} \text{ Net Annual Public Cost (\$)} = \\ PV_{2010} \text{ Public Expenses} \\ - PV_{2010} \text{ Public Revenues}$$

where

(4) PV_{2010} *Public Revenues* ($) =
PV_{2010} *Base Rent* + PV_{2010} *Ticket Surcharges*
+ PV_{2010} *Share of Total Facility Revenues*
+ PV_{2010} *Share of Gate*
+ PV_{2010} *Share of Premium Seating*
+ PV_{2010} *Share of Concessions*
+ PV_{2010} *Share of Advertising*
+ PV_{2010} *Share of Naming Rights*
+ PV_{2010} *Share of Parking*
+ PV_{2010} *Share of Other ML Tenant Revenues*
+ PV_{2010} *Share of Other ML Revenues*
+ PV_{2010} *Share of Non-ML Revenues*

and where

(5) PV_{2010} *Public Expenses* ($) =
PV_{2010} *Share of Maintenance*
+ PV_{2010} *Share of Capital Improvements*
+ PV_{2010} *Municipal Services Expenses*
+ PV_{2010} *Share of Other Expenses*

Public cost outcomes across locations and facility types are compared by measuring the share of total costs paid by the public sector ("public share") relative to that paid by the private sector. Public share is calculated for both capital cost and total cost data, referred to as "public share, capital cost" (Equation 6) and "public share, total cost" (Equation 7).

(6)   *Public Share, Capital Cost* (%) = $\dfrac{PV_{2010}\ Public\ Capital\ Cost}{PV_{2010}\ Capital\ Cost}$

(7)   *Public Share, Total Cost* (%) = $\dfrac{PV_{2010}\ Total\ Public\ Cost}{PV_{2010}\ Capital\ Cost}$

where

(8) PV_{2010} *Capital Cost* ($) =
       PV_{2010} *Total Cost Building*
       + PV_{2010} *Total Cost Land*
       + PV_{2010} *Total Cost Infrastructure*

There are two important caveats to the use of the public share measure "public share, total cost." First, the numerator includes both capital and the present value of annual net operating costs, whereas the denominator includes only capital costs. The distinction arises from the overall objective of accounting for those instances where public participants earn net income from facility operations that are intended to either directly or indirectly service any publicly issued development debt, sometimes referred to as "lease givebacks." Our public-share formula takes into account the degree to which facilities "pay for themselves" from the public sector perspective. Consequently, the second caveat: Public-share outcomes can fall outside the range of 0 to 100 percent. Public shares less than 0 percent indicate that the public sector has more than offset its initial investment through annual revenues. Conversely, public shares greater than 100 percent indicate that the public sector has not paid back any of the upfront capital costs through facility operations and, instead, is continuing to pay out additional subsidies year after year.

Data Sources

Capital cost data build on earlier work by J. G. Long[5] and include new data for facilities opened between 2002 and 2010 as well as facilities under construction and in the discussion phase. Capital cost data are cross-referenced from different sources, including academic case studies,[6] industry publications,[7] general-interest publications,[8] and Lexis/Nexis searches of major newspapers and periodicals for each facility. Total public cost data, including annual public revenue and expense data, are cross-referenced from industry publications[9] and selected academic studies.[10]

Results

Table 6.1 presents our results on the long-term trend in capital expenditures (building, land, and infrastructure) and the associated public share. As expected, the average and median facility capital costs rise steadily from the 1950s to the first decade of the twenty-first century. In 2010 dollars, the average facility capital cost increases sevenfold from $69 million during the 1950s to $494 million during 2000–2009. Less expectedly, however, the average and median public capital cost were actually lower during the 1980s than during the 1970s and just slightly higher in the 1990s than the 1970s.[11] The public share falls from the 1950s to the 1960s before rising again in the 1970s, if either a simple or weighted average is used.[12] The public share then falls in the 1980s and again in the 1990s in all three measures (simple average, median, and weighted average). The public share in capital costs, however, does not continue to fall during 2000–2010: It basically stagnates using either the weighted average (going from 59 percent in the 1990s to 62 percent during 2000–2010) or the median (going from 74 percent to 72 percent), but it increases modestly (from 58 percent to 66 percent) using the simple average. This somewhat surprising result—that the downward trend in the public share from the 1970s through the 1990s is halted or reversed in the 2000s—is interpreted in the next section.

The capital cost of stadium (as opposed to arena) construction trends upward through the 1980s, but the public capital contribution rises into the 1970s and then falls in the 1980s. In consequence, the weighted average public share of stadium capital costs falls from 100 percent during the 1950s to 84 percent in the 1960s and rises back up to 96 percent in the 1970s before falling to 49 percent in the 1980s, rising to 79 percent in the 1990s, and falling again to 52 percent during 2000–2009.[13] The public shares for arena construction display an even more erratic pattern, again rising from 52 percent in the 1960s to 93 percent in the 1970s, falling to 73 percent in the 1980s and to 41 percent in the 1990s, and rising again to 67 percent during 2000–2009.

TABLE 6.1 Capital costs only, all facilities in use for the big four major leagues, 1950–2010 (millions of 2010 dollars)

	1950–1959	1960–1969	1970–1979	1980–1989	1980–1984	1985–1989	1990–1999	1990–1994	1995–1999	2000–2009	2000–2004	2005–2009	2010+
All facilities													
Facilities opened	5	21	26	13	5	8	53	15	38	38	27	11	5
Average capital cost	69	158	177	210	174	233	299	283	305	494	435	641	647
Median capital cost	74	207	147	185	185	166	290	290	293	467	422	505	488
Average public cost	69	116	169	128	155	111	178	181	176	305	271	386	274
Median public cost	74	65	134	98	150	73	164	214	146	266	255	347	321
Simple average public share (%)	100	73	90	63	88	48	58	60	58	66	64	70	56
Median public share (%)	100	100	100	81	100	38	74	82	73	72	74	69	77
Weighted average public share (%)	100	73	96	61	89	48	59	64	58	62	62	60	42
Stadiums													
Facilities opened	4	12	15	4	2	2	22	5	17	30	18	12	2
Average capital cost	67	186	230	348	172	524	350	343	352	592	517	651	980
Median capital cost	77	215	213	216	172	524	345	326	359	502	502	571	980
Average public cost	67	156	221	170	124	216	276	325	262	309	322	283	315
Median public cost	77	179	213	124	124	216	288	326	279	320	333	249	315
Simple average public share (%)	100	87	90	50	71	29	79	95	74	60	64	56	46
Median public share (%)	100	100	100	57	71	29	93	95	88	69	70	68	46
Weighted average public share (%)	100	84	96	49	72	41	79	95	74	52	62	43	32
Arenas													
Facilities opened	1	9	11	9	3	6	31	10	21	12	9	3	3
Average capital cost	74	121	106	149	176	136	262	253	267	294	270	390	426
Median capital cost	74	94	82	130	202	119	250	264	246	291	228	390	468
Average public cost	74	63	99	109	176	76	108	109	107	196	170	254	247
Median public cost	74	39	82	98	202	73	80	56	85	223	191	254	321
Simple average public share (%)	100	54	91	69	100	54	44	42	44	69	66	69	63
Median public share (%)	100	83	100	100	100	62	24	31	23	82	82	69	90
Weighted average public share (%)	100	52	93	73	100	56	41	43	40	67	63	65	58

The public share in arena capital and total costs, however, is consistently below that for stadiums. Because arenas can be used 200 to 350 days a year—sometimes twice in one day—arenas can be cost-effective private investments. The same is rarely true for stadiums, which are used less than thirty days a year in the case of football facilities and less than one hundred days a year in the case of baseball stadiums. For these reasons, private capital is more forthcoming for arenas than for stadiums, particularly arenas that host more than one major league team.

Table 6.2 shows our results when capital and operating public costs (total public costs) are included. Data limitations restrict these results to the 1990–2009 period. For most measures, when net operating costs are included, the public share goes up. For instance, the weighted average public share of total costs exceeds that of capital costs for all facilities by 12 percentage points for 1990–1994, by 11 percentage points for 1995–1999, by 21 percentage points for 2000–2004, and by 10 percentage points for 2005–2009. This means that, on average, the public sector spends more on the operation of the sports facilities than it receives back, raising the overall public subsidy.

The average total public contribution per facility increases slightly from $210 million during 1990–1994 to $218 million during 1995–1999 but then increases sharply to $360 million during 2000–2004 and to $477 million during 2005–2009. The sharp increase during 2000–2009 holds for stadiums and arenas and runs counter to prevailing notions of an ongoing diminution in the public contribution.

The public share in total costs also decreases from 76 percent to 69 percent for all facilities, stadiums, and arenas between 1990–1994 and 1995–1999, but then increases rapidly to 83 percent during 2000–2004 before falling back during 2005–2009 to 70 percent.

We include data on the median expenditures and shares to elucidate whether outliers are distorting our average results. Not only are the medians not suggestive of such distortion, but the consideration of individual facilities prior to the 2000s reinforces this view.[14] For stadiums, there are five significant outliers during 2000–2009: AT&T in San Francisco, Gillette in Foxboro, new Busch in St. Louis, Citi Field in Queens, and Yankee Stadium in the Bronx, each funded

TABLE 6.2 Capital and operating costs, all facilities in use for the big four
major leagues, 1990–2009 (millions of 2010 dollars)

	1990–1994	1995–1999	2000–2004	2005–2009
All facilities				
Facilities opened	14	36	28	10
Average capital cost	283	305	435	641
Median capital cost	290	293	422	505
Average public cost	210	218	360	477
Median public cost	196	191	341	515
Simple average public share (%)	73	70	87	78
Median public share (%)	82	71	89	76
Weighted average public share (%)	76	69	83	70
Stadiums				
Facilities opened	5	16	20	8
Average capital cost	343	352	517	651
Median capital cost	326	359	502	571
Average public cost	346	311	419	517
Median public cost	338	291	436	547
Simple average public share (%)	101	88	82	77
Median public share (%)	101	93	87	76
Weighted average public share (%)	102	86	77	68
Arenas				
Facilities opened	9	20	8	2
Average capital cost	253	267	270	390
Median capital cost	264	246	228	390
Average public cost	135	144	239	318
Median public cost	117	120	252	318
Simple average public share (%)	57	57	88	85
Median public share (%)	47	36	87	85
Weighted average public share (%)	55	52	83	81

overwhelmingly with private funds that led to the drop in the public share for stadiums, although not the share for all facilities (stadiums and arenas) together.

Analysis of Results

Our finding of a stagnant or upward share of public contribution to facility financing since 2000 deviates from the general perception. One standard treatment, arguing a steady downward trend in the public share since the mid-1980s, is provided by Dennis Howard and John Crompton.[15]

Howard and Crompton offer four explanations for this trend. First, the Deficit Reduction Act of 1984 prohibited the use of tax-exempt bonds to finance the construction of luxury boxes. Although this act may have been modestly related to the growing private share, it is unlikely to have caused a break in 1985, because facilities under construction at the time were grandfathered. Further, the act may be seen as an intermediate variable, itself the result of a growing wariness about public financing subsidies to privately owned sports teams.

Second, the Tax Reform Act of 1986 provided inter alia that stadium revenues could not contribute more than 10 percent of facility debt service for the financing to benefit from tax-exempt debt. The provisions of this act, too, were grandfathered, and many loopholes were identified by teams, municipalities, and the investment bankers who counseled them. The most prominent loophole enabled teams to make upfront contributions to construction costs instead of paying higher rent or doing more sharing of stadium revenues with the public coffers. Many teams made deals with concession companies wherein the companies made upfront payments for concession rights and lowered the share of sales revenue shared with the teams. The teams used this upfront money to help finance their capital contributions. Similarly, teams sold naming rights, pouring rights, permanent-seat licenses, and long-term suite leases to raise initial capital for construction. Thus, the 1986 act incentivized teams to substitute lower rent (and stadium revenue sharing) payments for higher initial contributions to facility capital costs. Other things being equal, then, the act would lower the public share in capital costs but have no impact on the public share in total costs.

Our data set does not permit us to analyze years prior to 1990 for total costs, but the capital cost data in Table 6.1 are consistent with this expectation. Public contributions to facility capital costs drop appreciably after 1985. It is difficult to attribute this drop off, however, to the Tax Reform Act of 1986, because facilities under construction at the time were grandfathered. It is likely that the trend in the late 1980s had more to do with critical attitudes toward public stadium subsidies at the time.

Third, Howard and Crompton argue that the lower public or higher private share is a product of the fact that new sports facilities provided such enhanced revenues from premium seating, signage, catering, and concessions, team owners could afford to make larger contributions.

Fourth, Howard and Crompton posit that the inauguration of President Ronald Reagan in 1981 coincided with a new ideology that favored a smaller government involvement in the economy. It would not be surprising if this attitude extended to the sports industry, especially in the context of growing fiscal problems in the 2000s. Yet Howard and Crompton also suggest that more critical attitudes toward facility subsidies flowed from the growing academic literature that found the lack of an economic impact from sports teams and facilities. This literature did not emerge until the early 1990s and did not gain wide recognition until the end of the decade.

Our results do not support the contention of a significant impact of this literature. The public capital share for all facilities between the 1980s and 1990s remains basically the same and then rises after 2000. (The share falls between 1990–1994 and 1995–1999, but it is problematic to attribute this drop to the academic literature, because most of the financing for the deals between 1995 and 1999 was put in place during 1993–1996, before the academic literature gained prominence.) The public share in total costs displays a similar pattern, falling modestly from 1990–1994 (76 percent) to 1995–1999 (69 percent), but then rising sharply to 83 percent during 2000–2004 before falling back to 70 percent during 2005–2009.[16]

This pattern becomes more striking when it is recalled that since the late 1990s, the NFL and MLB have had subsidy programs to help teams contribute to stadium-construction expenses. The NFL's G3 program has, in essence, provided league grants of between $50 million and $150 million (in proportion to the size of a team's market) to help fund owners' private contributions to stadium costs.[17]

Since the introduction of its luxury tax and revenue-sharing program in 1997, MLB has also subsidized the private team contribution to stadium construction.[18] In MLB, teams share revenue based on their "net local revenue," or their local revenue minus their stadium capital and operating expenses. Because between 2002 and 2006 the top half of teams faced an effective marginal tax rate of approximately 39 percent, every dollar a team spent on building or renovating its stadium essentially was refunded by MLB by 39 cents—that is, the team's revenue-sharing obligation was reduced by 39 cents.[19] In MLB's 2007–2011 collective bargaining agreement, the marginal rate is reduced to 31 percent, lowering the implicit subsidy.[20]

Although these substantial league subventions assist the team's upfront capital contributions and would be expected, other things equal, to lower the public share of initial stadium investment, they may also lead to the team's paying lower rent and sharing less stadium revenue. In the case of the Yankees' new stadium, for instance, the team will pay no rent to New York City.

The question then remains: Why does the public share in facility finance not continue its steady decline after 2000? One possible response is that the leagues are using their monopoly power more effectively, helping offset other factors. As urban populations and incomes have continued to grow, the big three leagues in the United States have not increased the number of franchises commensurately. The last expansion in MLB was in 1998, while the NBA and NFL each have only added one franchise since 1995. MLB even waived the contraction flag in 2001 and 2002, threatening to eliminate teams in several cities if they did not build new publicly financed stadiums.

Another, albeit related, possible explanation is that demand for the major spectator sports is growing rapidly. As fans grow more intense, their willingness to support public subsidies to attract a new or to retain an existing team increases. Even if a sports team cannot be counted on to generate new jobs or higher incomes, it can yield a variety of important benefits that are not directly registered in the marketplace in the form of consumer surplus, externalities, and public goods. The median public total cost to build a sports facility during 2000–2009 was $467 million. This amounts to approximately $30 million per year of debt service over thirty years. For an urban area that has a population of three million, this subsidy amounts to a meager $10 per person per year.[21] Given the small tax burden per capita, the popularity of sports teams, the large amount of money that is dedicated to the lobbying effort to get new facilities approved, and the powerful political and business forces that line up behind a new facility, it is perhaps not so surprising that on average the public share of financing has been maintained at such a high level.

Confounding the interpretation of trends is the presence of special factors and idiosyncrasies that affect each facility deal. These special factors become more important during quinquennia or decades when the number of new facilities is small (e.g., 1980–1984, when only six facilities, including two stadiums, were built). Because large cities have more bargaining leverage than small cities, other things equal, we expect to observe lower public shares in large cities. Indeed, for the two decades (1990–2009) and eighty-eight facilities covered in our data set, the simple average public share in capital costs is 87 percent for cities with below-median population and 67 percent for cities with above-median population.[22] Hence, we would expect that periods when a disproportionate share of new facilities is being built in small cities would exhibit higher public shares.[23] However, the flattening of the trend toward smaller public shares after the 1990s does not appear to be affected by this factor. The percent of facilities opened in cities with above-median population was 45 percent in the 1990s and 49 percent in the 2000s.[24] If anything, this slight increase would lead to the expectation of a drop in the public share between these two decades.

Another anomaly appears in the 2000s, as the public capital share for arenas rises above that for stadiums by 10 percentage points. One of the reasons for this is that, unlike the 1990s, when eleven joint NBA/NHL arenas opened, during 2000–2009, five solo NBA arenas, four solo NHL arenas, and one joint arena opened. When an arena has only one top-level professional team, it is more difficult for a private investor to achieve a positive return; this compels the team to seek a larger public contribution.

The local idiosyncrasies of politicians, the political culture, sports history, the personalities of team owners, the relationships between politicians and team owners, the fiscal situation, and the real estate market, among other conditions, also affect the terms of facility deals. It would be difficult to conclude, for instance, that, absent the fawning behavior of Mayor Anthony Williams, Washington, D.C. could not have bargained a more favorable stadium deal with MLB. As the nation's capital and eighth-largest media market, the Washington market was in a strong position to negotiate with MLB. This position was enhanced by the absence of concrete stadium proposals from any other city and MLB's desperately needing to move the Expos, whose Montreal market had been despoiled. Had Rudy Giuliani remained as New York City mayor rather than being replaced by Michael Bloomberg, it is likely that the Yankees, Mets, and Nets would have received substantially higher public subsidies for their new facilities. Such subjective factors undermine any attempts to identify the systemic forces that underlie trends in facility financing.

Conclusion

We have presented comprehensive summary data for capital and total costs for all professional sport facilities built since the 1950s. Most of our evidence accords with conventional views about the public contribution and the public share over time. We find, however, that the trend toward a lower public share that began in the 1980s does not continue into the 2000s. Because facility financing deals are generally set two to three years prior to the opening of the building, and because the academic literature finding that a city cannot expect a positive economic contribution from a new facility (or a new team) does not become extant until the late 1990s, it is problematic to attribute a significant political impact to this literature. It is, of course, possible that, absent this literature, the average public share would have risen further in the 2000s. The hiatus in the downward trend in the public share in the early 2000s seems to be attributable to the growing popularity of sports, the growth of U.S. cities, the ongoing monopoly power of sports leagues, and idiosyncratic factors.

7 Going for Gold

The Financing and Economic Impact of the Olympic Games

T HE OLYMPIC GAMES are among the largest and most visible athletic events in the world. Every two years, the world's best athletes from some two hundred countries come together to compete in lavish new venues in front of thousands of spectators. Hundreds of millions of sports fans worldwide watch the Games on television.

The "Olympic Movement," which the International Olympic Committee (IOC) defines as "all those who agree to be guided by the Olympic Charter and who recognize the authority of the International Olympic Committee," is the driving force behind the Olympic Games. The stated goal of the Olympic Movement is to help build a better world. Although Pierre de Coubertin, who founded the modern Olympic Games in the nineteenth century, may have had altruistic, idealistic notions of pure amateur competition, unsullied by

---

This essay is based on Brad Humphreys and Andrew Zimbalist, "The Financing and Economic Impact of the Olympic Games," in *The Business of Sports*, ed. Brad R. Humphreys and Dennis R. Howard (Westport, CT: Praeger, 2008), 101–124.

financial motivations in mind, the Olympic Games have become a big business. The participants are effectively professional athletes; the organizers are highly compensated, professional bureaucrats; hosting the Games involves huge construction and renovation projects that may take over a decade to complete; and these expenditures are usually justified by claims of extraordinary economic benefits that will accrue to the host city or region as a direct result of hosting the Games.

This essay examines the financing of the Olympic Games, the sordid details of how the awarding of the Games became a high-stakes contest to see which country could shower the IOC with the most gifts and perks, and the economic impact of the games. We focus primarily on the evolution of the financing of the Olympic Games over the past thirty-five years and the assessment of the economic impact of the Games.

Financing the Olympic Games

The modern Olympic Games began in 1896, but it was not until 1976 that a watershed event shook up the financing model for the Games and set them on their current economic course. In that year, the city of Montreal hosted the Summer Games. Montreal incurred a debt of $2.8 billion (approximately $10 billion in 2010 dollars) that was finally paid off in 2005.[1] Annual debt service created a large budgetary hole for the city for three decades.

By the end of the Montreal Games, the 1980 Summer Olympic Games had already been set for Moscow, but no city wanted to bid for the right to host the 1984 Summer Games.[2] After some scrambling, Los Angeles agreed to host the 1984 Summer Games, but only on the condition that it took on no financial obligation. With no alternative, the IOC accepted this condition, and Los Angeles was awarded the 1984 Summer Games on July 1, 1978.

1978 also marked the first significant relaxation of Olympic amateur rules under then–IOC president Lord Killanin. In that year, Rule 26 of the Olympic Charter was modified so that athletes were allowed openly to earn money from endorsements, if the money went to their national sports federations or their countries' National Olympic Committees (NOCs). The receiving organization was then permitted to pay the athlete's expenses, including "pocket money." "Broken-time" payments for time away from the athlete's regular job were also authorized if the athlete had a regular job. But the rule continued to declare that professional athletes were ineligible.

During the 1980–2001 reign of IOC President Juan Antonio Samaranch, the complete professionalization and commercialization of the Olympic Games were promoted by further liberalizing the amateur regulations. In 1982, the amateur rules were revised to permit payments into a trust fund that provided expenses during the athlete's active career—and substantial sums thereafter. Eventually, decisions about accepting professionals were left to the International Federation (IF) of each sport. The new professional era was heralded during the 1992 Summer Games in Barcelona, when the United States sent its dream team of NBA stars, which, unlike their more recent incarnations, went on to win the gold medal. Nominally, for the 2004 Summer Games in Athens, boxing was the only sport that did not accept professionals, but even this distinction is dubious, because the NOCs of many countries gave their boxing medalists cash prizes.

These changes also led to increased commercialization and increased TV and sponsorship money, which, in turn, led to corruption and scandal within the IOC. Samaranch set a new tone for the IOC when he began his reign in 1980. He insisted on being referred to as "His Excellency" and being treated as a head of state. Before he took over in 1980, the 112 IOC representatives had to pay their own way to cities bidding for the Olympic Games. Within a year, they were getting not one but two first-class tickets, plus all expenses paid for as well as lavish entertainment. Samaranch himself always insisted on limousine service and the best suite in the best hotel in any city. In Lausanne, Switzerland, home to the IOC headquarters, he had the IOC rent him a massive penthouse suite at the Palace Hotel for $500,000 per year.

IOC representatives who voted on the host city followed Samaranch's lead, and payoffs grew by leaps and bounds. Outrageous tales of excesses abounded. One surrounds the selection of Nagano, Japan, to host the 1998 Winter Games. The son of Samaranch's close adviser Artur Takacs was a lobbyist for Nagano's organizing committee, for which he was paid a salary of $363,000, plus a bonus if Nagano won the Games. A consortium of Japanese businessmen promised $20 million for the construction of an Olympic Museum in Lausanne if Nagano got the Games, which, not surprisingly, it did. Salt Lake City lost out, but the city learned a lesson.

The previous Winter Games were in Albertville, France. Most observers believed that Falun, Sweden, had a better bid. Samaranch, however, prevailed upon the IOC members, the large majority of whom he appointed, to select Albertville for 1992; that way, Paris would be effectively eliminated from competition for the 1992 Summer Games, which instead went to his hometown, Barcelona.

Gifts to IOC members ranged from free first-class trips to college entrance and tuition, room and board for children, rent-free apartments, free shopping expeditions, sexual favors, and tens of thousands of dollars in cash. All this fun came to a head with revelations around the Salt Lake City bid for the 2002 Winter Games. Since then, the IOC has supposedly reformed itself, inter alia, by reducing the number of voters and by officially declaring an outright ban on gifts.

Meanwhile, the modest financial success of the 1984 Summer Games in Los Angeles led to a new era of international competition among cities to host the Games. The relative success of Los Angeles, however, was sui generis. Los Angeles incurred very little construction expense, and the chair of the Los Angeles Organizing Committee for the Olympic Games (LAOCOG), Peter Ueberroth, was able to raise substantial sums by selling sponsorships to corporations. LAOCOG generated a modest surplus (just over $300 million) and reset the Olympic Games financial model for less public and more private financing.

Nonetheless, other host cities found it impossible to procure the same proportion of private support and, instead, relied upon large public expenditures. Several billions of dollars of public monies were committed in Seoul (1988), Barcelona (1992), Nagano (1998), Sydney (2000), Athens (2004), and Beijing (2008). In some cases, the local OCOG ran a modest surplus (20 percent of any surplus must be shared with the IOC),[3] but the local government laid out billions of dollars to help finance the activities of the OCOG. In the case of Athens, for instance, the public investment exceeded $10 billion; some of this public investment resulted in improved, more modern infrastructure for the city, but some of it resulted in white elephants. Many facilities built especially for the Games go un- or underutilized after the sixteen- or seventeen-day period of the Olympic Games competition itself while requiring tens of millions of dollars annually to maintain and occupying increasingly scarce real estate. Public investment for the 2008 Beijing Summer Olympics exceeded $40 billion.

Salt Lake City Olympiad chief and former governor of Massachusetts Mitt Romney questioned whether U.S. cities should enter bids to host the Olympic Games, stating that they were increasingly driven by "giganticism" with the addition of new sports and more frills. Romney said, "It's a fair question to ask, 'Is it worth it or not?' My own position is that the Games make sense, not as a money-making enterprise but as a statement for peace."[4]

The IOC presents the financing of the Olympic Games in terms of the related organizations: the local organizing committee (OCOG), the NOC, the IFs, and itself. The OCOG's budget is not the same as the budgetary impact on the local city that hosts the games. The local city, its regional government, and its national government may provide billions of dollars of subsidies to the OCOG, and the OCOG may report a surplus.[5] This surplus has little meaning regarding the budgetary impact on public bodies from hosting the Games. Moreover, it is common practice for the OCOG budget to consist entirely (or almost entirely) of operating, as opposed to capital, expenditures.[6] Nonetheless, to the extent that the OCOG receives funding from the IOC or from private sources, the lower will be the financing burden that falls on the local, state, and national governments that host the Games. What follows, then, is a discussion of how the IOC

TABLE 7.1   Olympic movement revenue (millions of current US$)

Source	1993–1996	1997–2000	2001–2004	2005–2008
Broadcast	1,251	1,845	2,230	2,570
TOP program	279	579	663	866
Domestic sponsorship	534	655	796	1,555
Ticketing	451	625	411	274
Licensing	115	66	87	185
Total	2,630	3,770	4,187	5,450

Sources: IOC, *2006 Olympic Marketing Fact File,* available at www.olympic.org, 16; IOC, *2008 Media Marketing Guide,* 4; IOC, *2010 Olympic Marketing File,* 26.

distributes the revenue that is collected from the staging of each Olympic Games.

Table 7.1 presents the total revenue that accrues to the IOC or any of its constituent organizations during each quadrennial Olympic Games cycle, consisting of one Winter and one Summer Games. It shows a healthy revenue growth in each of the major categories, with television revenues the largest single source of revenue by a factor of three. The TOP Program consists of eleven companies that hold exclusive category sponsorships as the official Olympic companies.

TOP Program revenues go 50 percent to the local OCOGs, 40 percent to the NOCs, and 10 percent to the IOC.[7] Broadcast revenue goes 49 percent to the host OCOG and 51 percent to the IOC, which, in turn, distributes the lion's share of this revenue to the NOCs and IFs. Prior to 2004, the host OCOGs received 60 percent of broadcast revenue. Beginning in 2012, it has been determined that OCOGs will receive a fixed number, rather than a fixed percentage, as broadcast revenues continue to rise.[8] Overall, the IOC has retained 8 percent of Olympic revenue; the remaining 92 percent has been shared by the OCOGs, NOCs, and IFs.

Table 7.2 depicts the astronomical growth in television broadcasting revenue for the Summer and Winter Games since 1960. Not surprisingly, the largest share of broadcast revenue comes from the United States. For instance, for the 2004 Athens Summer Games, the IOC contract with NBC yielded $793.5 million, or 53.1 percent of

TABLE 7.2 Broadcast revenue history

Summer		Winter	
Olympic Games	Broadcast revenue (millions of current US$)	Olympic Games	Broadcast revenue (millions of current US$)
1960 Rome	1.2	1960 Squaw Valley	0.1
1964 Tokyo	1.6	1964 Innsbruck	0.9
1968 Mexico City	9.8	1968 Grenoble	2.6
1972 Munich	17.8	1972 Sapporo	8.5
1976 Montreal	34.9	1976 Innsbruck	11.6
1980 Moscow	88.0	1980 Lake Placid	20.7
1984 Los Angeles	286.9	1984 Sarajevo	102.7
1988 Seoul	402.6	1988 Calgary	324.9
1992 Barcelona	636.1	1992 Albertville	291.9
1996 Atlanta	898.3	1994 Lillehammer	352.9
2000 Sydney	1,331.6	1998 Nagano	513.5
2004 Athens	1,494.0	2002 Salt Lake	736.1
2008 Beijing	1,737.0	2006 Torino	833.0

Sources: IOC, *2006 Marketing Fact File,* 46; IOC, *2008 Media Marketing Guide,* 4, 6.

the total. Following the U.S. rights fee were Europe ($394 million), Japan ($155 million), Australia ($50.5 million), Canada ($37 million), and South Korea ($15.5 million). All told, eighty rights holders televised the Athens Summer Games to 220 countries and two billion potential viewers worldwide.[9] Ten thousand media personnel were on hand to cover the Games.[10]

OCOGs do not cover all their expenses from the above sources. For instance, the Nagano OCOG in 1998 had revenues of $990 million, of which approximately $435 million came from the IOC. Similarly, the Salt Lake City OCOG had revenues of $1.348 billion, of which approximately $570 million came from the IOC.[11]

Results

Economic theory would suggest that any expected local economic benefit would be bid away as cities compete with each other to host the Games. More precisely, with perfect information, the city with the highest expected gain could win the Games by bidding $1 more than the expected gain to the second-highest city. Such an outcome could yield a small benefit to the winning city, but this would require perfect information and an open market bidding process. In fact, the bidding process is not done in dollar amounts but comes rather in the form of providing facilities and guaranteeing financing and security.[12] In the post-9/11 world, security costs are far from trivial. Total security costs in Athens in 2004 came to $1.4 billion, with forty thousand security people; Beijing in 2008 was projected to have over eighty thousand security personnel working the Games.

It is also widely acknowledged that the bidding process is laden with political considerations. Moreover, the bidding cities are more likely to be motivated by gains to particular private interests within the city (developers, construction companies, hotels, investment bankers, architects, real estate companies, and so forth) than by a clear sense that the city as a whole will benefit economically.

In contrast, the IOC views its principal role as promoting sport, not economic development. It requires buildings and infrastructure to be financed with non-Olympic money.[13]

Accordingly, even though a local OCOG may break even or have a small surplus,[14] the greatest likelihood is that the city itself (and state and national governments) experiences a fiscal deficit from the Games. On the one hand, the only tax revenue that would accrue to host governmental bodies would be from incremental sales and income resulting from hosting the Olympic Games.[15] The evidence on this score is not encouraging. On the other hand, hosting governmental bodies, together with any private support, must pay for facility construction and upgrade and infrastructural improvements necessitated by the Games. They must also pay for the opening and award ceremonies, transportation of the athletes to the various venues, entertainment, telecommunications/broadcasting centers, and security, among other things.

The initial publicized budgets of the OCOGs invariably understate the ultimate cost to the OCOG and, to a much greater degree, the total cost of staging the Games. The former escalates for several reasons. First, construction costs inflate significantly as land values increase with growing scarcity during the roughly ten-year cycle of Olympic Games host selection and preparation. Second, the early proponents of hosting the Games in a particular city find it in their interest to underrepresent the true costs as they seek public endorsement. Third, as the would-be host city enters into competition with other bidders, there is a natural tendency to match its competitors' proposals and to add bells and whistles to its plan. The latter escalates, because it includes infrastructure and facility costs, while the publicized OCOG budget includes only operating costs. The infrastructure and facility costs usually form the largest component of total expenses, often by a substantial margin.

Thus, Athens initially projected that its Games would cost $1.6 billion, but they ended up costing closer to $16 billion (including facility and infrastructure costs). Beijing projected costs of $1.6 billion, but ended up paying over $40 billion.[16] The 2014 Winter Games in Sochi, Russia, were initially budgeted at around $12 billion; the projected price tag in late 2009 reached $33 billion. Of this, $23 billion would come from public sources.[17]

London expected its 2012 Games to cost under $4 billion, but they are now projected to cost $19 billion.[18] To be sure, as expenses have escalated for London, some of the projects have been scaled back, such as the scratching of the planned roof over the Olympic Stadium. The stadium was originally projected to cost $406 million and will end up costing over $850 million. Further, its construction will be financed by taxpayers, and the government has been unsuccessful in its effort to find a soccer or a rugby team to be the facility's anchor tenant after the 2012 Games. This will saddle the British taxpayers with the extra burden of millions of dollars annually to keep the facility operating. It is little wonder that the London Olympics Minister stated, "Had we known what we know now, would we have bid for the Olympics? Almost certainly not."[19]

In a world where total revenue from the Games is in the neighborhood of $4 to $5 billion for the Summer Games and roughly half that for the Winter Games, costs above these levels mean that someone has to pay.[20] Although private companies often contribute shares of the capital costs (beyond the purchase of sponsorships), host governmental bodies usually pick up substantial parts of the tabs. Moreover, as we have seen, not all the money generated at the Games stays in the host city to pay for the Games; rather, close to half the money goes to support the activities of the IFs, the NOCs, and the IOC itself.[21]

Thus, although the Sydney OCOG in 2000 reported that it broke even, the Australian state auditor estimated that the Games' true long-term cost was $2.2 billion.[22] In part, this was because it now costs $30 million per year to operate the ninety-thousand-seat Olympic Stadium.[23]

Similarly, the 1992 Olympics in Barcelona generated a reported surplus of $3 million for the local organizing committee, but it created a debt of $4 billion for the central Spanish government and of $2.1 billion for the city and provincial governments.[24] The Nagano Organizing Committee (1998 Winter Games) showed a $28-million surplus, but the various units of Japanese government were left with an $11-billion debt.[25]

For all the foregoing reasons, if there is to be an economic benefit from hosting the Olympic Games, it is unlikely in the extreme to come in the form of improving the budgets of local governments. This raises the question of whether broader, longer-term, or less-tangible economic gains accrue from hosting the Olympic Games, and it is to this question that we now turn.

How Do the Olympic Games Affect the Economy?

In general, sporting events produce two types of economic benefits: direct economic benefits and indirect economic benefits. Direct economic benefits include net spending by tourists who travel from out of town to attend the event; spending on capital and infrastructure construction related to the event; long-run benefits—for example lower transportation costs attributable to an improved road or rail network—generated by this infrastructure; and the effect of hosting a sporting event on local security markets, primarily stock markets. Indirect benefits include possible advertising effects that make the host city or country more visible as a potential tourist destination or business location in the future and increases in civic pride, local sense of community, and the perceived stature of the host city or country relative to other cities or countries. The Olympic Games are much like other sporting events, except that the Games involve many more participants, officials, and fans; involve more infrastructure construction; induce many more visitors from out of town; and have a much higher profile than most other sporting events.

Because of the larger size and profile of the Olympic Games, they have a greater potential to generate economic benefits than smaller sports events. However, the criticisms about overstatement of economic benefits made about smaller sporting events also apply to the Olympic Games, as we shall see.

Among the direct economic benefits generated by the Olympic Games, tourist spending is probably the most prominent. From Table 7.3, an average of 5.1 million tickets was sold for the past six Summer Games, including almost 6 million tickets to the 1984 Games in Los Angeles. The Winter Games are considerably smaller, averaging 1.3 million tickets over the past five Games. Even though selling five million tickets does not mean that five million spectators attend, and many of the tickets are sold to local residents, especially for the Summer Games, which typically take place in large metropolitan areas, a sporting event of this size and scope has the potential to attract a significant number of visitors from outside the host city. Also, because the Games are often spread over more than two weeks, these visitors may spend a significant amount of time in the host area, generating substantial spending in the lodging, food, and beverage sectors.

The Olympic Games require large spending on constructing and updating venues. These include facilities for the actual competition, accommodations for the participants and visitors, and facilities for the army of media covering the Games. Many of these venues are specific structures, such as a velodrome for bicycle racing, a bobsled/skeleton/luge run, and so forth, that involve costly construction due to their specialized natures. According to one report, twenty-one of the twenty-two stadiums erected for the 2004 Summer Games in Athens were unoccupied in 2010.[26]

In addition, Olympic venues typically have huge seating capacities. The stadiums that have hosted the opening and closing ceremonies for the Summer Olympic Games often seat one hundred thousand spectators. The iconic, ninety-one-thousand-seat capacity Bird's Nest in Beijing, built for the 2008 Summer Games, has been underutilized in the extreme: "In the year after the Olympics, [the facility] hosted a Jackie Chan concert, an Italian soccer match, an opera, and a presentation of Chinese singing standards. But the local soccer team declined a deal to make it their home field, and the only tenants now are tourists who pay $7 to visit the souvenir shop. By most accounts, the vendors hawking trinkets outside the stadium outnumber the foreigners who go there to gawk."[27]

In addition to venue construction, hosting the Olympic Games often requires expansive infrastructure to move the participants, officials, and fans to and from the venues. A majority of past transportation infrastructure construction has been on roads. But host cities and regions have also spent considerable sums on airport construction as well as on the renovation and construction of public transportation systems.[28] In less-developed cities, the building of a modern telecommunications capacity also represents a substantial investment.

The construction of this infrastructure generates appreciable economic activity in the host community. Large numbers of construction workers must be hired, and large quantities of construction materials must be purchased and transported.

Beyond the construction period, Olympic Games–generated infrastructure can provide the host metropolitan area or region with a continuing stream of economic benefits. The venues built for Olympic Games events can be used for years or decades after the Games are over. The existence of these venues can generate some ongoing economic benefits. But, more importantly, upgrades to the transportation infrastructure can provide significant benefits to the local and regional economy, if local businesses are able to make use of the improved transportation infrastructure. These benefits take the form of reduced production costs and prices charged by local businesses.[29]

The economic benefits to local securities markets are typically associated with the announcement of the awarding of the Olympic Games and not with the actual hosting itself. If the awarding of the Games generates significant expected future profits in the host economy, then this could lead to a current increase in stock returns in the host country. A permanent increase in wealth, generated by increases in returns to stock shares, could lead to increases in current consumption and investment. However, the magnitude of these wealth effects is likely to be small, and a temporary increase in stock returns associated with the Olympic Games selection decision may indicate, at best, a small increase in future profits by firms in specific industries or, alternatively, spurious correlation.

The indirect economic benefits generated by the Olympic Games are potentially more important than the direct benefits and also more difficult to quantify. One possible indirect benefit is the advertising effect of the Olympic Games. Many Olympic Games host metropolitan areas and regions view the Games as a way to raise their profile on the world stage. Cities and regions compete intensely for a share of international tourism spending, and the Olympic Games are possibly one way to make the host stand out in this crowded marketplace. In this sense, the intense media coverage before and during the Olympic Games is a form of advertising. If hosting the Olympic Games is an effective form of advertising in that it leads tourists who would not have otherwise considered this to be a destination to visit the host city or region, then this advertising effect can generate significant economic benefits over a long period of time. These potential economic benefits take the form of increased tourist spending, just like the direct benefits discussed above. The difference is that these potential benefits may be long lasting and may be spread more diffusely over the host city or region, not concentrated in and around the Olympic Games venues like the direct benefits associated with hosting the Games.

Types of Evidence

Hosting the Olympic Games may produce a variety of benefits in the host economy. However, just because hosting the Games can produce economic benefits does not imply that hosting the Games actually generates economic benefits. A thorough assessment of the economic benefits generated by hosting the Olympic Games should include evidence about the size of their economic impact. A considerable body of evidence on past economic impacts, as well as some prospective evidence about the potential impact of future Olympic Games, exists. Before reviewing this evidence, it is useful to discuss the types of evidence that are available.

The evidence on the economic impact of the Olympic Games falls into four categories: retrospective evidence based on econometric analysis; case studies of individual Olympic Games; evidence derived from computable general equilibrium (CGE) models; and "multiplier-based" estimates of future economic impact. Note the important temporal element associated with each of these types of evidence. The "multiplier-based" estimates are prospective; these studies are basically forecasts of economic benefits that will take place at some time in the future. Because this type of evidence is a forecast, it should be judged by the same criteria as any other economic forecast. The other three types of evidence are retrospective. They are based on an examination of what actually happened in the past when a metropolitan area or region hosted the Olympic Games. This fundamental difference between "multiplier-based" estimates and other types of evidence is sometimes not clearly delineated in the popular press or among careless analyses of economic impact, but it is critically important for understanding the differences in estimates of the economic impact of the Olympic Games.

Econometric-based evidence on the economic impact of sporting events uses historic data on the performance of the local economy before, during, and after the event. This approach uses statistical methods to determine how much of the past local economic activity could be attributed to the sporting event and how much would have taken place without the sporting event occurring. The most commonly used statistical methods are reduced form or structural regression models.

Case studies of the economic impact use a similar approach to the econometric method. This approach examines past indicators of economic activity but does not use sophisticated regression techniques. Case studies often examine a broader set of economic indicators than econometric studies and use unconditional statistical tests, such as tests of differences in means, cross-tabs, or chi-square tests of statistical independence.

CGE models are complex representations of the entire economy, including sectors that are not related to sporting events. These models explicitly account for the interconnected nature of the economy. Because the Olympic Games are large-scale events, involving significant numbers of participants, officials, staff, and spectators, the effects of the Games may spread beyond the immediate area and affect a number of distinct sectors of the economy in different ways. CGE models can account for complex economic effects, such as, for example, the effect of the additional borrowing needed to finance venue and infrastructure construction on the availability (or price) of funds to finance other construction projects in the economy. CGE models can also explicitly account for long-run economic effects.

The basic idea behind multipliers is straightforward and emerges from input-output models of the economy. When a consumer purchases a $1 pack of gum at a local store, the economic effects of that transaction extend well beyond the consumer handing a dollar to the cashier, who places that dollar in the till. Some of that $1 in spending finds its way into the pocket of the cashier in the form of wages, some finds its way into the pocket of the store owner, some into the pocket of the driver who delivered the gum, and so on. If the clerk, store owner, and delivery person live in the local community, this money is further distributed in the local economy as these individuals pay rent, buy groceries, and so on. A multiplier is an analytical device used to estimate the broad economic impact of each dollar spent in the local economy, in terms of the total amount of additional revenues earned by firms, the total amount of personal income, and the number of jobs generated.

Estimating the economic impact of a sporting event using the multiplier approach is relatively simple in theory. First, estimate the number of people who attend the sporting event; second, estimate the amount of spending by these attendees; third, apply a multiplier to this spending to estimate the broad, overall impact of this spending on the economy. However, upon closer examination, this process requires a significant amount of discretionary input on the part of the researcher, and coming up with accurate estimates of several of these components is not a straightforward process.

The Problem with Multipliers

Multiplier-based estimates of the economic impact are subject to a number of potentially damaging criticisms.[30] Although these criticisms are widely known in academic circles, the continued use of multiplier-based estimates of the economic impact of sporting events suggests that these limitations are not understood in other settings.

One important problem with multiplier-based estimates stems from the estimate of the number of attendees. New economic impact can only be generated by the spending of spectators, participants, and officials from outside the host area. Spending by local residents does not represent new economic impact—it represents spending that would have taken place in the host area even if the Olympic Games were held elsewhere. Therefore, this spending needs to be removed from the estimate.[31] However, estimating the total number of attendees is much easier than estimating the number of attendees from outside the host area. From Table 7.3, 8.3 million tickets were sold to events at the 1996 Atlanta Summer Games. Some of these tickets were clearly sold to residents of Atlanta, but how many of these

TABLE 7.3   Ticket revenues (current $)

Olympic Games	Tickets sold	% of capacity	Revenue to OCOG (millions of current US$)
1984 Los Angeles	5.7 million	83	156
1988 Calgary	1.6 million	78	32
1988 Seoul	3.3 million	75	36
1992 Albertville	0.9 million	75	32
1992 Barcelona	3.0 million	80	79
1994 Lillehammer	1.2 million	87	26
1996 Atlanta	8.3 million	82	425
1998 Nagano	1.3 million	89	74
2000 Sydney	6.7 million	88	551
2002 Salt Lake	1.5 million	95	183
2004 Athens	3.8 million	72	228

Source: IOC, *2006 Marketing Fact File*, 60.

8.3 million tickets were purchased by Atlantans? This number is difficult to estimate accurately.

Further complicating the process are time switchers and casuals. "Time switchers" are attendees who would have visited the host area at some other time, for some other reason, but instead choose to visit the host area during the sporting event. "Casuals" are attendees who visit the host area at the same time as the sporting event for some other reason and decide to attend the event out of convenience. The spending by both types of attendees needs to be removed from the economic impact estimate, as it cannot be directly attributable to the sporting event. This spending would have taken place regardless of whether the sporting event was in the area. Failure to remove this spending leads to overestimating the economic impact generated by the event.

A second important problem with multiplier-based economic impact estimates is their failure to account for crowding out. In many cases, the host area for the Olympic Games is a tourist destination in its own right; tourists would visit this area even if the Olympic Games were held elsewhere (London, for example, is a major tourist destination). "Crowding out" takes place when outside visitors attending the Olympic Games buy hotel rooms, meals, and other travel-related goods and services that would have been purchased by other visitors absent the Olympic Games. Crowding out implies that each dollar of new economic impact estimated by multiplier-based methods needs to be offset by some corresponding lost economic impact that was crowded out, or else the net economic impact will be overstated.

It is extremely difficult to determine how much crowding out actually takes place when an area hosts the Olympic Games. However, one study found that gate arrivals at the Atlanta airport during the 1996 Summer Games was identical to gate arrivals in the same months in 1995 and 1997, implying that quite a few tourists to Atlanta were crowded out by the 1996 Games.[32] In late 2004, Athens tourism officials were estimating about a 10 percent drop in summer tourism that year due to the Olympics. The Utah Skier Survey found that nearly 50 percent of nonresidents would stay away from Utah in 2002 due to the expectation of more crowds and higher prices. The Beijing Tourism Bureau projected that the number of visitors to the city in August 2008 during the Games would not be greater than in August 2007.[33]

Even though the size of crowding out is difficult to determine, it exists, and multiplier-based estimates of economic impact typically ignore it and, consequently, overestimate the actual economic impact.

A third problem with multiplier-based estimates is the displacement phenomenon. Some local residents may choose to leave town to avoid the congestion during the Games. The displaced people spend money outside the local area that they would have spent locally absent the Games. For instance, a survey in Barcelona indicated that fully one-sixth of the city's residents planned to travel outside the city during the 1996 Olympic Games.

A fourth important problem with multiplier-based estimates of the economic impact of sporting events is the selection of the multiplier. Economic theory does not provide exact guidance on the size of the multiplier to use in any particular application. The size of the multiplier used is at the discretion of the analyst. More importantly, the larger the multiplier used, the larger the estimate of the economic impact. This creates an incentive for researchers to systematically choose large multipliers to generate large estimates of the economic impact of sporting events.

Despite all these problems, the majority of published estimates of the economic impact of the Olympic Games come from multiplier-based estimates. Multiplier-based estimates are widely used, because, relative to the other approaches discussed above, this approach requires little data, little technical expertise, and very little in the way of computing power. Multiplier-based estimates are relatively cheap to produce and easy to manipulate.

Evidence on the Economic Impact of the Olympics

Considering the size and prominence of the event, relatively little objective evidence on the economic impact of the Olympic Games exists. Much of the existing evidence has been developed by the host cities or regions, which have vested interests in justifying the large expenditures on the Games that are documented above. These "promotional" studies suffer from a number of the flaws discussed in the previous section and must be taken with a very large grain of salt. Given these caveats, Table 7.4 shows some estimates of the economic impact of past Olympic Games as well as some published estimates of the number of outside visitors who attended the Games. In all cases, the estimated dollar values of the economic impacts have been converted to 2006 U.S. dollars using contemporaneous exchange rates.

Column four on Table 7.4 contains the published estimated economic impact generated in eight past Olympic Games. In all cases, these impacts were generated using multiplier-based economic impact estimates. In all but one of these Games, the estimated economic impact was significant, ranging from US$1.5 billion to nearly US$17 billion. The time frame for these economic impacts varies significantly, from a single year to a thirteen-year period. Because the

TABLE 7.4 Total estimated economic impact of various Olympic Games

Olympic Games	Period	Real millions of 2006 US$	Visitors	Notes
1964 Tokyo	1964		70,000	Actual
1972 Munich	1972		1,800,000	Estimated
1976 Montreal	1976		1,500,000	Estimated
1980 Moscow	1980		30,000	Actual
1984 Los Angeles	1984	4,488.5	600,000	Multiplier
1988 Calgary	1988		1,339,000	Unknown
1988 Seoul	1982–1988	4,598.0	279,332	Multiplier
1992 Albertville	1992		942,000	Estimated
1992 Barcelona	1987–1992	42.8	400,000	Multiplier
1994 Lillehammer	1994		1,208,000	Estimated
1996 Atlanta	1991–1997	6,526.8	1,100,000	Multiplier
2000 Sydney	1994–2006	1,565.4	700,000	Multiplier
2002 Salt Lake	1996–2003	1,696.5	850,000	Multiplier
2004 Athens	1998–2011	16,983.1	5,900,000	Multiplier
2006 Turin	2006	2,000.0	1,500,000	Multiplier

Source: Compiled from various media sources; author's calculations.

actual underlying economic impact is not constant across time, it does not make sense to express these figures on an annual basis. The extremely large estimated impact from the Athens Games, for instance, is in part due to the exceptionally long period of analysis used.

Because these estimates of economic impact are all based in part on spending by tourists who attend the Games, the information on estimated tourist attendance shown in column five of Table 7.4 is also interesting. Like the economic impact estimates, the visitor estimates show a wide amount of variation, ranging from a low of thirty thousand for the 1980 Moscow Games to a high of nearly six million, over a thirteen-year period, for the 2004 Athens Games. Again, the host cities or regions have incentives to overstate these estimates to justify their large expenditures on the Games.

The figures for the 1964 Tokyo Games and the 1980 Moscow Games are interesting, in that these are actual visitor totals based on the number of tourist visas issued by these two countries. The Moscow Games are clearly an outlier, because of the boycott of those

Games by the United States and some other countries over the ongoing war in Afghanistan and because of the difficulties of travel behind the Iron Curtain at that time. The Tokyo Games took place far from Europe and North America, which meant considerable travel costs in the early 1960s.[34] But still, the modest size of these two actual visitor counts, even given these caveats, makes some of the larger estimates in the table questionable.

Estimates of the economic impact of the Olympic Games derived from academic research published in peer-reviewed journals are more reliable types of evidence than the figures from promotional studies shown in Table 7.4, because the researchers who develop these estimates have no vested interest in the economic success of the Games and also because the peer-review process provides an important check on the methods and assumptions used to generate these estimates.

Only a few such studies exist. One study focused on the effect of the 1996 Atlanta Summer Games on the economy in Georgia.[35] The paper, which employs a difference-in-difference model, concludes that hosting the games increased employment in Georgia by 17 percent, or approximately 293,000 new jobs in the counties that contained Olympic venues or were contiguous to counties with Olympic venues in the four-year period 1996–2000, but had no effect on real wages. This result implies new employment but no benefit for the existing workers in these counties in Georgia.

This paper uses a novel, high-frequency panel data set for counties in Georgia over the period 1985–2000. The results, based on estimates of reduced-form econometric models of the determination of county-level employment and real wages, are interesting because of the length and breadth of this panel data set and the careful econometric analysis. However, the paper suffers from various deficiencies. It uses an arbitrary and misleading definition of the treatment counties, which, when adjusted, removes the employment effect. Further, the authors test for a level shift without controlling for the underlying trends, and the reduced-form nature of the analysis does not identify a particular mechanism through which hosting the Olympic

Games raises employment in the counties in and near the venues.[36] In the end, when appropriate adjustments are made, the positive employment effects from the Atlanta Games disappear.[37]

A second paper examines the effects of hosting the Olympic Games on migration into North American regions.[38] This paper examines population and employment in the regions surrounding Lake Placid, New York (1980); Los Angeles, California (1984); Calgary, Alberta, Canada (1988); and Atlanta, Georgia (1996). The results indicate a 1 percent increase in employment in these regions in a variable period following the Olympic Games along with a decline in per-capita income in this period after controlling for other factors that affect employment and income.

The evidence in this paper is based on estimated reduced-form econometric models of migration into these four regions using pooled data. Although the econometric approach is appropriate, the study uses relatively little data from before the Lake Placid and Los Angeles Games and after the Atlanta Games. This data limitation reduces the strength of the results.

These two papers find evidence that hosting the Olympic Games increases employment in the host region but do not contain any evidence that hosting the Olympic Games increases compensation in the host region. The lack of an effect on compensation implies that the distributional effects of the overall impact of hosting the Olympic Games may be different than the employment effects, if local prices and the local cost of living rose as a result of hosting the games. This could be the case even in Atlanta, where local wages were deflated by a national price measure, the Consumer Price Index for All Urban Consumers (CPI-U). If prices and the cost of living in Atlanta increased more than national average prices reflected in the CPI-U, then real wages in the Atlanta region could have declined as a result of hosting the 1996 Games.

A third paper examines the effects of the 2000 Sydney Games in the context of a multiregional CGE model. CGE models consider the broad impact of the Olympic Games across many different sectors of the economy, including labor and capital markets, as well as across different regions of a country. This study concludes that the Sydney Games increased real gross domestic product in Australia by A$6.5 billion (in 1996 dollars), or about 0.12 percent, each year over a twelve-year period. The study also concluded that the Sydney Games increased employment in Australia by 7,500 jobs per year over this twelve-year period. However, these results depended critically on the assumptions made about the Australian labor market. In particular, if wages actually rose in response to this increase in employment (rather than a constant wage), then the net impact of the Games in Australia was zero, with a negative effect in states outside New South Wales (the host region) being offset by a positive effect in the host state. This effect is due to the equilibrium labor-market response to a change in employment. If the effect of the new jobs created by the Games is to raise wages in all sectors of the economy, some of the jobs created by the Games will be offset by other jobs destroyed because of higher prevailing wages.

A retrospective study of the long-term economic impact of the 1994 Winter Olympic Games in Lillehammer, Norway, found little long-term benefit.[39] Despite extremely optimistic predictions from local and national authorities about the impact of the Lillehammer Games on local tourism, within a few years, 40 percent of the hotels built in and around Lillehammer for the Games had gone bankrupt, and two large Alpine skiing facilities built for the Games had been sold for less than $1 to prevent bankruptcy. In general, the long-term effects on tourism in the Lillehammer area were a fraction of the impact forecasted by planners. Even the Games themselves were something of a disappointment in Lillehammer: "February 1994 became a major disappointment for many hotels in the host region."[40]

The results in these studies present a consistent picture of the economic impact of hosting the Olympic Games on regions. Some jobs will be created as a result of hosting the Games. However, there appears to be no detectable effect on income, suggesting that existing workers do not benefit from the Games. Moreover, as the CGE results highlight, the total economic impact of hosting the Games depends on the overall labor-market response to the new jobs created by the Games. When taking into account the full labor-market situation, the net impact of the Games on a region may not be positive. The negative impact on regional income found by the study that examined four North American regions is consistent with a negative overall labor-market response to hosting the Games. Furthermore, the long-run impacts on tourism in the host region may be overstated, based on evidence from Lillehammer.

Clearly, the results from academic research on the economic impact of hosting the Olympic Games call into question the reported economic impact from the promotional studies shown in Table 7.4. Economic impacts on the order of $5 to $10 billion should be easily detectable in retrospective economic data from a geographic region. The fact that no peer-reviewed research published in a scholarly journal has found any evidence of billions of dollars of new income in any Olympic Games host regions suggests that the promotional studies vastly overstate the economic impact of hosting the Games.

The Lillehammer region is not the only one to experience a disappointing lack of post-Olympic surge in tourism. Recall that one of the economic benefits allegedly generated by the Olympic Games is an increase in the worldwide profile of the host city or region, leading to a long-run increase in tourism. One study examined the awareness of former Olympic Games host sites in Europe and North America.[41] Based on several thousand telephone interviews carried out over the period 1986–1989, less than 10 percent of the North American residents surveyed and less than 30 percent of the Europeans could correctly recall where the 1976 Winter Games were held (Innsbruck, Austria). Only 28 percent of the North Americans and 24 percent of the Europeans surveyed could recall that the 1980 Winter Games took place in Lake Placid, New York. These low recall numbers are not consistent with a large, long-lasting "advertising effect" generated by hosting the Olympic Games. Further, to the extent that the Games are accompanied by bad weather, pollution, unsavory politics, or terrorist acts, the Games may actually damage a city's or an area's reputation.

Economists have looked beyond income and employment measures for evidence that hosting the Olympic Games has an economic impact on the host economy. One area examined is stock markets.[42] The relationship between hosting the Olympic Games and stock markets is straightforward. To the extent that hosting the Olympic Games generates any benefits, including tangible economic benefits associated with increased tourism or intangible benefits, such as national pride, sporting benefits, increased visibility, and so forth, stock markets should be efficient mechanisms for valuing these benefits far into the future and discounting them back to the present. Positive benefits, if present, may be capitalized into stock prices at the time that the Games are awarded. Research on the effect of hosting the Olympic Games on stock markets exploits the nature of the process through which the Games are awarded. A large number of potential applicants are winnowed down to a small number of candidate hosts, and an announcement of the winner is made. Until this announcement is made, considerable uncertainty exists about who will be awarded the games, and the contest is winner-take-all. The announcement about the winner of the Games takes place at a specific time (seven years prior to the Games) and represents a natural experiment in stock prices.

The existing evidence is mixed. The announcement that Sydney would host the 2000 Summer Olympic Games produced modest increases in stock returns in a limited number of industries: building materials, developers and contracts, and engineering. The announcement that Athens would host the 2004 Summer Olympic Games produced a short-term, significant increase in overall stock returns on the Athens Stock Exchange but had no impact on the Milan Stock Exchange. Milan was one of the cities in the running for the 2004 Summer Games. Stock returns in construction-related industries on the Athens Stock Exchange increased more than other sectors following the announcement, suggesting that much of the economic benefit accrues to this sector.

This evidence is limited to only two Olympic Games, and the increases in stock returns reported in the studies are modest, short term, and primarily limited to the construction industry and related sectors of the economy. The empirical model used to analyze stock returns on the Athens Stock Exchange explains only 6 percent of the observed variation in returns. Overall, the evidence from this literature suggests that stock markets do not forecast large positive economic impacts flowing from the Olympic Games. Although the idea that hosting the Olympic Games affects stock returns may appear important to the general public, a careful reading of this literature reveals that the underlying effects are small, transitory, and limited to a few sectors of the economy. This evidence does not support net economic impact on the order of those reported on Table 7.4 accruing to the host city or region.

Can the Olympic Games Be an Economic Success?

Our review of the existing peer-reviewed evidence on the economic impact of the Olympic Games reveals relatively little evidence that hosting the Games produces significant economic benefits for the host city or region. If the economic gains are modest, or perhaps nonexistent, what can host cities and regions do to leverage hosting the Olympic Games? A careful examination of past experiences suggests two important avenues for leveraging the Olympic Games: Host cities or regions need to make careful land-use decisions and maximize the post–Olympic Games use of new and renovated facilities and infrastructure.

Land is an increasingly scarce resource in large urban areas that typically host the Summer Games and in the mountainous areas that host the Winter Games. Hosting the Olympic Games requires a significant amount of land for facilities, the Olympic Village, housing for the media and staff, accommodations for spectators, and parking. Unsuccessful Games leave behind legacies of seldom- or never-used structures taking up valuable land. For example, one recent study concluded that the primary legacy of the Nagano Games are a rarely used bobsled track and a huge speed-skating venue that has generated significant operating losses since the Games. Likewise, the long-term impact of the Calgary Games is seen as less important than the annual rodeo, the Calgary Stampede, and the signature venue in Calgary, the Saddledome, is viewed as obsolete and in need of replacing less than twenty years after the end of the Games.[43] Although it was used for years following the 1976 Montreal Games, the Olympic Stadium was widely perceived as one of the worst facilities in Major League Baseball, and many "features," such as the retractable roof, never worked. Many of the venues used in the 2004 Athens Games are either vacant or seldom used and occupy valuable land in a crowded urban center.[44] The Beijing Games left a legacy of several expensive buildings, including the elaborate Water Cube swimming facility. Early reports suggest a severe underutilization of the Water Cube. London's Olympic Stadium threatens to create similar problems.

Successful Games, such as the 1984 Los Angeles Summer Games, utilize existing facilities as much as possible and consume scarce urban land as little as possible. The stadium used for the opening and closing ceremonies in the 1996 Atlanta Games was reconfigured to a baseball stadium immediately following the conclusion of the Games. The bullet train built for the Nagano Games greatly reduced the travel time between that city and Tokyo.

Tying up scarce land for seldom-used Olympic Games venues in urban areas and Alpine recreation areas cannot be an optimal use of this valuable resource. Olympic Games planners need to design facilities that will be useful for a long time after the Games are over and are constructively integrated into the host cities or regions.

Clearly, the impact of the Olympic Games varies according to the differing levels of development in the host city and country. Properly planned, hosting the Games can catalyze the construction of a modern transportation, communications, and sport infrastructure. Such a potential benefit is bound to be greater for less-developed areas. But even in such areas, hosting the Games requires a significant outlay of public funds to finance the infrastructural improvements. These improvements can also be made without hosting the Games.

Thus, it is relevant to ask whether planning for the Olympic Games is an optimal use of scarce public monies. It is also relevant to consider that in many circumstances the public policy process is so gridlocked that needed infrastructural investments may be delayed for years, if not decades, without the Olympic Games catalyst and that the Games do provide at least some capital to facilitate the completion of desirable projects.

Conversely, in more-developed regions, where land is even scarcer during the initial bid planning (and destined to become scarcer still over the ten-year period of Olympic selection and preparation) and labor and resource markets are tight, hosting the Games can occasion a gross misuse of land as well as provoke wage and resource price pressure, leading to higher inflation.

Finally, it is important to recognize that hosting the Olympic Games may generate significant nonpecuniary benefits to the host city or region. The residents of the host city or region are likely to derive significant pride and sense of community from hosting the Games. Their home is the focus of the world's attention for a brief but intense period. The planning and work required to host the Games takes considerable time and effort, and much of the hard work is done by volunteers. Pulling off such a huge endeavor is a source of considerable local and national pride. These factors are important and valuable, even though researchers find it difficult to place a dollar value on them.

Some recent research has attempted to quantify the value of the nonpecuniary benefits generated by the Olympic Games.[45] Economists have used the Contingent Valuation Method (CVM) to place a dollar value on such diverse intangible benefits as cleaning up oil spills in pristine wilderness areas and preserving green space in urban areas. The basic approach in CVM is to elicit people's willingness to pay for some intangible through hypothetical questions involving referendum voting or changes in taxes. A recent estimate of the total willingness to pay for the intangible benefits generated in the United Kingdom from hosting the 2012 Summer Games was in excess of £2 billion sterling.

In the end, the economic and noneconomic value to hosting the Olympic Games is a complex matter, likely to vary from one situation to another. Simple conclusions are impossible to draw. Prospective hosts of future Games would do well to steer clear of the inevitable Olympic Games hype and to take a long, hard, and sober look at the long-run development goals of their regions.

8 Performance-Enhancing Drugs and Antidoping Policy in Major League Baseball

Experience, Incentives, and Challenges

THE PROBLEM with performance-enhancing drugs (PEDs) in professional sports has many dimensions. It is commonly agreed that the use of PEDs by professional athletes needs to be combated for the following reasons: (1) It creates unfair competition, (2) it distorts records, (3) it instigates PED use by formerly clean athletes, (4) it endangers the health of users,[1] and (5) it encourages youth to emulate the examples of their favorite players.

The response to these problems in the United States has been reluctant. The U.S. public, like sports fans around the world, lives vicariously through its teams and its heroes. Star athletes push the known boundaries of speed, endurance, and strength. Sports fans are understandably enthralled when records are broken. Top athletes not only produce a piece of history; they push out the boundaries of human achievement. Symbolically, by doing so, they appear to chal-

This essay is based on "Performance Enhancing Drugs and Antidoping Policy in Major League Baseball: Experience, Incentives, and Challenges," in *Threats to Sports and Sports Participation,* ed. P. Rodriguez, S. Kesenne, and J. García (Oviedo, Spain: Universidad de Oviedo Press, 2009).

lenge our greatest limit, our mortality. The Greeks invented stories about demigods to imagine the transcendence of human performance. If PEDs promote record-breaking performance, then the first reaction of most fans is to be excited.

It is not until the publicity around PEDs passes a threshold of scandal and unacceptability that an expectation of policies to control the abuse emerges. Even then, there is a strong tolerance of rule breaking, as long as the violators do not get caught and the executives give the appearance that they are forthrightly attempting to curb the problem.

In the United States, an additional peculiarity exists. Professional baseball has been around since the formation of the National League in 1876, when the records of individual players and teams began to be kept.[2] Baseball was unchallenged on the pedestal of spectator sports until at least 1958 by the NFL and some twenty-five years later by the NBA. The production function of baseball is much more individualistic than that in football or basketball, and, as such, the records of individual players stand out more. Most individual player records in baseball are hallowed in U.S. culture. Almost any baseball fan can tell you who hit the most home runs in a single season and how many home runs were hit; indeed, many nonfans can also answer those questions. It is probable, however, that very few basketball fans can tell you which player scored the most points in a single NBA season and how many points he scored.

Thus, if a defensive lineman uses steroids, and this enables him to set the record for tackles per season, the feat is barely noticed.[3] But if an outfielder uses steroids, and it is presumed that this enables him to hit seventy-three instead of sixty-three home runs, then every baseball writer, radio or television commentator, and blogger in the country has something to say about whether the record should count.

Finally, it is important to remember that baseball and other unionized sports must negotiate any antidoping policies with their players' associations. Drug policy is a mandatory subject for collective bargaining in the United States. Thus, unlike the International Olympic Committee (IOC), the International Tennis Federation (ITF), or NASCAR,[4] which can unilaterally set drug policies without player approval, baseball, football, basketball, hockey, and other team sports are obligated to set policy bilaterally. It is against this backdrop that the evolution of baseball's experience with PEDs should be analyzed.

National Legislation

The Federal Food, Drug, and Cosmetic Act of 1938 prohibited the distribution of all prescription drugs unless authorized by a physician. In 1970, Congress enacted the Controlled Substances Act, which stipulated criminal penalties for drug offenses, but steroids were not specifically mentioned as a controlled substance. However, in 1988, an amendment to the Controlled Substances Act was passed that made the distribution of anabolic steroids illegal unless authorized by a physician. A further amendment in 1990, known as the Anabolic Steroids Control Act, set stricter controls with tougher criminal penalties (up to five years in prison) for the distribution of steroids and human growth hormone (HGH). Penalties were also established for the possession of anabolic steroids, but not for the possession of HGH. Steroid precursors, such as androstenedione, were not covered by the 1990 act. In October 2004, Congress again amended the Steroids Control Act, adding certain steroid precursors (including androstenedione or "andro") and granting the Food and Drug Administration (FDA) authority to add other substances in the future.

It is noteworthy that DHEA is not on the controlled substances list. DHEA is a precursor to testosterone and is regarded to be anabolic. DHEA was omitted from the Steroid Control Act of 2004 as a result of pressure from key senators, including Orrin Hatch (R-Utah). Further, creatine, regarded by some to have muscle-building qualities, also does not appear on the controlled substances list. Although creatine may be an effective body-building supplement, it is not helpful with performance endurance. Thus far, only minimal side effects from creatine use have been identified. More significantly, creatine is practically ubiquitous in everyday foods, including fish and meat, making it very difficult to test for excessive levels from artificial use. Artificial creatine supplements are widely used by professional athletes and others to build muscle.

Baseball Policies Regarding PEDs

The first known PED to make an appearance in baseball clubhouses was amphetamines. According to the account in the 1970 bestseller *Ball Four* by former Yankee pitcher Jim Bouton, amphetamines were readily and freely available in locker rooms during the 1960s. According to various sources, speed continued to be widely dispensed in clubhouses until just a few years ago. Although Bouton himself describes these speed pills as "enablers" (enabling a player to recover from a late night of partying), ample evidence shows that amphetamines are quite capable of enhancing performance for many players. They can improve one's energy, focus, and confidence.[5] Although Bouton's party antidote claim may have been true for some players, the larger and more general point is that amphetamines facilitated making it through a long, grueling season where players had 162 games in 180-odd days. According to the 2007 Mitchell Report, MLB commissioned a survey of drug use in baseball in 1990 that found that amphetamine use was then prevalent in the game.[6]

To be sure, when MLB added amphetamines to the banned substances list before the 2006 season, the number of players who arranged to get doctor's prescriptions for the attention deficit disorder (ADD) drugs Ritalin and Adderall suddenly jumped from 28 to 103 in 2007.[7] The number continued to increase, albeit slightly, to 106 in 2008 and to 108 in 2009.[8] Ritalin and Adderall are known stimulants. The widespread availability of amphetamines over four-plus decades, of course, raises endless issues for those who like to debate the legitimacy of baseball records during the steroid era.

Following the 1970 Drug Abuse Act of Congress, Commissioner Bowie Kuhn issued a drug policy memo in 1971 stating that possession or distribution of amphetamines or barbiturates was a violation of the law and could be the basis for discipline. In 1984, following cocaine incidents with several players, the commissioner's office arranged with the Players Association a system for testing players when a "reasonable cause" existed. First-time offenders would not be subject to discipline but would be required to enter a counseling and treatment program. Neither steroids nor amphetamines were on the list of controlled substances in that accord.[9] In May 1985, then-Commissioner Peter Ueberroth unilaterally declared a mandatory drug testing program to cover all MLB employees in the major and minor leagues, but the program did not include major league players. The Players Association resisted mandatory testing then and continued to do so for the next seventeen years, arguing that it was a violation of the players' privacy rights. Namely, a player's privacy rights required there to be reasonable cause before a player or his possessions could be searched. If all players, regardless of cause, were mandatorily tested, this policy would undermine such rights, according to the union.[10]

Following the passage of the Anabolic Steroids Control Act in 1990, then-Commissioner Fay Vincent issued a memorandum in June 1991, expressly declaring the use of anabolic steroids to be prohibited in baseball. In early 1994, Commissioner Bud Selig put forth an antidoping proposal as part of the collective bargaining discussions. The proposal, however, was apparently never seriously discussed, because the owners and the players were deadlocked over more immediate economic issues that preceded the strike of 1994–1995.[11] In May 1997 and again in March 2001 and April 2002, Commissioner Selig issued memos that essentially reiterated the language of Vincent's 2001 memorandum.

In 2001, Selig unilaterally imposed an antidoping policy with testing and penalties for minor leaguers. In that year, 4,850 tests were administered, and 9.1 percent came back positive for steroid use. In 2002, the number of positive tests almost fell by half, with the proportion of positives being 4.8 percent.[12] Also in 2002, the owners and major leaguers agreed to incorporate a testing and penalty policy in their new collective bargaining agreement. The drug policy provided for random, anonymous testing of major leaguers in 2003; if more than 5 percent of the players tested positive, then in 2004 there would be random testing of all major leaguers. In the 2003 pretest, between 5 and 7 percent of players tested positive.[13] Those players testing positive were subject to discipline, but first-time offenders only received a warning. Thus, the twelve undisputed positive tests in 2004 resulted in no suspensions.

As a result of various events discussed below, the owners and players agreed to enhance baseball's antidoping policy twice during 2005. In January, they agreed to include HGH on the controlled substances list and to penalize first-time offenders.[14] There were again twelve positive tests in 2005, and the transgressors were suspended for ten days each. In November 2005, the two sides agreed to impose stiffer sanctions: a fifty-game suspension for the first offense, a one hundred–game suspension for the second offense, and a permanent suspension for the third offense. Any positive test and sanction could be appealed to an arbitration board. In 2006, two players tested positive for steroids and were suspended for fifty games each, and in 2007, three players tested positive and were suspended for fifty games each. In addition, one player in 2006 and one player in 2007 were suspended fifty games each, based on "nonanalytic" evidence— that is, the players did not fail a test, but other convincing evidence was adduced.

Finally, following the release of the Mitchell Report in December 2007, Selig announced that he would begin implementing some of the report's recommendations unilaterally and that other suggestions would be discussed in a new round of negotiations with the Players Association. These measures are outlined below.

Events Shaping the Evolution of MLB Policy

Although public awareness of widespread steroid use in baseball did not materialize until after 2000, there is now significant, though largely anecdotal, evidence of extensive use as early as the late 1980s. Other than Jose Canseco's allegation that more than three-quarters of major league ballplayers have used steroids, which, to be sure, seems to be on the high side, there is the estimate by Dave McKay, longtime coach for the St. Louis Cardinals and Oakland A's, that 30 percent of players used steroids at one point. Former Cincinnati Reds pitcher Jack Armstrong estimated that between 20 percent and 30 percent of players were serious users between 1988 and 1994.[15]

The first known public accusation of a baseball player using steroids was made by journalist Tom Boswell in an episode of *60 Minutes* that aired on September 28, 1988, just weeks after Canadian sprinter Ben Johnson was stripped of his gold medal in the 100-meter dash for testing positive at the 1988 Summer Olympic Games. At the time, however, and throughout the 1990s, the extent of use and the impact of use were far from clear. Indeed, as baseball's power numbers began to creep up during the 1990s, there were other ready explanations: Strength programs were in vogue; hitter-friendly ballparks were being built; expansions by two teams in 1993 and 1998 brought lesser pitchers into the majors; bat design was improved; and some argued that the ball was livelier.

Nonetheless, each year seemed to bring new evidence for anyone who cared to inquire. Philadelphia Phillies outfielder Len Dykstra showed up at spring training in March 1990 with thirty pounds added to his frame and a few inches to his neck. Dykstra credited his heft to "real good vitamins."

The drug survey commissioned by MLB and the Players Association was implemented during spring training in 1991. Of the 880 players who participated, including many on the 40-man rosters, 1.5 percent reported having used anabolic steroids at some point during their lifetimes, and 0.5 percent (or 4 players) reported using them within the previous twelve months.[16] It is likely, of course, that use was underreported in the survey; yet it is significant that the incidence of amphetamine use was acknowledged at much higher rates.

As incremental evidence mounted and suspicions surfaced, some prominent baseball writers began to raise the issue of steroid use among players. Peter Gammons, for instance, wrote in the *Boston Globe* in August 1992 regarding steroid use in baseball that "there's a growing suspicion that it's much greater than anyone lets on."[17] Bob Nightengale wrote in a July 1995 article, "Come on, you know there's steroid use in baseball." Then several weeks later, he followed with a story that quoted several players and team executives expressing concern about the prevalence of steroids in baseball, and in a third piece he referred to steroid as "baseball's deep, dark sinister secret."[18] In the latter article, Nightengale quotes Randy Smith, then general manager of the San Diego Padres, saying, "We all know there's steroid use, and it's definitely become more prevalent." Smith estimated that 10 to 20 percent of the players were users.

The 1996 season began with a burst of power that Commissioner Selig described as "startling." Pitcher Tim Belcher was quoted as saying, "Everybody's blaming the pitchers, but it's smaller strike zones, smaller parks, and steroids. That's not a good combination."[19]

Prior to the 1997 season, Gammons made some more trenchant observations: "Physicians and GMs are increasingly concerned about steroid use in baseball. As one team physician said last week, 'The owners won't do anything about it, because the cost of testing for steroids is very high, and they don't want to face the costs or the circumstances.'" Gammons went on to criticize the commissioner's office for "turning its back on such issues."[20]

Journalistic wake-up calls continued to be sprinkled in the media throughout 1997 and 1998, but public awareness was not really jolted until the McGwire/Sosa home run record chase during the summer of 1998. During the home run drama, a bottle of androstenedione was found in Mark McGwire's locker in August. McGwire admitted to using "andro" and also the over-the-counter amino-acid supplement creatine. His admission was widely reported in articles toward the end of the month. Although awareness was raised, the general public commentary was still in support of McGwire. Andro was not banned by baseball, nor was it a controlled substance under federal steroid law, and McGwire had been a great power hitter since his rookie year when he hit forty-nine home runs in 1987. Furthermore, the general gestalt was that steroids and bulky muscles were good for football players but were of dubious value in baseball, where speed, good hand-eye coordination, balance, and strong wrists were commonly seen to be the sources of hitting prowess. Nonetheless,

Commissioner Selig and Don Fehr jointly decided to fund a study on androstenedione and its effects following the 1998 season.

Meanwhile, McGwire's heroics and connection to andro served as a potent example for America's youth. By 2001, according to the National Institute on Drug Abuse, 8 percent of male high school seniors were using andro.[21]

In June 2000, Boston police found steroids and hypodermic needles in a car belonging to a Boston Red Sox infielder, and in the same month a clubhouse attendant found six vials of steroids and syringes in the locker of a Florida Marlins pitcher. In September 2000, an Arizona Diamondback clubhouse employee discovered a package of steroids and several hundred diet pills mailed to an infielder on the team, among other similar incidents.[22]

The rest of the story is pretty well known. According to the argument in *Game of Shadows*,[23] Barry Bonds observed the power-inducing results of performance enhancers after the 1998 season and decided that he, too, wanted to benefit. Bonds hit a record seventy-three home runs in 2001.

In a June 2002 article in *Sports Illustrated*, 1996 MVP Ken Caminiti admitted using steroids.[24] These comments led to a U.S. Senate Subcommittee hearing later that month. At the hearing, Rob Manfred, MLB executive vice president for labor relations, testified that there had been a 16 percent jump of the number of players going on the disabled list over a three-year period and that the lengths of their stays on the list had grown longer. The consensus of team physicians was that steroids had been an important contributing factor. A *USA Today* study found that between 1992 and 2001, trips to the disabled list for major leaguers increased by 32 percent, or double the increase identified in the three-year period considered by Manfred.[25] At the Senate hearing, Fehr told Senator Byron Dorgan (D-North Dakota) that the issue of steroid testing of players would be on the collective bargaining agenda.

On July 8, 2002, a piece in *USA Today* reported that 79 percent of active players at the time were in favor of drug testing.[26] Later that month, the players and the owners agreed to the first mandatory, random-testing drug program in MLB, as part of the 2002 collective bargaining agreement. On September 3, 2003, federal agents raided the offices of the Bay Area Laboratory Cooperative (BALCO) in Burlingame, California. On the day of the raid, BALCO's president told the agents that the laboratory distributed performance-enhancing substances to dozens of elite athletes, naming Barry Bonds, Jason Giambi, and Gary Sheffield, among others. This information led to a grand jury probe and the eventual testimony of Bonds and the others named. Although these testimonies were supposed to be confidential, some of their content was leaked to Lance Williams and Mark Fainaru-Wada, who began to publish a series of articles in the San Francisco Chronicle in early December 2004. These articles, in turn, spawned a never-ending saga of "he said, he said" that continues in differing contexts to this day. In January 2005, the players and owners agreed to tighten the penalties of their antidoping policy, but events would soon outstrip the acceptability of the new program.

In February 2005, Jose Canseco published his memoir, Juiced. Canseco alleged that over three-quarters of major leaguers took steroids, and he offered a long list of names. The opportunity was too good for the members of Congress to pass up. In March 2005, there was another hearing, this time before the House Committee on Government Reform, with legislators pressing for still tougher standards and discipline in baseball's program. Obligingly, MLB issued the three-strikes-and-you're-out policy, described above, in November 2005.

The November 2005 policy shift seemed to silence the skeptics. Apart from a raging debate about how records during the "steroid era" should be counted or discounted and whether users should be admitted into the Hall of Fame, the issue of steroid policy faded into the background for the next two years. Then, in December 2007, after more than twenty months of investigation and reportedly between $10 and $20 million of expense, former Senator George Mitchell issued his commissioned report on steroid use in MLB.

The report chronicled the history of PED use in baseball and the evolution of programs to deal with it. It also accused over ninety

major leaguers, including roughly thirty-five active players, of being
users. Some of the names, such as Roger Clemens and Andy Pettitte,
had not previously surfaced. Importantly, the report concluded by
making various recommendations for the improvement of baseball's
program, based on standard World Anti-Doping Agency (WADA)
protocols for effectiveness in antidoping policy.

Among the recommendations were the following. First, MLB's
program should have an independent program administrator. Second, the program needed more transparency and accountability,
including the issuance of periodic reports on the program's operations with aggregate data on testing and regular audits. Third, the
program needed to have more effective, year-round testing. Fourth,
the program needed to strengthen some of its procedures. Notably,
in 2007, testers called ahead for parking permits and ballpark passes.
Thus, it was possible that players received advance warning of the
tests and could take appropriate masking measures. There were also
issues of monitoring the player before and during the taking of the
sample. In addition, Mitchell called for due process for the players,
adequate funding for all aspects of the program, and a robust educational effort.

Commissioner Selig pledged to carry out all the Mitchell Report's
recommendations that he could on his own and to bargain with the
Players Association on the others. On April 11, 2008, the commissioner's office and the Players Association announced that they had
agreed on a set of measures to fortify the antidoping program. These
changes followed closely the spirit of the Mitchell Report recommendations. The main points in the new agreement are as follows:

1. Although not completely independent, the oversight and administration process has been made substantially more independent.[27] The Independent Program Administrator (IPA) is
   appointed for a multiyear term and can only be dismissed by
   an independent arbitrator under very narrow circumstances.
2. There will be increased transparency via the IPA releasing an
   annual report on the testing results.

3. There will be increased testing, adding at least six hundred tests (20 percent increase) each year and doubling the number of off-season tests. Several additional drugs are added to the banned substances list.
4. There will be increased adaptability via an annual review process that allows the parties to respond to new developments.
5. There will be a mandatory education program for all players, and today's players will engage in a community education program regarding the dangers of PEDs.
6. The testing program will be expanded to include baseball's top prospects in each year's amateur draft.

The Misleading Claims of Eric Walker

Eric Walker is a sabermetrician who was hired by Sandy Alderson in the early 1990s as a team consultant to the Oakland A's. Walker was one of the main forces behind the redirection of team player strategy that was made famous in Michael Lewis's *Moneyball.* Walker has developed a Web site, Steroids-And-Baseball.com, where he rants about the deceptions in the Mitchell Report and in the popular media discussion of PEDs' effect on power in baseball. Walker's Web site gained some notoriety early in 2008, when the *New York Times* published an article dedicated to elaborating its argument and evidence.[28] Walker contends that commonly used metrics, such as home runs per game, are not the proper measurement of increased power from steroids:[29]

> To understand that, realize that power determines how far a ball will go when struck well; for a given level of power, *with all other factors constant,* a certain **proportion** of all hits will be home runs. Still keeping all else fixed, more power means more home runs, less means fewer. But suppose all else is *not* constant. Suppose, for example, that the strike zone as called by umpires were to change materially one way or the other over time (which has actually happened, as with the rapid

and substantial 2001 expansion); clearly, the number of hits gotten would also change materially. So, even with no change in actual power, batters would get materially more or fewer home runs as a consequence.

Moving from a straight crude count to a rate measure is no improvement. If hits were to go up for reasons unrelated to power—as, for example, by strike-zone size changes—so would the *rate* of home runs as measured by home runs per plate appearance or home runs per at-bat. (So also, we must remember, would total scoring.)

To successfully measure power *per se*, what we need to do is relate well-powered balls to **hit totals**. We could use the ratio of home runs to hits, and that works pretty well. But not all "well-powered" balls necessarily leave the yard: doubles and triples are also, to some extent, indicators of power. Thus, the best measure of sheer power is Total Bases per Hit, a figure aptly known as **the Power Factor**. (emphasis in original)

Walker goes on to show that his variable, the Power Factor (PF), has trended slowly upward over the entire period from 1900 to the present, roughly from 1.3 to 1.6. The gradual increase was fed by three enduring spikes: the first in the early 1920s, when a livelier ball (the "rabbit" ball) was introduced; the second in 1977, when the Rawlings ball replaced the Spalding ball; and the third in 1993–1994, when, he says, a change was made in the ball-manufacturing process. That is, all three positive discontinuities in PF were brought about by a bouncier ball. When Walker subtracts the impact of the ball metamorphoses, he finds that the PF did not show any increase at all during the "steroid era" (roughly late 1980s to the present, in his conception).

Walker basically argues that steroids may allow a well-struck ball to go farther, but they do not help a batter make solid contact with a pitch. Thus, if the strike zone shrinks, batters will make solid contact more often and get more hits. Because, as Walker writes, "a certain proportion of hits will be home runs," a smaller strike zone will cause more home runs per game. It will not, however, change the ratio of home runs to hits. In such a case, the extra home runs do not result from more power but from a smaller strike zone. Hence, reasons Walker, the PF ratio controls for exogenous factors and is a better measurement of power than total home runs or home runs per game.

But is Walker correct when he asserts that steroids will not help a batter make solid contact more often? If steroids help increase muscle strength—in wrist muscles, tricep muscles, hip muscles, thigh muscles, and so forth—then they should also give the hitter more control over the bat and even allow the hitter to begin his swing later or to take a shorter swing yet generate the same bat speed.[30] They can also give the hitter more confidence, which could improve performance.

Another issue is that Walker's PF measure reflects factors other than power. Doubles and even triples do not necessarily emanate from power. A line drive in the gap or a ground down the line can result in an extra base hit, particularly if the batter has speed. PF, then, contains "noise" as a power measure.

The most important issue, however, is that Walker looks only at the average PF each year in the major leagues. He does not consider the distribution of PF. Consider a simple example. If half the pitchers and half the batters use PEDs, then the half of the batters who do will potentially be able to hit the ball farther, so a higher share of their hits (assuming that steroids do not increase their number of hits) will be home runs. If some of those batters are home-run hitters, then the extra lift may lead to their hitting over fifty, over sixty, or over seventy home runs. The 50 percent of batters who do not use steroids will face pitchers, half of whom use PEDs. These batters may lower their share of hits that are homers, either because it is more difficult for them to put a home run stroke on the stronger pitches, or because they are called upon to play different offensive roles with more power hitters in the team's lineup. In this circumstance, the average PF ratio for all baseball would stay more or less the same, but the steroid users would hit more home runs.[31]

Walker purports to offer solid statistical evidence to back up his claims, but he fails to control for more than one variable at a time, ignores the fact that his assertion that a livelier ball was introduced in the middle of the 1993 season is coterminous with the two-team expansion that year and with the growing use of steroids in the game, and never tests for anything but average power performance. I ran a variety of tests that take a closer look at the evidence.

Let us first consider the econometric evidence when we use either the average leaguewide PF or homers-to-hits (HTH) ratio as the dependent variable. Walker contends that PF is a purer measure of power than the HTH ratio, but, as discussed above, this is far from clear. Walker also anticipates that some will disagree and points out, via overlaid graphs, that the two are nearly identical anyway. Herein lies the first major problem with Walker's statistical argument. When I consider data from 1901 through 2007, the correlation coefficient between leaguewide PF and HTH is indeed very high (.9818), but the correlation coefficient between PF and homers per game is even higher (.9912). Because the entire basis for Walker's argument is that homers per game is a misleading power statistic, the almost perfect correlation between PF and homers per game suggests that Walker may be engaging in much ado about nothing. But let us look further,[32] considering a regression of PF on various factors with data from 1901 through 2007.

(1) $$PF = 1.29*** + .002\ Time*** - .033\ WWI$$
$$- .078\ WWII*** + .071\ Rabbit***$$
$$- .034\ Rawlings*** + .039\ MfgCh**$$
$$+ .021\ Exp98 + .019\ SteroidEra$$

Adj R^2 = .88

This regression suggests that baseballwide PF increased over time at a rate of .002 per year at a .01 significance level; that WWI did not have a statistically significant impact on PF; that WWII had a negative, statistically significant impact; that the end of the dead-ball era had a very positive and significant effect on PF; that the change from Spalding to Rawlings in 1977 had a negative and statistically significant impact, which was roughly offset by either the manufacturing change or the expansion in 1993 or the growing use of steroids at that time; and that the effects of the expansion in 1998 and of the steroid era were positive but not statistically significant.[33]

Walker maintains that the introduction of the Rawlings ball in 1977 resulted in an increase in PF. For instance, citing a Pennsylvania State University study, Walker states, "They say they found that the density of the materials used to make official major-league baseballs has increased several times throughout history—for example, that the core density increased rapidly after Rawlings became the ball maker in 1977. Because there is a direct relationship between increases in density and a ball's capacity to travel when struck, a denser ball means more apparent batter power (and more home runs)."[34] The evidence here, controlling for more factors than does Walker, suggests clearly that the contrary is true—there was a highly significant, negative impact on power (using Walker's PF) in 1977 when Rawlings began to manufacture the baseball. Apart from this, however, these results neither affirm nor disprove the Walker hypothesis. The same model was tested on HTH ratio as the dependent variable, and the results are shown in Equation 2.

$$(2) \quad HTH = .009^{***} + .001 \text{ Time}^{***} - .013 \text{ WWI}$$
$$- .022 \text{ WWII}^{***} + .011 \text{ Rabbit}^{***}$$
$$- .023 \text{ Rawlings}^{***} + .004 \text{ MfgCh}$$
$$+ .001 \text{ Exp98} + .009 \text{ SteroidEra}$$

Adj R^2 = .90

Not surprisingly, the HTH regression results are similar to those of PF, but there are a few notable differences. First, the MfgCh variable is no longer statistically significant (P value = .461), casting doubt on Walker's theory that the ball was juiced in that year by a change in the manufacturing process at Rawlings.[35] Second, the SteroidEra variable, although still insignificant, is just barely so, reaching significance at the .13 level. Third, the adjusted R^2 actually rises .02 in this model, using HTH as the index of power hitting. Walker's juiced ball hypothesis is his explanation for the increase in PF after 1993. If this is disproved, then Walker's argument suffers.

Next, consider a third model that addresses the distribution of power hitting, not the aggregate level across all major leaguers. As explained above, one would not necessarily expect to see the *league-wide average* PF or HTH to rise with steroid use; rather, the increased power may instead show up in superior figures from the league's leading power hitters. In the third model, I construct two new dependent variables, which are the PF and the HTH of the top five home-run hitters in each league. The variable combines the PF and HTH numbers of these top ten home-run hitters in MLB each year.

(3)   Top 10 PF = 1.45*** + .003 Time*** − .048 WWI
                  − .140 WWII*** + .221 Rabbit***
                  − .075 Rawlings*** + .046 MfgCh
                  + .017 Exp98 + .056 SteroidEra**

Adj R^2 = .91

When I consider the top ten PF hitters, the Walker argument that steroids do not promote power withers further. First, the MfgCh variable remains insignificant. Second, the SteroidEra variable becomes significant at the .05 level. Lastly, the explanatory power of the model increases to 91 percent of the variance in the dependent variable.

In the final model, I run the top ten HTH ratio hitters on the same independent variables. The results are similar, but stronger, against the Walker hypothesis.

(4)   Top 10 HTH = .041*** + .002 Time*** − .016 WWI
                  − .044 WWII*** + .069 Rabbit***
                  − .040 Rawlings*** + .005 MfgCh
                  + .001 Exp98 + .020 SteroidEra**

Adj R^2 = .93

The MfgCh variable drops further out of the range of statistical significance (P-value = .924), and the P-value of the SteroidEra variable improves to .046.[36]

I also ran all the above tests using a quadratic specification for time—that is, including both "Time" and "Time-Squared" as explanatory variable. This modeling, wherein "Time-Squared" is significant and negative, allows later period variables to display greater significance. In Equation 5, for instance, the binary variable denoting league expansion in 1998 is significant at the 1 percent level. This result could signify either that the expansion by two teams in that year itself had an impact or that the growing use of PEDs had an impact, or both. The ball change in 1920 ("Rabbit") loses statistical significance in this specification, but this appears to be a function of collinearity with the WWI variable. When the WWI dummy is dropped, the Rabbit dummy becomes significant at the 1 percent level.[37]

(5) $PF = 1.26^{***} + .006\ Time^{***} - .000004\ Time\text{-}Sq^{***}$
$- .057\ WWI^{**} - .088\ WWII^{***} + .022\ Rabbit$
$+ .009\ Rawlings + .078\ MfgCh^{***}$
$+ .007\ SteroidEra + .051\ Expan98^{***}$

Adj $R^2 = .89$

Thus, my foregoing arguments that Walker runs the wrong tests, muddies the measurement of power, misidentifies a manufacturing change impact, and focuses improperly on average overall power rather than the distribution of power seem to be supported by the econometric tests. Hence, Walker's claims to the contrary notwithstanding, I conclude that the use of anabolic steroids can increase the output of power hitters.

Analysis

The soap opera elements of the struggle against PEDs seem always to dominate the public discussion and the media portrayal of the issue. Thus, there is always more coverage of the latest Bonds rumor or Clemens press conference than there is of the social problem of steroids, the specifics of program procedures, or the physical effects of PEDs. Accordingly, it is not surprising that much of the discourse seems to be focused on finding a villain. The unspoken premise seems to be: If only we can blame it all on Selig, or on Fehr, or on an evil player or two, then we can wash our hands, and the issue will go away. Of course, nothing could be further from the truth.

Moreover, a fair reading of the history of PEDs in baseball shows that, although exemplary leadership behavior may have been lacking, there are no sinister villains. Bryant's 2005 book *Juicing the Game* is prototypical of the approach that chose to blame Commissioner Selig for conspiratorial and cynical behavior.[38] Bryant's basic argument is that Selig and his lieutenants believed that the home-run feats of McGwire and Bonds had rescued baseball from the fan alienation that followed the cancellation of the 1994 World Series. Selig, Bryant alleges without evidence, knew all about steroids and purposefully did nothing about it.

The problems with this interpretation are manifold. As shown above, Selig, in fact, took various initiatives beginning in 1994 and continuing to this day to confront the steroid issue. He, however, could not act unilaterally and, to say the least, had difficulty convincing the Players Association that a mandatory random-testing program was acceptable. Moreover, despite mounting evidence of steroid use in baseball, during the 1990s, most observers still believed that big muscles did not enhance performance on the ball field. Further, any student of baseball economics in the 1980s and 1990s knows that the financial issues behind free agency and collective bargaining dominated the mentality of the owners and players. Other issues, however worthy, took a back seat to the issue of salaries and keeping the game on the field. Finally, if trips to the disabled list increased by 32 percent between 1992 and 2001, as reported in *USA Today,* and the average stay on the list increased as well, then PEDs impose an obvious and significant cost on owners who sign players to guaranteed, long-term contracts, where players receive full salary no matter how long they are on the disabled list or even if they become permanently disabled.

Selig, of course, could have done more, and he could been more forceful. Criticizing Selig for early lack of effective leadership on the issue, however, is very different than accusing him of snickering behind the curtain and laughing on the way to the bank.

More writers today are likely to point their fingers at Fehr and/or Gene Orza, the leaders of the Players Association, as the villains in this drama. Fehr and Orza have taken the position all along that the Fourth Amendment protects the privacy rights of all citizens, including ballplayers, and that drug testing was acceptable as long as there was reasonable cause—that is, a sound basis for suspicion. Mandatory, random testing, however, does not meet this Fourth Amendment standard, according to Fehr and Orza, and, therefore, they maintained that it was improper. Legally, their argument may be sound,[39] and, as trade union leaders, it was understandable for Fehr and Orza to insist upon the protection of the civil rights of their membership.[40]

Yet the reality is more complicated for a variety of reasons. First, and perhaps most basically, if fewer than half the players used PEDs, then the majority of players (and union members) was directly disadvantaged by the presence of PEDs in the game. Indeed, from a longer-term perspective, even the users themselves may have been disadvantaged by the presence of PEDs. Fehr and Orza could have taken a position that it was in their membership's interests to allow for mandatory random testing, perhaps after an initial hiatus or adjustment period. This argument gains greater credibility in light of the 2002 *USA Today* poll that found 79 percent of players favored such steroid testing.

Second, even if testing was appropriate and players supported it in the abstract, there was still the question of trust. At the time of its 2002 poll, *USA Today* also interviewed a number of players in depth. Here is what it learned about player concerns: "According to numerous interviews, players want to know before they agree to testing how the tests will be administered and by whom. They worry about privacy matters and what the punishment would be for players who test positive. And they worry that owners might manipulate careers with control over drug testing, voiding contracts of undesired players and looking the other way with stars."[41] Given the historical nature of labor relations in baseball, one has to give deference to such concerns. Nevertheless, as we have seen in the testing protocols established in 2002, amended twice in 2005 and again in 2008, it is possible to stipulate safeguards around most of these issues.

Third, major leaguers have reason to be concerned that if PEDs are banned at their level, then potential replacement players from the minor leagues, college, and high school baseball must also be prevented from using artificial enhancers. Since 2001, MLB has had mandatory random testing of minor leaguers, but there have been questions about how effective this program has been, especially in its early years.[42] Similar questions exist for college baseball, where the NCAA has testing, but its effectiveness is in doubt.[43] New Jersey was the first state in 2006–2007 to begin testing high school athletes; only five hundred athletes were tested in the first year. Since then, Texas and Florida have started programs, and other states are contemplating doing so.

That said, in hindsight, it seems that Fehr and Orza fell into a typical trade union leader trap of being concerned only with the apparent, narrow economic interests of the membership. Many find the argument persuasive that a greater good exists than protecting the Fourth Amendment rights of millionaire ballplayers and that this greater good should have been the central focus of baseball's labor leaders. Fehr and Orza *may* have been acting as responsible union leaders, but they were certainly not acting as effective statesmen.

Finally, there is the player-as-villain hypothesis. If the public delights at the prosecution of its heroes, then somehow it is a form of exculpation. A fair perspective on player users, however, is that the players have been part of a baseball culture that has protected, if not endorsed, the use of PEDs and of a marketplace that provides stronger incentives to indulge than to refrain.[44] None of the media or congressional critics can say with certainty that he or she would not have indulged were he or she in the position of a major league ballplayer.

There is also the view that it is understandable if a player is a user, but it is unforgivable for an accused player to lie about his behavior, especially under oath. But accused players, however good they are on the ball field, are just mortals. Once accused, they are scared, and they receive legal advice about how best to protect their reputations. Perhaps they should know better and behave differently, but it is a stretch to villainize them under the circumstances.

The larger point about finding villains is that it has little to do with the very bumpy road ahead. First, we still do not know enough about the magnitude and the mechanisms of the enhancing effect of steroids and other drugs. Although it is clear, for instance, that because no urine test available detects HGH,[45] players have migrated away from steroids to HGH (and from HGH to creatine), it is not clear what effect HGH has on performance. The Mitchell Report states, "A number of studies have shown that use of human growth hormone does not increase muscle strength in healthy subjects or well-trained athletes. Athletes who have tried human growth hormone as a training aid have reached the same conclusion."[46] HGH does, however, promote tissue growth, which, in turn, aids in recovery from injury. This latter characteristic may also facilitate longer workouts in the gym, which promotes muscle strength. To be sure, it is difficult to separate the impact of steroids on muscle-mass development, because the same players who have used steroids have also dedicated themselves to lengthy, rigorous training programs. It appears to be the case that steroids, HGH, and amphetamines enable these more intense workouts.[47]

Another issue is that without more effective regulatory controls from the FDA or other government agencies, it will be impossible to eliminate the use of stimulants and enhancers. This problem is illustrated in a December 2007 study that found nearly 15 percent of fifty-eight sampled dietary supplements contained steroids or prohormones that were not disclosed on the label.[48]

Beyond that, there is the more complicated problem that cheaters will probably always find ways to stay ahead of the curve. Just as HGH today can be used with impunity in team sports, new compounds and masking agents will be developed over time that will enable players to avoid detection. It appears that the only possible way to combat this dynamic is to arrange for the freezing of urine or blood samples for future testing. Issues here regarding practicality, cost, chain of custody, and general reliability still provoke heated debate among experts in the field.[49] Presumably, the terrain will become yet more complex in the next five to ten years as opportunities for gene doping present themselves.[50] In any event, what appears clear is that there will be no quick fixes, and, indeed, the doping challenge is likely to be with us for decades to come.

What also appears to be clear is that MLB has become proactive and is on the right course. MLB lagged behind the individual sports and even the other team sports in introducing mandatory random testing with sanctions for PED use. The NBA, the NFL, and the NHL all had random-testing programs in place before MLB's first program was agreed upon in 2002.[51] Although the effectiveness of antidoping programs lies in the details of implementation (year-round testing, independence, auditing, sampling controls, and so forth), in its structure, MLB appears to have a stronger testing program in 2008 with stiffer penalties than the other U.S. team sports.[52]

Baseball fans have shown themselves to be resilient. Not only do they have ambivalent feeling toward the use of PEDs; they are willing to forgive as long as MLB is making a forthright effort to confront the problem. Indeed, unless the underlying integrity of baseball's governance is under challenge, it might even be the case that all the extra publicity for the game serves only to grow baseball's mystique and cachet.

To be sure, the ongoing trickle of implicated players from the infamous list of the 104 players who tested positive in 2003 does have a wearying effect. In 2009, first Alex Rodriguez's and then David Ortiz's names leaked out.[53] The testing results from 2003 were supposed to be anonymous, but they were seized by federal agents during the BALCO investigation. Someone with access to the results appears to be determined to release individual player names, drip by drip. Presumably, dozens of prominent names have yet to be leaked, providing years of grist for the sports pages and blogs. The issue is not going away.

What remains for baseball is to develop a policy toward the records set during the "steroid era." It seems to this observer that only one sensible choice exists. If amphetamines are considered to be performance-altering drugs, then the PED era has been in effect for approximately half a century. It likely will persist in various intensities for years to come. To single out particular records or individuals, when we do not know the effect of the PEDs on the performance in question and when the record breaker played with and against others who were also users, seems unrealistic. Moreover, if we were to nullify a particular record, then by implication it should nullify the performance of that player's team and, hence, wipe out the standings of the season in question. There is no logical place to stop.

Baseball fans know that many elements of the game have changed over the years and will continue to change: the ball, the stadium dimensions, the travel, the height of the mound, the size of the glove, the share of non-U.S. players, the bat design, the workout regimes, and so on. Baseball fans also have their own opinions about the use and impact of PEDs. Fans have always discounted and debated the effects of these changes and, hence, the comparability of records over time. That is one of the joys of baseball fandom. Asterisking or expunging records will just dilute the enjoyment of this vaunted baseball tradition.

Notes

Chapter 1

1. Moag & Company, "The Sports Industry's Resistance to Bear Markets," Winter 2002. Although the report was written during the 2001 recession, Moag sent it around to the firm's clients again in 2008 as a guide to the resilience of the sports industry.

2. In early June 2003, the FCC voted 3–2 to allow networks to increase their ownership of local affiliates. The new rules allow a network to own a newspaper and television station in the same city (up to three television stations in the same city) and to reach up to 45 percent of U.S. households via its owned affiliates.

3. See, for instance, the testimonies of James Gleason, COO of Cable Direct and chair of the American Cable Association, and of James Robbins, CEO of Cox Communications, before the U.S. Senate Committee on Commerce, May 6, 2003.

4. Comcast, the telecommunications conglomerate and nation's largest cable company, is buying NBC Universal, so it will be negotiating with itself when fees for carriage of NBC are set. Comcast also owns the emerging national sports channel Versus.

5. It is, of course, possible that competing broadband systems will emerge along with new aggregating companies. Such a development would alter the sales chain, but it would still represent a fundamental challenge to

the existing cable distributors' ability to sell packages to the household. Accordingly, it would also disrupt the present relationship that RSNs have, via the cable distributors, to the consumer.

6. These estimates are based on the annual estimated franchise valuations that appear in *Forbes* magazine.

7. Martin Shubik, "The Dollar Auction Game: A Paradox in Noncooperative Behavior and Escalation," *Journal of Conflict Resolution* 15, no. 1 (1971): 109–111. This discussion also borrows from Robert Frank, "Challenging the Myth: A Review of the Links among College Athletic Success, Student Quality, and Donations" (paper from the John S. and James L. Knight Foundation Commission on Intercollegiate Athletics, Miami, FL, 2004).

8. To be sure, it is a tendency that professors should readily recognize in these times of grade inflation. A "C" grade is supposed to be average; in many classes, all students receive above a "C," and, hence, the entire class is above average.

9. Of course, if owners behave strictly as rational profit maximizers and are unaffected by the special features of sports leagues, they will not be influenced by higher offers from competitive teams, and they will simply offer players salaries up to their expected marginal revenue product.

10. In the formal jargon of the NFL CBA, these items would be referred to as Defined Gross Revenue (DGR) and spillover.

11. Paul Brown, Mike Brown's father, was a long-time owner of the Bengals.

12. The NFL's salary-cap system contains a player payroll minimum for each team in addition to a maximum for each club. The salary cap for the 2009–2010 season was approximately $128 million per team. The player payroll minimum was 87 percent of that, or about $111 million per team. The payroll minimum also will disappear in 2010, and, thus, it is possible that overall spending on players would decrease despite the absence of a salary cap for the 2010 season. New free-agency rules would also go into effect automatically for an uncapped season. A player would need six seasons of NFL service time to be eligible for unrestricted free agency instead of the four seasons now required. (According to the most recent figures available, 237 players are eligible for unrestricted free agency during the 2010 off-season in an uncapped system. An additional 203 are restricted free agents under an uncapped system—enabling their teams to retain them by matching any contract offers from other clubs—instead of being eligible for unrestricted free agency this off-season.) Further, each team is allowed an

additional transition-player tag to use, along with its current allotment of one franchise player or transition-player designation, to restrict the mobility of its players in free agency. And the top eight play-off teams can sign free agents only to replace lost players.

13. Lester Munson, "Antitrust Case Could Be Armageddon," *ESPN.com*, July 17, 2009, available at http://sports.espn.go.com/espn/columns/story ?columnist=munson_lester&id=4336261 (accessed July 18, 2009).

14. MLS is structured such that operators of each team jointly own the entire soccer league. On appeal, the U.S. Court of Appeals for the First Circuit raised questions about whether MLS was indeed a single entity. Nonetheless, the district court finding on behalf of MLS was upheld on the grounds that the players' association failed to define a relevant market.

15. More precisely, it asserted that the antitrust laws in baseball's labor relations would apply in the same manner as they do in other team sports. The Flood statute reads as follows: "The conduct, acts, practices, or agreements of persons in the business of organized professional major league baseball directly relating to or affecting employment of major league baseball players to play baseball at the major league level are subject to the antitrust laws to the same extent such conduct, acts, practices, or agreements would be subject to the antitrust laws if engaged in by persons in any other professional sports business affecting interstate commerce."

16. The year 1973 also marked the first time that the NCAA placed limits on the number of scholarships that could be awarded in each sport. For elaborations on the contradictions of the NCAA's policies toward amateurism, see Allen Sack and Ellen Staurowsky, *College Athletes for Hire* (Westport, CT: Praeger, 1998); Michael Oriard, *Bowled Over: Big-Time College Football from the Sixties to the BCS Era* (Chapel Hill: University of North Carolina Press, 2009); Walter Byers, *Unsportsmanlike Conduct: Exploiting College Athletes* (Ann Arbor: University of Michigan Press, 1995); Andrew Zimbalist, *Unpaid Professionals: Commercialism and Conflict in Big-Time College Sports* (Princeton, NJ: Princeton University Press, 2001).

17. For a full listing of the 2009 bowl gifts, as approved by the NCAA, see the December 7–13, 2009, issue of *Sports Business Journal*, p. 32. These gift items and/or debit cards are also often provided to a school's VIP guests.

18. Page 1 of the Keller complaint.

19. In a setback to the NCAA, on February 8, 2010, a district court judge in San Francisco denied the NCAA's request to dismiss the two lawsuits and, instead, ruled that the two suits be combined into one. This ruling opens the multibillion-dollar NCAA licensing contracts to discovery.

20. In 2008, former NCAA president Myles Brand stated: "I see nothing wrong with selling jerseys with just numbers on them. But I would draw the line at selling names." The sale of actually worn jerseys, often with players' names on them, appears to contravene the principle in Brand's attempted demarcation.

21. Some believe that the new generation, so enamored with the manifold digitalized opportunities for consuming sports, will no longer put a premium on the live event. Although anything is possible, early evidence does not indicate any diminution in the excitement of consuming sports live and in person.

Chapter 2

Acknowledgments: The author wishes to thank Amy Perko, Mary Jo Kane, and Jeff Orleans for their comments on an earlier draft of this paper.

1. Only eighteen schools generated a net operating surplus over the five-year period 2003–2004 through 2007–2008. These figures do not include most or all capital spending on the cost side, nor do they include all the indirect costs associated with running the athletics program, among other problems.

2. Dan Fulks, *NCAA Revenues and Expenses of Division I Intercollegiate Athletics Programs Report, 2004–08* (Indianapolis: NCAA, August 2009). For more analysis of the trends for athletic expenses to grow more rapidly than athletic revenues or university educational expenses, also see Robert Litan, Jonathan Orszag, and Peter Orszag, Sebago Associates for the NCAA, "The Empirical Effects of Collegiate Athletics: An Interim Report," August 2003; Jonathan Orszag and Peter Orszag, Compass for the NCAA, "The Empirical Effects of Collegiate Athletics: An Update," April 2005; and Jonathan Orszag and Mark Israel, Compass Lexicon for the NCAA, "The Empirical Effects of Collegiate Athletics: An Update Based on 2004–07 Data," February 2009.

3. University of California, Berkeley, *Information Sheet on Intercollegiate Athletics and Faculty Resolution,* November 2009. Meanwhile, the Berkeley faculty senate, in the face of academic cuts, voted to end all subsidies to the school's athletics department. A month later, the faculty senate at the University of Texas issued a similar protest after the football coach's contract was renegotiated upward to exceed $5 million annually.

4. Interestingly, Alabama reported $123.8 million in operating revenue and $123.4 million in operating expense for 2007–2008 to the NCAA. However, university spokesperson Deborah Lane told *USA Today* that a transfer

of $25.3 million from the Alabama boosters club to the athletic department was double-counted and that the department's report to the NCAA in 2007–2008 was apparently overstated by this amount. Jodi Upton, Steve Berkowitz, and Jack Gillum, "Big-Time College Athletics: Are They Worth the Big-Time Costs?" *USA Today,* January 13, 2010.

5. Jonathan Orszag and Peter Orszag, "The Physical Capital Stock Used in Collegiate Athletics: Report to the NCAA," April 2005.

6. If no beds are empty, then there is an opportunity cost to giving an athlete a scholarship: Namely, the place could have been occupied by a student paying the face value (or a portion thereof) of the school's tuition, room, and board.

7. Such claims often begin with the invocation of the legendary Flutie effect, named for Doug Flutie's dramatic 1984 touchdown pass that lifted Boston College over the University of Miami. The Flutie effect, however, is chimerical. Boston College's application increases of 16 percent in 1984 and 12 percent in 1985 (not the 30 to 40 percent often cited in media reports) were consistent with the underlying trend rate at the school. Bill McDonald, "The 'Flutie Factor' Is Now Received Wisdom. But Is It Real?" *Boston College Magazine* (Spring 2003).

8. Devin Pope and Jaren Pope reviewed the literature and ran additional tests. They found that certain types of athletics success appear to increase interest in a school from applicants with high, low, and medium SAT scores; they did not find, however, that the initial interest translates into more applications or admits from the high SAT group. In the end, they conclude that the "summary data . . . would suggest that athletically successful schools actually saw slightly slower long-run growth in applications and enrollments." Devin Pope and Jaren Pope, "The Impact of College Sports Success on the Quantity and Quality of Student Applications," *Southern Economic Journal* 75, no. 3 (2009): 776. Robert Frank reviewed the literature as well and arrives at a similar conclusion. Robert Frank, "Challenging the Myth: A Review of the Links Among College Athletic Success, Student Quality, and Donations" (report prepared for the Knight Foundation Commission on Intercollegiate Athletics, May 2004); also see Andrew Zimbalist, *Unpaid Professionals: Commercialism and Conflict in Big-Time College Sports* (Princeton, NJ: Princeton University Press, 2001), chap. 7; and Orszag and Orszag, "The Physical Capital Stock Used in Collegiate Athletics."

9. The 2009 study by Orszag and Israel for the NCAA, for instance, reaches the following conclusions: "In our previous reports we found no evidence to establish a pattern, positive or negative, between athletic expenditures

and academic quality. . . . Our updated results continue to show no consistent support for such a relationship. . . . In our previous reports, we found no consistent evidence for a relationship between operating expenditures on sports and alumni giving. Using data from 2004–07, . . . we do not consider the observed statistical relationship between athletic expenditures and alumni giving to be robust enough to suggest a causal relationship." Orszag and Israel, "The Empirical Effects of College Athletics," 10–11; also see Frank, "Challenging the Myth."

10. See Jeffrey Stinson and Dennis Howard, "Athletic Success and Private Giving to Athletic and Academic Programs at NCAA Institutions," *Journal of Sport Management* 21, no. 2 (2007): 237–266; and Brad Humphreys and Michael Mondello, "Intercollegiate Athletic Success and Donations at NCAA Division I Institutions," *Journal of Sport Management* 21, no. 2 (2007): 265–280.

11. See, for instance, T. A. Rhoads and S. Gerking, "Educational Contributions, Academic Quality, and Athletic Success," *Contemporary Economic Policy* 18, no. 2 (2000): 248–258.

12. This theoretical expectation is consistent with the empirical findings in Orszag and Israel, "The Empirical Effects of Collegiate Athletics," 6, where they find that an additional dollar of athletic spending leads to an additional dollar of revenue—that is, there is a zero net return to the spending.

13. Jay Weiner, *College Sports 101* (Miami, FL: Knight Foundation Commission on Intercollegiate Athletics, 2009), available at www.knight commission.org (accessed January 6, 2010).

14. Fulks, *NCAA Revenues and Expenses of Division I Intercollegiate Athletic Programs Report, 2004–08,* 19.

15. Gary Brown, "Refined Reporting Shines Brighter Light on Spending," *NCAA News,* April 17, 2008.

16. This growing divide occurs both across and within conferences. When it is within conferences, competitive balance of the on-field competition is threatened. Iowa State, Nebraska, and Texas all play football in the Big 12 conference, one of the six BCS conferences. According to data from the most recent EADA reports, Iowa State's football revenue was $17 million, while that of Nebraska was $49 million and that of Texas was $73 million. See http://ope.ed.gov/athletics.

17. See the *O'Bannon* and *Keller* law suits.

18. For a discussion of some of these measures and where they have been implemented, see Michael Smith, "Must Win Situation," *Sports Business Journal,* August 24–30, 2009.

19. It may also be the case that some of the AD's proposed reforms, such as eliminating certain teams or restricting the number of scholarships, will provoke antitrust challenges from affected athletes. In this case, an antitrust exemption would be protection for the NCAA.

20. In a sample of forty-five Division I public universities, Duke economist Charles Clotfelter found that between 1986 and 2007, the average compensation of full professors rose 30 percent, while that of university presidents grew 100 percent, that of head basketball coaches jumped 400 percent, and that of head football coaches increased 500 percent. (Clotfelter, unpublished research. Clotfelter had full data on basketball salaries for twenty-two schools and on football salaries for forty-five.)

21. Pete Carroll's compensation at USC in 2009–2010 reportedly was $4.4 million. Alabama's football coach Nick Saban had his $4-million-annually contract extended and enriched in 2009. The new contract, in addition to endless, handsome perquisites and a variety of bonuses, guarantees him $44 million through 2018. Mack Brown, the football coach at the University of Texas, did Saban one better: Signed later in 2009, Brown's new contract provides for a guaranteed $5-million salary in 2010, with annual increases of $100,000 through 2016. Brown's contract is even more fabulous, because Texas has no state income tax. In December 2009, the University of Texas Faculty Council voted informally to call the salary "unseemly and inappropriate."

22. The sources for these figures are discussed in the statistical section of the text that follows.

23. One eye-popping severance clause appears in the contract of Mike Sherman, Texas A&M's football coach, who, if he is terminated, will be paid $150,000 a month for the remainder of his contract, which runs through March 2015. Thus, if his contract is terminated after the 2009–2010 season, he will receive a $7.8-million golden handshake.

24. As it turns out, Kiffin did finish the regular season at Tennessee—but just barely. On January 12, 2010, he and his son (Lane Kiffin, the head coach) decided to leave Tennessee after one year to follow a better offer from the University of Southern California (USC), replacing Pete Carroll, who had departed for the NFL's Seattle Seahawks amid various investigations around improprieties of the program at USC. Meanwhile, Lane Kiffin leaves behind his own mess of at least six secondary NCAA violations and an ongoing NCAA review of the Tennessee football program regarding the use of "hostesses" to attract recruits. The departure of 34-year-old Lane Kiffin sparked a near-riot in Knoxville. He needed a police escort to get off campus,

and it only got worse when it was learned that his assistant, Ed Orgeron, also leaving for USC, had contacted Tennessee-committed recruits to remind them that USC was now an option. The jilted Vols immediately tried to steal Duke's head coach before settling for Louisiana Tech's.

25. Steve Wieberg, "Top Assistants Command Big Pay," *USA Today*, November 10, 2009, available at www.usatoday.com/printedition/sports/20091110/coachpay10_st.art.htm.

26. James Johnson, "The Suicide Season," *Shreveport Times*, September 4, 2008.

27. Allen Barra, *The Last Coach: A Life of Paul "Bear" Bryant* (New York: W. W. Norton, 2005).

28. See Andrew Zimbalist, "Gender Equity in Intercollegiate Athletics: Economic Considerations and Possible Solutions," in *Sports Economics*, ed. Leo Kahane and Stephen Shamske (New York: Oxford University Press, 2010). Orszag and Israel reach similar conclusions in "The Empirical Effects of Collegiate Athletics."

29. To be sure, as with any piece of legislation circumscribing the market, there will be efforts to avert the controls. That is, if compensation limits are imposed, schools will look for ways to indirectly remunerate coaches. The U.S. Congress need not concern itself with these details if it grants the NCAA a partial antitrust exemption; if the NCAA takes advantage of such an exemption, the association will have to detail the regulation so as to minimize transgression. It would probably be unwise to apply a Bryant Rule, limiting coach's pay to that of the university president, because this would likely engender significant inflation in presidents' pay. An alternative would be to limit head coaches' pay to, say, 300 percent above that of the average salary of all assistant professors at the school or in the conference. A limit would also have to be imposed on the value of all benefits and perquisites at, say, 40 percent of the compensation maximum, as well as a restriction on outside income, requiring most of it to be channeled through the university.

30. College coaches have protested that college football teams cannot be properly compared to professional teams. The latter, they say, can always call up reserves when players get injured, but college teams must have players on their rosters to replace the injured. First, NFL teams have a maximum of sixteen players on reserve and practice squads to complement their forty-five-men active rosters. Second, the NCAA Injury Surveillance System Summary reports that for the 2000–2001 season, the serious-injury rate during games in football was 14.1 per 1,000 exposures, while the rate in football practices was 1.6 per 1,000. If we assume that sixty players enter a game and

the team plays thirteen games during the year (that is, including a post-season game), then the average total number of serious injuries (where a player is out seven or more days) from games is eleven per year. If on average each such player misses two games, then the average number of game-injured players is 1.69 per game. Performing a similar calculation for practice-injured players yields 1.48 per game for a combined average of 3.17 injured players per game. This hardly constitutes a justification for carrying 85 scholarship and 117 total players on an FBS team.

31. Teams are also allowed to carry up to eight additional players on their practice squads.

32. NCAA, *Gender Equity Report, 2005–06*, October 2008, 27.

33. This number is based on twenty-five men's scholarships at $30,000 each, plus the possibility of savings on women's scholarships and the probable reduction in athletic support staff and equipment.

34. Fulks, *NCAA Revenues and Expenses of Division I Intercollegiate Athletics Programs Report, 2004–08*, 37.

35. See the next essay in this book for an elaboration on this analysis.

36. If two or more non-BCS teams satisfy the "automatic berth" provisions, then the team with the highest BCS rank will receive the automatic berth, and the remaining teams will be considered for an at-large selection (i.e., chosen at the discretion of the host bowl committee). As always, Notre Dame gets special treatment as an independent: It receives an automatic berth if it finishes in the top eight in the BCS standings. In 2009, the BCS is working with another tweak in its selection formula. As explained on the Bowl Championship Series FAQ page of the BCS Web site: "Each conference will be evaluated over a four-year period based on the [*sic*] three elements: the average rank of the highest ranked team; the average rank of all conference teams; and the number of teams in the top 25." As explained in the text, a number of factors rigidify the status of automatic berth conferences. In the extremely improbable event that during the course of a four-year cycle one of the automatic berth conferences is threatened, the BCS conferences can always modify the procedures again, as it is the BCS conferences that govern the system.

37. BCS conferences actually earn additional revenue. Under BCS rules, BCS conferences are required to purchase 50 percent of the seats at BCS bowls, but they pay only 60 percent of each ticket's face value. Schools apparently sell discounted tickets to students but sell full-price tickets to alumni, to boosters, and to other fans. Of course, for some matchups, such as the 2008–2009 contest between Cincinnati and Virginia Tech, the BCS

schools have to sell most of their tickets at the discounted prices, and their revenue gains are more modest.

38. Of course, a sixteen-team play-off, which is practiced in the FCS and Division III football, would generate even more excitement and revenue. One plausible selection process for an eight-team play-off would be to choose the conference champions from the FBS conferences that had the eight best records. Jim Delaney, the commissioner of the Big Ten conference, told the House Subcommittee on Commerce, Trade, and Consumer Protection on December 7, 2005, that a play-off system would increase television rights fees by hundreds of millions of dollars. Darren Rovell estimates that rights fee would go up 2.5 times initially and even more after the Rose Bowl is collapsed into the mix. Darren Rovell, "College Football Playoffs: I'll Say They're Worth $160 Million a Year," *CNBC.com*, January 9, 2008, available at www.cnbc.com/id/22570730. University of Tulane President Scott Cowen cites Neil Pilson, who estimates that there would be a big boost in TV rights fees from a play-off structure. Scott Cowen, "BCS or Bust: Competitive and Economic Effects of the Bowl Championship Series On and Off the Field," testimony before the U.S. Senate Committee on the Judiciary, October 29, 2003. DeLoss Dodds, AD at the University of Texas, believes that a play-off system would be so popular that it would add at least an extra $1 million in revenue for every team playing Division IA football. Others have offered similar estimates; see the next essay in this book.

39. This survey is available at www.knightcommission.org. College presidents have been historically loathe to address the need for athletic reform. The average tenure of a college president is around six years; building a coalition for reform takes a long time and risks incurring the wrath of the trustees, the local boosters, many alumni, and students. Several college presidents who have been outspoken about the need to reform found themselves pushed out of office. Given that no effective reform has thwarted the commercial juggernaut of college sports in over a century and given the long list of pressing matters concerning college governance, it is simply not in a president's interest to concentrate on athletics.

40. Machen was previously president of the University of Utah, sensitizing him to the perspective of the nonequity conferences in the FBS.

Chapter 3

1. In its first eleven years, the BCS championship game has involved only eleven different teams. Oklahoma has been invited four times; Ohio State and Florida State have been invited three times each. For a discussion

of these skewed results, see Woody Paige, "NCAA Playoff System Still Far from Reality," *Denver Post,* November 27, 2009.

2. "Obama Renews Plea for College Football Playoff," *MSNBC.com,* January 9, 2009, available at http://nbcsports.msnbc.com/id/28579044 (accessed January 10, 2009).

3. About the July 7, 2009, hearings called by Senator Orrin Hatch (R-Utah) before the Senate Judiciary Committee, *Wall Street Journal* columnist William McGurn wrote, "In terms of popularity, it's a contest more evenly matched than any Rose Bowl. In one corner there's Congress with its 18 percent approval rating, according to the latest Rasmussen poll. In the other sits the BCS, whose system makes tons of money from television for its members but is preferred by just 15 percent of fans, according to a 2007 Gallup poll. No real winner here." William McGurn, "College Football Goes Down the Hatch," *Wall Street Journal,* July 7, 2009.

4. DIA has been infelicitously renamed Football Bowl Subdivision (FBS) and DIAA is now Football Championship Subdivision (FCS), leaving the linguistic puzzle: Why does the championship game occur in the FBS and not the FCS?

5. "Ari Fleischer Puts the BS in the BCS," *PERRspectives.com,* November 25, 2009, available at www.perrspectives.com/blog/archives/001677.htm (accessed December 10, 2009).

6. *Sports Business Daily,* November 25, 2009. *Sports Illustrated*'s Stewart Mandel quipped on Fleischer's appointment: "I love that the BCS, the most unpopular entity in sports, hired a guy who worked under the most unpopular president in history." Ibid. Nine former Heisman Trophy winners attended the 2009 Orange Bowl game. Each agreed that the current BCS system needed to be changed. Former Boston College quarterback Doug Flutie opined, "We need a different system. Ninety-five percent of the fans want to see a play-off of some kind." Mark Blaudschun, "It's a 2-Team Playoff," *Boston Globe,* January 9, 2009.

7. Interestingly, early on, the bowl organizing committees claimed their purpose was to raise money for charity. Murray Sperber describes the situation in the late 1940s: "In reality, the bowls ran a huge financial shell game. The top tier—Rose, Sugar, Orange, and Cotton—paid well, but almost all of the others kept most of the revenue or never made any. Furthermore, according to a *Collier's* investigation, even though all of the bowls claimed that they 'are conducted for the benefit of local charities . . . the [bowl] contributions to charities are inconsequential.' Figures revealed that only $5,000, or .003 percent of the gross receipts, had been donated to charity by 16 bowls in 1947." Murray Sperber, *Onward to Victory: The Crises That Shaped*

College Sports (New York: Macmillan, 1998), 179. The charitable claim remains on the BCS Web site today.

8. Cited in Jim Naughton, "Debate over the Championship Game in Football Reflects Larger Tensions in College Sports," *Chronicle of Higher Education,* September 19, 1997.

9. *BCS Chronology.*

10. Several long-term agreements between major bowls and conferences expired at this time, enabling the adjustment. Regional affiliation was restored to the major bowl games in 1998.

11. Naughton, "Debate over the Championship Game in Football Reflects Larger Tensions in College Sports."

12. These three conferences are Big West, WAC, and Mid-American. Today, the University of Louisville belongs to the Big East, a BCS conference, and Senator McConnell's interest in an antitrust investigation predictably seems to have waned.

13. Another WAC team, Wyoming, finished with an impressive 10–2 record and number-twenty-two ranking and was also not afforded an opportunity to play in an alliance bowl. One of Wyoming's two losses was to BYU in overtime.

14. Andrew Zimbalist, *Unpaid Professionals: Commercialism and Conflict in Big-Time College Sports* (Princeton, NJ: Princeton University Press, 2001), 106.

15. Reputations have a way of outliving the underlying reality and, thereby, being self-perpetuating. In 2010, for the first time, two non-BCS schools made it to a BCS bowl in the same year. Oddly, the two teams, Boise State and Texas Christian University, both undefeated in the regular season, were paired against each other in the Fiesta Bowl. Many predicted disastrous ratings for the FOX broadcast, and, it seems, FOX's own expectations were low. FOX assigned two obscure broadcasters, Sam Rosen and Tim Ryan, to cover the event. As it turned out, however, the overnight ratings for the 2010 Fiesta Bowl were 8.6 (and Boise State's home territory is not wired on the Nielsen overnights). Meanwhile, two BCS schools, Iowa and Georgia Tech, teamed up in the Orange Bowl the following night and scored only a 7.1 overnight rating.

16. For instance, in 2007, the New Mexico Bowl paid $180,000 to each team. Paul Rogers, "The Quest for Number One in College Football," *Marquette Sports Law Review* 18 (2008): 285.

17. In 2006–2007, the five non-BCS conferences together were granted one vote to share on the BCS board. The BCS conferences have one vote

each. As a result of this token change, some now refer to all eleven FBS conferences as BCS conferences, with the distinction that the original six BCS conferences are now referred to as the "automatic qualifier" (AQ) conferences. In this essay, I continue to use the traditional nomenclature, treating the BCS and AQ conferences as one and the same.

18. If two or more non-BCS teams satisfy the "automatic berth" provisions, then the team with the highest BCS rank will receive the automatic berth, and the remaining teams will be considered for an at-large selection (i.e., chosen at the discretion of the host bowl committee). As always, Notre Dame gets special treatment as an independent: It receives an automatic berth if it finishes in the top eight in the BCS standings. In 2009, the BCS is working with another tweak in its selection formula. As explained on the *Bowl Championship Series FAQ* page of the BCS Web site: "Each conference will be evaluated over a four-year period based on the [*sic*] three elements: the average rank of the highest ranked team; the average rank of all conference teams; and the number of teams in the top 25." As explained in the text, a number of factors rigidify the status of automatic berth conferences. In the extremely improbable event that during the course of a four-year cycle one of the automatic berth conferences is threatened, the BCS conferences can always modify the procedures again, because the BCS conferences govern the system.

19. According to the testimony of Michael Young, president of the University of Utah, before the Senate Judiciary Committee on July 9, 2009, "the Mountain West, the ACC, the Big East, and the Pac-10 each had exactly one team play in a BCS bowl game [in 2008–2009]. Yet, the three AQ [automatic qualifying or BCS conferences] conferences each received $18.6 million from the BCS for that year, whereas the Mountain West received only $9.8 million." Senate Subcommittee on Antitrust, Competition Policy and Consumer Rights, "The Bowl Championship Series: Is It Fair and in Compliance with Antitrust Law?" available at http://judiciary.senate.gov/hearings/hearing.cfm?id=3951 (accessed November 20, 2009). Further, according to Dr. Rob Spear, athletic director at the University of Idaho, each of the six BCS conferences received a base share of $9.5 million in 2008–2009, while only one base share of $9.5 million was sent to the five non-BCS conferences to share among them. Rob Spear, *Idaho Vandals*, entry posted November 19, 2009, available at www.govandals.com/ViewArticle.dbml?DB_OEM_ID=17100&ATCLID=204836943 (accessed November 20, 2009). Utah, which led the Mountain West Conference with a regular season record of twelve wins and no defeats, played in a BCS bowl in 2008–2009 but did not play in the

national championship game. Significantly, during the years 2007–2008 and 2008–2009, the schools of the Mountain West Conference had better interconference records with the schools from the BCS conferences than the schools from any of the eleven FBS conferences.

20. Under the BCS Agreement, Notre Dame gets an automatic $1.3 million payout each year, whether it makes it to a BCS bowl game or not. See, for instance, Nicholas Bakalar, "In BCS, Dollars Are the Only Relevant Numbers," *New York Times,* January 4, 2009. If Notre Dame participates in a BCS game, its take rises to $4.5 million—a sum that it does not have to share with any schools, as it operates as an independent in football. *BCS Chronology.* Notre Dame's guaranteed take roughly equaled Utah's net take in 2008–2009. Utah had an undefeated season (13–0), including a sound defeat of Alabama in a BCS bowl. After sharing with the other non-BCS conferences, Utah received gross revenues of approximately $3.1 million for its BCS bowl appearance, which, after expenses, came to a net of $1.5 million.

21. The payout from the 2009–2010 BCS was slightly lower, as it depends on the steady TV contract and game-day revenues at the bowls. The guaranteed payout to each BCS conference was $17.7 million, with the SEC and Big Ten each receiving $22.2 million for having two teams in BCS bowls. The non-BCS conferences for the first time had two teams in BCS bowls (although none in the championship game) and received a total of $24 million to divide among themselves. They did this as follows: Mountain West, $9.8 million; Western Athletic, $7.8 million; Conference USA, $2.8 million; Mid-American, $2.1 million; and Sun Belt, $1.5 million. The non-BCS conferences use a performance-based formula, agreed upon among themselves, to divide their total BCS revenues. The current four-year TV contract with FOX provides a yearly average of $82.5 million in revenue to the BCS; the new contract four-year deal with ESPN, beginning in 2010–2011, will average $125 million annually.

22. BCS conferences actually earn additional revenue. Under BCS rules, BCS conferences are required to purchase 50 percent of the seats at BCS bowls, but they pay only 60 percent of each ticket's face value. Schools apparently sell discounted tickets to students, but sell full price tickets to alumni, to boosters, and to other fans. Of course, for some matchups, such as the 2008–2009 contest between Cincinnati and Virginia Tech, the BCS schools have to sell most of their tickets at the discounted prices, and their revenue gains are more modest.

In addition, each year, the BCS makes a total $1.8 million payout to the FCS conferences. *2008–09 BCS Media Guide,* 10 (2008), available at http://

msn.foxsports.com/id/8765284_37_1.pdf. According to Tulane University President Scott Cowen, during the first five years of the BCS, sixty-three BCS schools earned approximately $500 million, while fifty-two non-BCS schools in DIA earned $17 million. Scott S. Cowen, president of Tulane University, testimony before the U.S. House of Representatives, Committee on the Judiciary, Oversight Hearing on "Competition in College Athletic Conferences and Antitrust Aspects of the Bowl Championship Series," September 4, 2003. Part of the payouts to non-BCS schools now come in the form of a *de minimis* payment to a school for "making itself available to participate in a BCS bowl." Thus, Temple University, Army, and Navy were each granted a $100,000 participation fee in 2005 and 2006. BCS Chronology. Temple is no longer independent and, hence, no longer receives the separate fee.

23. The ratio in 2007–2008 was a bit more unequal, with forty-four BCS teams and twenty non-BCS teams. In 2006–2007, it was forty-three BCS to twenty-one non-BCS; in 2005–2006, it was thirty-nine to seventeen; in 2004–2005, thirty-six to twenty; and in 2003–2004, forty to sixteen.

24. The BCS conferences use somewhat different formulas in dividing the bowl revenues among the schools in the conference. The most common system is to provide a travel budget for the participating school and then to divide the balance equally among the schools in the conference. This practice is followed in the Big Ten, the ACC, and the Pac-10. The Big East pays schools that make a BCS bowl game $2.4 million, with decreasing amounts for lesser bowls. In 2007, West Virginia received the most total revenue from the Big East conference (from all sources, including conference media deals and March Madness) at $4.66 million, and Syracuse received the least at $2.53 million; in the Big 12, the top recipient was Texas at $9.5 million, and the bottom was Oklahoma State at $6.6 million; in the SEC, the top recipient was Alabama at $13.2 million, and the bottom recipients were Auburn and Mississippi each at $10.6 million. This data are from 990 Forms obtained from *GuideStar Non-Profit Reports and Forms 990 for Donors, Grantmakers, and Businesses,* available at www.guidestar.org/index.jsp.

25. This pattern has been in place at least since the beginning of the BCS. According to Tulane President Cowen's 2003 congressional testimony, during 1999–2002, the top ten BCS teams played sixty-five home games against non-BCS schools but only eleven road games.

26. In the forty-five bowl matchups between BCS and non-BCS schools over the 2002–2003 to 2008–2009 period, the BCS schools won thirty games for a .667 winning percentage. During the period 1998–1999 to 2002–2003,

BCS and non-BCS schools met in sixteen postseason bowl games, and the record was an even eight and eight. Thus, despite the occasional standout performance, the non-BCS schools appear to have become less competitive with the BCS schools on the gridiron—again, reinforcing the notion that the BCS is maintaining a caste system in FBS football.

27. Indeed, during the four-year span 2006–2007 through 2009–2010, Boise State had three undefeated regular seasons yet received only one BCS bowl invitation and, not surprisingly, no invitations to the "national title" game.

28. *Bowl Championship Series FAQ.*

29. See the statement of Paul Michael Kaplan to the Senate Judiciary Committee, Hearings on the BCS, July 7, 2009.

30. In a rather odd twist to the normally stringent strictures of NCAA amateurism, gifts are also provided to players at the bowl games. For instance, players participating in the 2008–2009 national championship game in Miami were able to go to a suite at either the Westin Diplomat or the Fontainebleau to pick out $300 of Sony Electronics products of their choice. The players left mailing addresses, and the goods were shipped for them. Lesser bounties were provided to players in the other BCS and non-BCS bowl games. See, for instance, Danielle Oliver, "2008 Bowl Gifts to Participants," *Sports Business Journal,* December 8, 2008.

31. Alternatively, and especially in a sixteen-team play-off, the first-round games could be hosted by the higher seeded teams at their home stadiums.

32. The claim is sometimes made that the lesser bowls would lose their corporate sponsors, who would all flee to the play-off bowls. To the extent that this is so, it would only occur because the corporations believed that they were attracting more eyeballs to the play-off bowls than they were to the non-BCS bowls. Thus, more money would be spent by corporations on bowl sponsorships. Further, as prices for sponsoring a play-off bowl rise, some corporations will return to the non-BCS bowls until the cost per thousand viewers (or some other metric) equalizes. In the end, the BCS apologists wind up making an argument against the free market—perhaps not so unusual for cartel defenders.

33. For a concise explanation on the facts surrounding the CFA and its antitrust problems, see John Siegfried and Molly Gardner Burba, "The College Football Association Television Broadcast Cartel," *Antitrust Bulletin* 49 (2004): 799. The CFA schools do not overlap perfectly with the current BCS schools. For instance, the Big Ten and Pac-10 did not join the CFA, and several schools were in the CFA that are not in the BCS.

34. The *2008–09 BCS Media Guide* explains that the non-BCS schools receive a guaranteed 9 percent of BCS *net* revenue and an additional 9 percent of *net* revenue if one of the non-BCS schools plays in a BCS bowl (p. 10). It also states that 9 percent of net revenue in 2008–2009 was equal to approximately $9.5 million. Net revenue is not defined in the *BCS Media Guide*, and I inquired of several ADs at non-BCS schools, but none knew how net revenue was reckoned. Bill Hancock, the BCS administrator, e-mailed me, stating that the actual net revenue figures were confidential but that the formula was gross revenue (excluding the Rose Bowl revenue) less annual budgeted expenses (approximately $4.5 million), less annual payments to FCS conferences (total of $1.8 million), less annual payments to Army and Navy (total of $0.2 million). Thus, without the $22.5 million payout from the Rose Bowl, the BCS net revenue in 2008–2009 was $105.8 million.

35. Some of these changes include the following. In 1999, five computer rankings were added, making the total eight, with the policy to average the top seven ratings for each team. In 2001, two computer rankings were dropped, and two new ones were added, with the BCS taking an average of the middle six. Also in 2001, a fifth element was added—quality wins. This element added extra ratings points for victories against teams ranked in the top fifteen. In 2002, the margin of victory was dropped as an element in the ranking formula; there was also an adjustment, adding and subtracting computer ratings. In 2004, it was decided to remove the elements of strength of schedule, team record, and quality wins, because they were already reflected in the computer rankings—essentially admitting that these elements had been double counted in the past. The team rankings were now a product of the average of three elements: the average of the computer rankings, the AP media poll, and the *USA Today* coaches' poll.

36. These examples and much of this argument were first developed by Hal Stern in "Statistics and the College Football Championship," *American Statistician* 58 (2004): 179; and Hal Stern, "In Favor of a Quantitative Boycott of the Bowl Championship Series," *Journal of Quantitative Analysis in Sports* 2 (2006): 4. Also see Bill James, "Boycott the BCS!" *Slate.com*, January 7, 2009, available at www.slate.com/id/2208108 (accessed December 5, 2009). In 2001, Nebraska was trounced by Miami (37–14), while Oregon went on to dismantle the BCS number-three ranked Colorado. The anomalies did not stop there. In 2003, Oklahoma, LSU, and USC finished with one loss each. Oklahoma lost in the Big 12 championship game but remained number one in the BCS ranking. LSU edged out USC for a shot at the "title" and went on to beat Oklahoma. USC beat Michigan in the Rose Bowl and

finished number one in both human polls. The 2004 season ended with five undefeated teams. USC and Oklahoma were selected for the title game, and USC humiliated Oklahoma (55–19). Meanwhile, Auburn, the undefeated champion of the powerhouse SEC, was not given a shot at the title. In 2006, Florida, Michigan, Louisville, and Wisconsin had one loss apiece, and undefeated Boise State waited to see who would face number-one Ohio State. Florida was chosen and pounded the Buckeyes (41–14).

37. Graham Watson, "AD 'Very Hopeful That We'll Find a Game,'" *ESPN.com,* available at http://sports.espn.go.com/ncf/news/story?id=4642585 (accessed November 10, 2009).

38. David Harville, "A Penalized Maximum Likelihood Approach for the Ranking of College Football Teams Independent of Victory Margin," *American Statistician* 57 (2003): 241; and David Harville and Michael Smith, "The Home Court Advantage: How Large Is It, and Does It Vary from Team to Team?" *American Statistician* 48 (1994): 22.

39. See quotations from several voters displaying such a pattern of discrimination against non-BCS conference schools in the statement of Paul Michael Kaplan to the Senate Judiciary Committee, Hearings on the BCS, July 7, 2009.

40. Noel Campbell et al., "Evidence of TV Exposure Effects in AP Top 25 College Football Rankings," *Journal of Sports Economics* 8, no. 4 (2007): 425–434; and Rodney Paul et al., "Expectations and Voting in the NCAA Football Polls," *Journal of Sports Economics* 8, no. 4 (2007): 412–424. Yet another reinforcing effect of the BCS advantage was identified in a study that found that, all else equal, football recruits were 6 percent more likely to choose a BCS school over a non-BCS school. Michael Dumond et al., "An Economic Model of the College Football Recruiting Process," *Journal of Sports Economics* 9, no. 1 (2008): 67–87.

41. B. Jay Coleman et al., "Voter Bias in the Associated Press College Football Poll," *Journal of Sports Economics* 11, no. 4 (2010): 397–417. Also see Mark David Witte and McDonald Paul Mirabile, "Not So Fast, My Friend: Biases in College Football Polls," *Journal of Sports Economics* 11, no. 4 (2010): 443–455.

42. What follows in the text is not meant as a complete antitrust analysis. To do such an analysis would require a careful discussion of market definition as well as a consideration of each of the different markets impacted by the BCS cartel. These markets include the bowls, the television networks, and the advertisers; each is potentially negatively affected by the BCS monopoly. My discussion concentrates on the final consumers.

43. *NCAA v. Board of Regents of Univ. of Okla.*, 468 U.S. 85, 107 (1984).

44. *NCAA* 468 U.S. at 108. Notably, in another part of the decision, the Court gets its economic analysis wrong: "The television plan protects ticket sales by limiting output—just as any monopolist increases revenues by reducing output." *NCAA* 468 U.S. at 117. Monopolists operate on the elastic portion of their demand curves, so when they reduce output and raise price, their revenue declines. The trick is that costs decline more rapidly than revenue, enabling profit maximization.

45. *NCAA* 468 U.S. at 120.

46. Darren Rovell estimates that rights fees would go up 2.5 times initially and even more after the Rose Bowl is collapsed into the mix. Darren Rovell, "College Football Playoffs: I'll Say They're Worth $160 Million a Year," *CNBC.com*, January 9, 2008, available at www.cnbc.com/id/22570730 (accessed November 20, 2009). Cowen (2003 testimony) cites Neil Pilson, who estimates that a big boost in TV rights fees would result from a play-off structure. DeLoss Dodds, AD at the University of Texas, believes that a play-off system would be so popular that it would add at least an extra $1 million in revenue for every team playing Division IA football. Others have offered similar estimates. See, for instance, Keith Dunnavant, *The Forty-Year Seduction: How Television Manipulated College Football's Evolution from Sport to Big Business* (New York: St. Martin's Press, 1997), 187, who cites estimates of television revenues from a sixteen-team play-off of $200 million a year or more. Also see Jack Copeland, "Unbound," *NCAA Champion* 2, no. 3 (2009): 45, where he cites former NCAA executive director Richard Schultz's espousal of a two-week play-off in the early 1990s and his belief that such a play-off would increase revenues by three to four times. ACC Commissioner and former BCS coordinator John Swofford conceded before the 2009 Orange Bowl that a play-off system would generate more revenue than the BCS. See Blaudschun, "It's a 2-Team Playoff." Also see the testimony of Barry Brett before the Senate Judiciary Committee on July 7, 2009, available at http://judiciary.senate.gov/hearings/hearing.cfm?id=3951. Brett cites an estimate of $375 million in annual television rights fees for a play-off system. More generally, it would be of interest to essay an estimate of the anticompetitive harm from the BCS arrangement, but such an effort would take me too far afield from my present purpose.

47. BCS defenders have also argued that if the BCS is found in violation of the antitrust laws and forced to disband, the outcome would be no FBS championship system. Although there are legitimate questions about how

and by whom a postseason championship would be organized, it defies logic to think that a championship void would go unfilled.

48. The essential facility doctrine suffers from a lack of intellectual clarity and was dealt a blow by the Supreme Court in its 2004 *Trinko* decision (*Verizon Communications Inc. v. Law Offices of Curtis V. Trinko,* 540 U.S. 398 (2004)).

49. Gary Roberts, in his 1997 testimony before the Senate Judiciary Committee, argues that the formation of the Bowl Alliance was simply another form of restricting output. That is, it moved the postseason from a world where a dozen or so high-profile postseason games were played to one where four games were singled out as the only significant ones. Roberts states: "Payouts by the three alliance bowls (the Fiesta, the Sugar, and the Orange) after the 1994 season were less than half the $8.5 million payout they were forced to make after the 1996 season. These bowls, however, are merely the conduit, with the ultimate 'victims' of the monopoly pricing being the fans who had to pay dramatically higher prices for game tickets (Sugar Bowl ticket prices doubled from $50 to $100 in 1995, the first year of the alliance), corporate sponsors like Nokia (Sugar Bowl), and the networks [that] had to pay dramatically greater rights fees (which are then passed on to advertisers and eventually to consumers)." Gary Roberts, "On the Legal and Public Policy Effects of the College Football Bowl Super Alliance," testimony before the U.S. Senate Judiciary Committee, May 22, 1997. Of course, such a claim would need to provide empirical evidence that the dozen or so high-profile bowls were really at the same level of interest in the public's mind. Roberts does not provide this evidence.

50. In 1953, the NCAA passed a rule that schools could only participate in one postseason tourney. In 1961, it passed another rule that schools were "expected to participate" in the NCAA tournament. And in 1981, NCAA passed a "commitment to participate rule," obligating chosen schools to play in its March tournament. The NCAA settled the *MIBA* suit by buying out the NIT tournament for $40.5 million, plus $16 million to settle the suit.

51. Eric Thieme argues that if the NCAA were to organize its own postseason play-offs among the FBS schools, it would need to impose the "commitment to participate" rule, or the top football teams would not participate. Eric Thieme, "You Can't Win 'Em All," *Indiana Law Review* 40 (2007): 453. If this were true, the NCAA could presumably appeal to Congress for an antitrust exemption for this explicit purpose. However, several other scenarios seem plausible to avoid this problem.

52. Such a solution raises the question: Isn't one monopoly (the BCS) being substituted by another (the NCAA)? The answer is yes, but in the case of the NCAA, it would be a more inclusive monopoly that would enable an increase in output and a more legitimate process for determining the national champion. It would also enable a more equitable sharing of the postseason football revenue across the FBS conferences, the rest of Division I, and Divisions II and III. This more equal distribution would, in turn, reduce the incentive to a school to produce the national champion and may assist in controlling runaway program costs. Another option, a variant of which was suggested by Jeff Passan at Yahoo! Sports, would be to have a sixteen-team play-off, including the winners of each FBS conference and the five runners-up with the best records. The first- and/or second-round games would be hosted by the teams in each matchup with the better record—removing the potential problem of a team slacking off in its last game of the regular season. The losers in the first round could play in a bowl game, hosted by the current committees for the Orange, Sugar, and Fiesta bowls, with the championship game hosted by the Rose Bowl, the bowl game with the longest and most storied history.

Yet another less restrictive alternative would be to end the BCS system and throw the process open to the market, wherein particular bowl committees may be motivated to set up their own play-off systems. The bowl committees would have to induce schools to choose their bowl systems over others, which they would presumably do via higher rewards. The television networks may benefit from such competition among the bowls via lower rights fees (although there may also be disproportionately lower ratings). In such an arrangement, it is far from clear that consumers would benefit, as the determination of a national champion would be left largely unresolved.

53. Time periods and multiple other provisions are specified in this proposal. The details of the proposal raise a host of questions. First, the plan presently favors the MWC over the other non-BCS conferences. Second, the plan's ranking system still involves deliberation by a committee of interested parties, thereby extending the conflict of interest problem that inheres now to the coaches' poll. Third, the plan would require the NCAA to vote to lengthen the football season in the FBS; this, however, should be possible to do given that some FCS schools now play a fifteen-game season. Thus, although the details of the MWC plan may need to be reworked, they do suggest yet another alternative strategy: to keep the BCS but develop more inclusive rules and a play-off structure.

54. Antitrust claims against sports leagues are generally judged by the rule of reason rather than per se rulings. This is because sports leagues must engage in restraints of trade to exist (e.g., set a schedule of games, share revenue, impose labor-market rules). The NCAA would generally be assessed in a similar way. The BCS, however, does not need to exist for a national championship to occur. Accordingly, an argument can be made that an antitrust case against the BCS should be assessed on a per se basis, such as usually applies, for instance, in price-fixing cases.

55. Roberts, "On the Legal and Public Policy Effects of the College Football Bowl Super Alliance."

56. Of course, the sixty-five BCS schools also represent a majority of schools within Division IA (FBS) and are unlikely to vote away their privileged status.

57. These preferences are discussed in John Colombo, "The NCAA, Tax Exemption, and College Athletics," Illinois Public Law and Legal Theory Research Paper No. 08-08, February 19, 2009, available at http://papers.ssn.com/abstract=1336727; Congressional Budget Office, "Tax Preferences for Collegiate Sports," May 2009; and Zimbalist, *Unpaid Professionals,* chap. 6.

58. Mike Bianchi, "UF President Bernie Machen Talks Typical BCS Baloney," *Orlando Sentinel,* February 23, 2009, available at http://blogs.orlando sentinel.com/sports_bianchi/2009/02/uf-president-bernie-machen-displays -typical-bcs-hypocrisy.html (accessed November 22, 2009).

Chapter 4

1. A study published by the Women's Sports Foundation (*Her Life Depends on It,* May 2004) elaborates on some of the benefits from sports participation.

▪ Breast cancer risk: One to three hours of exercise a week over a woman's reproductive lifetime (the teens to about age forty) may bring a 20 percent to 30 percent reduction in the risk of breast cancer, and four or more hours of exercise a week can reduce the risk almost 60 percent. Leslie Bernstein et al., "Physical Exercise and Reduced Risk of Breast Cancer in Young Women," *Journal of the National Cancer Institute* 86 (September 1994): 1403–1408.

▪ Smoking: Female athletes on one or two school or community sports teams were significantly less likely to smoke regularly than female nonathletes. Girls on three or more teams were even less likely to smoke regularly. M. J. Melnick et al., "Tobacco Use among High School Athletes and Nonathletes: Results of the 1997 Youth Risk Behavior Survey," *Adolescence* 36 (Winter 2001): 727–747.

▪ Illicit drug use: Two nationwide studies found that female school or community athletes were significantly less likely to use marijuana, cocaine, or most other illicit drugs, although they were no less likely to use crack or inhalants. This protective effect of sports was especially true for white girls. K. E. Miller et al., *The Women's Sports Foundation Report: Health Risks and the Teen Athlete* (East Meadow, NY: Women's Sports Foundation, 2000).

▪ Sexual risk: Female athletes are less likely to be sexually active, in part because they tend to be more concerned about getting pregnant than female nonathletes. Tonya Dodge and James Jaccard, "Participation in Athletics and Female Sexual Risk Behavior: The Evaluation of Four Causal Structures," *Journal of Adolescent Research* 17, no. 1 (2002): 42–67.

▪ Depression: Women and girls who participate in regular exercise suffer lower rates of depression. George Nicoloff and T. S. Schwenk, "Using Exercise to Ward Off Depression," *Physician Sports Medicine* 23, no. 9 (1995): 44–58; Randy Page and L. A. Tucker, "Psychosocial Discomfort and Exercise Frequency: An Epidemiological Study of Adolescents," *Adolescence* 29, no. 113 (1994): 183–191.

▪ Suicide: Female high school athletes, especially those participating on three or more teams, have lower odds of considering or planning suicide attempts. Don Sabo et al., "High School Athletic Participation and Adolescent Suicide: A Nationwide Study," *International Review for the Sociology of Sport* 40, no. 1 (2005): 5–23.

▪ Educational gains: The positive educational impacts of school sports were just as strong for girls as for boys, including self-concept, educational aspirations in the senior year, school attendance, math and science enrollment, time spent on homework, and taking honors courses. H. W. Marsh, "The Effects of Participation in Sport during the Last Two Years of High School," *Sociology of Sport Journal* 10 (1993): 18–43.

A 2008 survey by Harris Interactive of over 2,000 third through twelfth graders also found significant psychological and social benefits from participation in organized sports. *Go Out and Play: Youth Sports in America* (East Meadow, NY: Women's Sports Foundation, October 2008).

2. The Department of Health, Education, and Welfare in 1980 was divided into two cabinet level departments: the Department of Health and Human Services and the Department of Education.

3. Clearly, a precise determination of whether the underrepresented gender is being provided equal opportunity will be elusive. The three-pronged test, where only one prong must be met for a subjective determination to be made that equal opportunity is being provided, was subject to an extensive period of public comment before it was promulgated. Since its promulgation, it has been extensively tested (and upheld) in the courts.

4. NCAA, *Gender Equity Report, 2005–06,* October 2008, 5, 10, 22.

5. In 2007, 4.32 million boys were participating in high school athletics (www.nfhs.org/custom/participation_figures/default.aspx; accessed January 1, 2009); thus, girls constituted 41.1 percent of all high school athletes— a slightly lower proportion than at the college level. The conversion of high school athletes into college athletes, then, was slightly more efficient for females than males. One possible inference here is that the provision of equal opportunity for female athletes in high school was more deficient at the secondary school than the university level.

6. General Accounting Office (GAO), *Intercollegiate Athletics: Recent Trends in Teams and Participants in NCAA Sports,* July 2007, available at www.gao.gov/new.items/d07535.pdf (accessed February 22, 2008).

7. To be sure, some methodological issues render the number of male and female participants less than perfectly precise. The GAO corrects for some of these issues. Other issues, such as when the schools count the number of athletes in each sport (e.g., when the team is first selected at the beginning of the season, at midseason, or at season's end), remain, because schools follow different practices. But no evidence suggests such irregularities bias the reported statistics in favor of one gender or the other.

8. Teams are also allowed to carry up to eight additional players on their practice squads.

9. NCAA, *Gender Equity Report,* 27.

10. See Andrew Zimbalist, "Gender Equity in Intercollegiate Athletics: Economic Considerations and Possible Solutions," in *Sports Economics,* ed. Leo Kahane and Stephen Shamske (New York: Oxford University Press, 2010); and a study performed for the NCAA by Robert Litan, Jonathan Orszag, and Peter Orszag, "The Empirical Effects of Collegiate Athletics: An Interim Report," August 2003, available at http://ncaa.org/databases/baseline study/baseline.pdf, section 4 and appendix I (accessed October 28, 2009). The authors used fixed effects models for Division IA football and found no

association between team spending and net revenue, no statistically significant relationship between spending and winning, no statistically significant relationship between winning and revenue, and a low correlation of a team's win percentage from one year to the next.

11. It is, of course, possible that if coaches' compensation was capped, the athletic departments would simply use the savings to seek other ways to attract the best athletes to the school (e.g., hiring more coaches, providing yet fancier facilities and travel amenities, and so forth). Although some such squandering of resources may occur, it is also likely that universities would be better able to control these forms of expenditure than they are coaches' salaries.

Chapter 5

1. Jeff Passan, "Comfortably Numb: Free Agents Paydays Should Grow," *Yahoo! Sports,* November 12, 2007, available at http://sports.yahoo.com/mlb/news?slug=jp-freeagency111307 (accessed November 12, 2007).

2. See, for instance, Pete Toms, "Beyond the Diamond," *Baseball Digest,* March 18, 2008; and Liz Mullen, "Flood of Talent Keeps Salaries in Check," *Sports Business Journal,* March 17, 2008.

3. It is particularly important to pay attention to this distinction when looking at the relationship between payroll and performance. Teams in the play-off hunt frequently add to their payrolls toward the end of the season, while teams out of the hunt unload players. This raises the payroll of successful teams (and vice versa), increasing the correlation between payroll and performance, but in this case it is performance that causes payroll rather than the other way around. Payrolls also differ in that they sometimes take the average annual value (AAV) of a contract over the length of a contract, and they sometimes take the amount actually paid out in a given year.

4. A Bird free agent is a player who is resigned by his former team. A non-Bird free agent is a player who is signed by a new team. Bird free agents not only can receive an extra year on their contracts; they can be offered salaries regardless of whether their salaries put the signing team over the salary cap.

5. The 60 percent, or roughly $12 million, does not include compensation to the players on the forty-man major league roster.

6. The NBA switched from DGR—basically media plus gate revenues—to BRI, including various categories of arena revenues, in 1999. In the 2005

CBA, it kept the BRI term but broadened the concept further to make it somewhat more inclusive. The NFL introduced its DGR with its salary cap in 1993. In that concept, a distinction was drawn between revenues supposedly directly generated by the players (media and gate), called DGR, and revenues not directly generated by the players, EDGR (excluded DGR). However, the 1993 CBA also stipulated that if the ratio of EDGR/DGR increased beyond its 1993 level, any overage (known as spillover) would be added into the revenue base for calculating the salary cap. Spillover did grow over time, until the NFL and the NFLPA decided to shift to the TR concept in 2006, which nominally includes all football-related revenues. When they made this switch, the league also lowered the designated percentage going to the players from 65.5 percent to 57 percent.

7. The G3 contribution is referred to as a loan, but it is paid back with funds (34 percent of club-seat revenue) that the team would transfer to the league in any event. So, it is more accurately described as a grant.

8. The actual computation of the credit is convoluted in the extreme. Fifty percent of up to a maximum of $300 million per project in present-value terms would be allocated over fifteen years, or a maximum of $20 million per year per project. On a per-team basis, this amounts to a $625,000 cap credit on each team's salary cap per project. Thus, in 2005, for instance, with the player share being 65.5 percent of DGR, this was the equivalent of a downward revenue adjustment of just over $954,000 per team, or $30.5 million leaguewide.

9. See previous endnote.

10. In 2007, for instance, the salary cap was set by taking 57 percent of "total revenue," subtracting benefits, and dividing by thirty-two to get the per team cap. Within this 57 percent, there is assumed to be a credit of 1.8 percent to cover the former G3 and security credit. If the G3 and security credit exceeds 1.8 percent, then the league, subject to union approval, is entitled to an additional credit up to 2.3 percent. Expenditures on G3 and security in excess of 2.3 percent can only be credited by decision of an arbitrator.

11. The source of this table is the author's communication with the NFL. As indicated in the table, TR exceeds DGR by between 11.8 percent and 14.7 percent, depending on the year.

12. It should be pointed out that the NFL's 2006 CBA allows for a deduction of 5 percent from total revenues as an adjustment for cost of goods sold (i.e., the difference between gross and net stadium sales), youth football, European football, charity, and some other items. It also allows for

a stadium-investment deduction of between 1.8 and 2.3 percent. So, the NFL's TR is really adjusted total revenue and is best understood in relation to its predecessor, DGR.

13. For the 2008–2009 season, the players' share of HRR was approximately 56 percent, or roughly $56.3 million per team, with a team payroll floor of $40 million. For the 2009–2010 season, HRR is projected to rise above $2.7 billion, lifting the players' share to the maximum 57 percent. Tripp Mickle, "NHL Expects Total Revenue to Top $2.7B," *Sports Business Journal,* June 28, 2010.

14. Ironically, the NFL displays a contrary pattern. One exception to the general pattern is the rapidly escalating cost of building stadiums and arenas. Insofar as new facility construction is funded by the team or the league (as in the NFL's G3 program), the tendency for rising salary shares to follow rising revenues may be attenuated or reversed.

15. For most MLB teams, the forty-man roster payroll is usually only $1 or $2 million above the payroll for the active twenty-five-man roster.

16. The posting system requires an MLB team to buy the right (via auction) to negotiate with the Japanese player. If the MLB team wins the auction and signs the player, the bid amount goes to the Japanese baseball team for which the individual played.

17. Or, to the extent it is known, $1 more than the player's MRP to the club with the next highest MRP for the player.

Chapter 6

1. This literature did not become publicly prominent until the late 1990s, after the Washington, D.C.–based Brookings Institution Press published *Sports, Jobs, and Taxes* in 1997. Naturally, the only relevant question is not whether a new team or facility will promote economic development. Among other things, a cost-benefit analysis of the project's fiscal impact and relevant opportunity costs should also be considered in the context of a decision to contribute public funds. Similarly, the intangible or nonpecuniary benefits are also pertinent.

2. We assume that 50 percent of the taxes are passed on by the team to the consumer for our estimate of the public capital share of the new Washington Nationals' stadium.

3. For example, earlier work by J. G. Long comes closest to achieving comprehensive and consistent measures across all facilities, including capital and operating costs, while still acknowledging that on a case-by-case

basis, significant subsidies remain uncounted. See J. G. Long, "Full Count: The Real Cost of Public Funding for Major League Sports Facilities and Why Some Cities Pay More to Play" (unpublished Ph.D. diss., Harvard University, 2002); and J. G. Long, "Full Count: The Real Cost of Public Funding for Major League Sports Facilities," *Journal of Sports Economics* 6, no. 2 (2005): 119–143.

4. A modified form of these measures was developed by Long in "Full Count" (2002) and based in part on the small number of financial analyses within the broader literature on the economics of sports facilities. See Dean V. Baim, *The Sports Stadium as a Municipal Investment* (Westport, CT: Greenwood Press, 1994); Rodney Fort and James Quirk, "Cross-subsidization, Incentives, and Outcomes in Professional Team Sports Leagues," *Journal of Economic Literature* 33 (September 1995): 31–54; B. A. Okner, "Subsidies of Stadiums and Arenas," in *Government and the Sports Business*, ed. Roger Noll (Washington, DC: Brookings Institute, 1974), 325–349; James Quirk and Rodney Fort, *Pay Dirt: The Business of Professional Team Sports* (Princeton, NJ: Princeton University Press, 1997); and Mark S. Rosentraub, *Major League Losers: The Real Cost of Sports and Who's Paying for It* (New York: Basic Books, Harper Collins, 1997).

5. Long, "Full Count: The Real Cost of Public Funding for Major League Sports Facilities and Why Some Cities Pay More to Play."

6. Baim, *Sports Stadium as a Municipal Investment*; Roger G. Noll and Andrew Zimbalist, *Sports, Jobs, and Taxes* (Washington, DC: Brookings Institution Press, 1997); Quirk and Fort, *Pay Dirt*; Rosentraub, *Major League Losers*; Raymond J. Keating, *Sports Pork: The Costly Relationship between Major League Sports and Government* (Washington, DC: Cato Institute, Policy Analysis 339, 1999).

7. Team Marketing Report (TMR), *Inside the Ownership of Professional Sports Teams* (Chicago: TMR, 2000); TMR, *Inside the Ownership of Professional Sports Teams* (Chicago: TMR, 2001); M. J. Greenberg, *The Stadium Game* (Milwaukee, WI: National Sports Law Institute, Marquette University, 2000); David C. Petersen, *Sports, Convention, and Entertainment Facilities* (Washington, DC: Urban Land Institute, 1996).

8. Michael Gershman, *Diamonds: The Evolution of the Ballpark* (Boston: Houghton Mifflin, 1993); Michael Benson, *Ballparks of North America: A Comprehensive Historical Reference to Baseball Grounds, Yards, and Stadiums, 1845 to Present* (Jefferson, NC: McFarland, 1989); Philip J. Lowry, *Green Cathedrals: The Ultimate Celebration of Major League and Negro League Ballparks* (Reading, MA: Addison-Wesley, 1986).

9. TMR, *Inside the Ownership of Professional Sports Teams* (2000 and 2001); TMR, *Stadium Revenue Agreements* (Chicago: TMR, 2005); TMR, *Fan Cost Index TM* (Chicago: TMR, 2006), available at www.teammarketing. com/fancost; TMR, *Fan Cost Index TM* (Chicago: TMR, 2009); Greenberg, *Stadium Game*; Petersen, *Sports, Convention, and Entertainment Facilities*.

10. Long, "Full Count: The Real Cost of Public Funding for Major League Sports Facilities and Why Some Cities Pay More to Play" and "Full Count: The Real Cost of Public Funding for Major League Sports Facilities"; K. C. Forsythe, "The Stadium Game Pittsburgh Style: Observations on the Latest Rounds of Publicly Financed Sports Stadia in Steeltown, USA; and Comparisons with 28 Other Major League Teams," *Marquette Sports Law Review* 10, no. 2 (2000): 237–310; Michael N. Danielson, *Home Team: Professional Sports and the American Metropolis* (Princeton, NJ: Princeton University Press, 1997); Noll and Zimbalist, *Sports, Jobs, and Taxes*; Rosentraub, *Major League Losers*.

11. These observed trends are not affected when we omit renovations from our data. Again, we only include renovations over $50 million in current dollars. The number of such renovations by decade is 1950s, zero; 1960s, zero; 1970s, two; 1980s, zero; 1990s, eight; 2000s, three.

12. The simple average takes the mean of the public shares for each facility during the decade. The weighted average sums all public capital costs over the decade and divides all public and private capital costs over the decade, giving more weight to more costly facilities.

13. The drop in the public share after 2000 for stadiums is affected by some notable outliers: AT&T Stadium in San Francisco, Gillette Stadium in Foxboro, new Busch Stadium in St. Louis, and Yankee Stadium and Citi Field in New York City. Because these outliers are all for stadiums, the public share for arenas rises after 2000, as does the overall share for arenas and stadiums.

14. The most significant outliers in our data set prior to the 2000s are as follows: Madison Square Garden from the 1960s cost $830 million in 2010 dollars and was entirely privately financed. Part of the deal, however, made the privately owned Garden exempt from city property taxes, which today provides a benefit of approximately $10 million annually to Cablevision Corporation. Montreal's Olympic Stadium from the 1970s with a cost of $2.05 billion in 2010 dollars and New Orleans' Superdome from 1975 at $662 million were each 100 percent publicly funded and among the first forays into domed roofs. In the 1980s, Toronto's SkyDome or, presently, Rogers Centre at $773 million in 2010 U.S. dollars and the first retractable

roof facility was largely privately funded. Lastly, when we run our data excluding renovations, all the observed trends remain.

15. Dennis Howard and John Crompton, *Financing Sport,* 2nd ed. (Morgantown, WV: West Virginia University Press, 2005), chap. 3.

16. In the case of stadiums alone, however, the weighted average public capital (total) share does fall steadily, from 102 percent during 1990–1994, to 86 percent during 1995–1999, to 77 percent during 2000–2004, and to 68 percent during 2005–2009.

17. The G3 transfer is referred to by the league as a loan, but the reality is that the team "pays back" this loan over time from its 34 percent sharing of club-seat premiums, and the latter sharing takes place with or without a G3 transfer. Hence, the loan is really a grant. The G3 program was formalized in 1999 but existed on an informal, ad hoc basis earlier in the 1990s as well. It formally ceased to operate in 2008, when the existing capitalization ran out.

18. Although the luxury tax component began in 1997 and lasted through 1999, the revenue-sharing (and, hence, indirect stadium subsidy) component did not begin until 2000.

19. In the NFL and MLB, the teams expect to generate a sufficient amount of extra revenues from their new facilities so that in net terms the leagues will benefit.

20. Other clauses and options were added to the 2007–2011 CBA that complicate the precise computation of the subsidy.

21. Of course, given the fiscal crisis that prevails in virtually all U.S. cities during 2006–2010, even spending small amounts per capita amounts to a challenge for most cities.

22. For cities below median population, the median public share in capital costs is 100 percent, and the weighted average public share is 90 percent. For cities above median population, the median public share in capital costs is 67 percent, and the weighted average is 63 percent.

23. Of course, it is also possible that some team owners will not perceive a large advantage to being in a big city if it means having to share the market with several professional teams from other sports and with a richer array of other cultural activities. In these instances, the expectation would not necessarily be for a lower public share.

24. The percent of facilities opened with above median population basically stays relatively constant between 1995–1999 (43 percent) and 2000–2009 (49 percent). Median population is defined by the Metropolitan Statistical Area (MSA) for 2008. The same cutoff is used for each period.

Chapter 7

1. Montreal city officials initially projected that the Games would only cost $124 million. Rick Burton, "Olympic Games Host City Marketing: An Exploration of Expectations and Outcomes," *Sport Marketing Quarterly* 12, no. 1 (2003): 38.

2. According to one report, the Soviet government spent $9 billion on facilities for the 1980 games. Burton, "Olympic Games Host City Marketing," 38.

3. Holger Preuss, *The Economics of Staging the Olympic Games* (Northampton, MA: Edward Elgar Publishing, 2003), 194.

4. Quoted in Burton, "Olympic Games Host City Marketing," 35.

5. For instance, in the recent Games hosted in the United States, the federal government provided $1.3 billion to Salt Lake City in 2002, $609 million to Atlanta in 1996, and $75 million to Los Angeles in 1984 (all reckoned in 1999 prices). Bernard L. Ungar, *Olympic Games: Federal Government Provides Significant Funding and Support* (Collingwood, PA: Diane Publishing, 2000), 5. For the 2010 Winter Games in Vancouver, in addition to the provincial government of British Columbia and the federal government of Canada each budgeting to contribute $9.1 million to help finance the bidding process, the provincial government was scheduled to put up an additional $1.25 billion to finance the Games (and to provide a guarantee to cover cost overruns), and the federal government was budgeted to contribute another $330 million. The city of Vancouver was budgeted to contribute $170.3 million. Available at www.mapleleafweb.com (accessed August 22, 2007). Not surprisingly, financing did not work out as planned, in part due to the worldwide recession of 2008–2009. In fact, the IOC provided a $22-million subsidy to the Vancouver Organizing Committee (VANOC), and "sources said that the IOC agreed to the first-of-its-kind bailout because without it, spending for the Games would have come to a screeching halt and major cutbacks would have been necessary." *Sports Business Daily,* October 27, 2009. VANOC also received an $87-million public bailout loan, and Standard & Poor's lowered the city of Vancouver's credit rating due to Olympic Games financing shortfalls, raising the city's borrowing costs.

6. Preuss, *Economics of Staging the Olympic Games,* 195.

7. International Olympic Committee, *2006 Olympic Marketing Fact File,* available at www.olympic.org/uk/organisation/facts/revenue/index_uk.asp. 23. (accessed October 28, 2007).

8. Preuss, *Economics of Staging the Olympic Games*, 110.

9. The U.S. share of total media rights has trended downward over time, from 83.4 percent during 1986–1989 to 60 percent during 2001–2004 to 52.6 percent during 2009–2012. *Sports Business Journal,* October 10–18, 2009. Because of the high U.S. share, the U.S. Olympic Committee (USOC) has received a disproportionate share of the total collected fees. Out of 205 NOCs in 2009, the USOC received 12.75 percent of all media rights fees from the Olympic Games. (This share had been 10 percent until 1996, when it was raised.) In 2009, after sharp disagreement, a negotiation between the USOC and the IOC led to a new agreement that, in 2020, the USOC share would be lowered again. The new level, however, was not agreed upon. Meanwhile, there appears to have been strong resentment among other NOCs about the high USOC share, and this may have contributed to the failed bids of New York for the 2012 Games and of Chicago for the 2016 Games. It may also have contributed to the peculiar decision to eliminate baseball and softball as Olympic Games competitions.

10. IOC, *2006 Olympic Marketing Fact File,* 51–54.

11. IOC, *2006 Olympic Marketing Fact File,* 82–83. From the Salt Lake City Games revenues, the IOC also provided $305 million to the NOCs.

12. In addition to providing for facilities, infrastructure, and security and to devoting large tracts of land on which to build the facilities, the eventual host city, along with its bidding competitors, typically spends $30 to $50 million to conduct its bid. Indeed, the failed Chicago bid for the 2016 Summer Games ran approximately a $100-million tab. Aaron Smith, "Chicago's Olympic Bid: An Expensive Proposition," *CNNMoney.com,* September 30, 2009, available at http://money.cnn.com/2009/09/30/news/economy/chicago_olympics_economics/index.htm (accessed October 1, 2009). The bidding process involves a roughly ten-year commitment for the eventual host city. Further, and as discussed elsewhere in this paper, host cities must maintain most Olympic Games facilities for decades into the foreseeable future.

13. Preuss, *Economics of Staging the Olympic Games,* 195.

14. Of course, not all OCOGs manage to break even; the Albertville OCOG lost $57 million. Burton, "Olympic Games Host City Marketing," 39.

15. Other taxes, such as real estate taxes, might come into play depending on the local tax system and whether the Games affected real estate values, positively or negatively. See, for instance, Gabriel Ahlfeldt and Wolfgang Maennig, "Impact of Sports Arenas on Land Values: Evidence from Berlin," *Annals of Regional Science* 44, no. 2 (2010): 205–227, which finds a

positive impact of sports facilities on real estate values within two miles of a new facility.

16. Herein lies another conundrum. The lower figure appears to include only operating costs or the budget of the Beijing OCOG. This is the figure that is generally publicized. The higher range also includes facility and infrastructure costs. The latter includes the expansion of the Beijing subway system and, hence, will likely serve the city productively well after the Games are over. Before and after comparisons are often plagued by this apples and oranges confusion.

17. *Sports Business Daily,* September 30, 2009.

18. Brendan Carlin, "Olympic Budget Trebles to £9.3bn," *London Telegraph,* March 15, 2007. Also see Bernard Simon, "Cost of Canadian 2010 Winter Olympics Escalates," *Financial Times,* February 6, 2006; and *Sports Business Daily,* November 14, 2008.

19. *Sports Business Daily,* November 14, 2008, citing a story in the *London Telegraph,* November 13, 2008. The Olympic Village was to be privately financed, but the plan fell through and will instead cost the taxpayers nearly $1 billion. The government hopes that the apartments will be sold after the Games, and the financing will be recouped.

20. To be sure, the Winter Games involve fewer participants, fewer venues, and less construction; hence, the cost of these Games is lower than for the Summer Games.

21. Not surprisingly, the PR hype does not always match this reality. For instance, the director of planning and budgeting of the Atlanta Games told Holger Preuss (author of the book *The Economics of Staging the Olympics*): "We can only give you the analyses which carry a positive image. Other analyses remain unpublished so as not to make our population insecure."

22. The Sydney bid cost $46.2 million, and its Games cost $3.24 billion. Preuss, *Economics of Staging the Olympic Games,* 233. The Sydney Games were originally projected to earn the Australian Treasury a surplus of $100 million. Burton, "Olympic Games Host City Marketing," 39. One of the goals of the Sydney Games was to generate increased tourism, yet Graham Mathews, a former forecaster for the Australian Federal Treasury, stated: "While having the Olympics may have made us feel warm and fuzzy and wonderful, in cold hard terms, it's actually hard in international experience to determine if there has been a positive, lasting impact on tourism from having that brief burst of exposure." Ibid., 40.

23. Similarly, maintenance costs on the Athens Olympic Games facilities in 2005 reportedly will come in around $124 million, and there appears

to be little to no local interest being expressed for the two Olympic soccer stadiums. "Cost of 2004 Athens Games Continues to Escalate," *Washington Post*, August 10, 2005. Torino had several white elephants, including its bobsled-run venue that cost $108 million to construct. Deputy President of Torino Games Evelina Christillin commented to a *Wall Street Journal* reporter, "I can't tell you a lie. Obviously, the bobsled run is not going to be used for anything else. That's pure cost." The speed-skating arena in Nagano (1998) is sometimes used for flea markets. Gabriel Kahn and Roger Thurow, "Quest for Gold—Torino 2006," *Wall Street Journal*, February 10, 2006.

24. The total reported cost of the Barcelona Games was $9.3 billion, of which private sources covered $3.2 billion and public sources covered $6.1 billion. See Burton, "Olympic Games Host City Marketing," 39. For a related account of large public expenditures on infrastructure for the Salt Lake City Olympic Games, see D. L. Bartlett and J. B. Steele, "Snow Job," *Sports Illustrated*, December 21, 2001, 79–98. Bartlett and Steele report that the U.S. government spent $1.5 billion of taxpayer money on the purchase of land, road construction, sewers, parking lots, housing, buses, fencing, a light rail system, airport improvements, and security equipment, inter alia. Some have argued that part of these expenditures would have occurred even if Salt Lake City did not host the Olympic Games.

25. Rick Burton and Norm O'Reilly, "Consider Intangibles When Weighing Olympic Host City Benefits," *Sports Business Journal*, September 7–13, 2009.

26. Michael Wines, "After Summer Olympics, Empty Shells in Beijing," *New York Times*, February 7, 2010.

27. Ibid.

28. Stephen Essex and Brian Chalkley, "Mega-sporting Events in Urban and Regional Policy: A History of the Winter Olympics," *Planning Perspectives* 19, no. 1 (2004): 205.

29. Terance Rephann and Andrew Isserman, "New Highways as Economic Development Tools: An Evaluation Using Quasi-experimental Matching Methods," *Regional Science and Urban Economics* 24, no. 6 (1994): 728.

30. John Crompton, "Economic Impact Analysis of Sports Facilities and Events: Eleven Sources of Misapplication," *Journal of Sport Management* 9, no. 1 (1995): 15.

31. This statement assumes that residents have fixed budgets for leisure spending. To the extent that they may expand their leisure spending or that they may substitute local leisure spending for leisure spending outside the local area, this claim must be modified.

32. Philip Porter, "Mega-sports Events as Municipal Investments: A Critique of Impact Analysis," in *Sports Economics: Current Research,* ed. John Fizel, Elizabeth Gustafson, and Lawrence Hadley (Westport, CT: Praeger, 1999), 61–74.

33. Victor Matheson, "Caught Under a Mountain of Olympic Debt," *Boston.com,* August 22, 2008, available at www.boston.com/sports/other _sports/olympics/articles/2008/08/22/caught_under_a_mountain_of _olympic_debt (accessed September 2, 2008). An additional problem for Beijing was that to abate the city's intense pollution during the summer months, the government ordered many of the city's factories closed leading up to and during the Games, and it imposed severely restrictive driving regulations.

34. Of course, the city of Tokyo may have benefited from Japanese tourists coming from other parts of the country. Any such benefit would have been at the expense of other places in Japan and would not have constituted a benefit to the whole country.

35. Julie L. Hotchkiss, Robert E. Moore, and Stephanie M. Zobay, "Impact of the 1996 Summer Olympic Games on Employment and Wages in Georgia," *Southern Economic Journal* 69 (2003): 691–704.

36. Stephanie Jasmand and Wolfgang Maennig use a difference-in-difference model to estimate long-term regional effects in Germany from the 1972 Munich Games. They do find regional income differences, but they identify no employment effects. Stephanie Jasmand and Wolfgang Maennig, "Regional Income and Employment Effects of the 1972 Munich Olympic Summer Games," *Regional Studies* 42, no. 7 (2008): 991–1002.

37. See Arne Feddersen and Wolfgang Maennig, "Regional Economic Impact of the 1996 Olympic Games in Atlanta—A True Olympic Effect?" (working paper, University of Hamburg, 2009).

38. Travis J. Lybbert and Dawn D. Thilmany, "Migration Effects of Olympic Siting: A Pooled Time Series Cross-sectional Analysis of Host Regions," *Annals of Regional Science* 34, no. 3 (2000): 405–420.

39. Jon Teigland, "Mega-events and Impacts on Tourism: The Predictions and Realities of the Lillehammer Olympics," *Impact Assessment and Project Appraisal* 17, no. 4 (1999): 305–317.

40. Teigland, "Mega-events and Impacts on Tourism," 309.

41. J. R. Brent Ritchie and Brian H. Smith, "The Impact of a Mega-event on Host Region Awareness: A Longitudinal Study," *Journal of Travel Research* 30, no. 1 (1991): 3–10. Other research showed that recognition of Calgary having hosted the 1988 Winter Games had almost entirely faded by 1991. See Matheson, "Caught Under a Mountain of Olympic Debt."

42. Gabrielle Berman, Robert Brooks, and Sinclair Davidson, "The Sydney Olympic Games Announcement and Australian Stock Market Reaction," *Applied Economics Letters* 7, no. 12 (2000): 781–784; Nikolas Veraros, Evangelia Kasimati, and Peter Dawson, "The 2004 Olympic Games Announcement and Its Effect on the Athens and Milan Stock Exchanges," *Applied Economics Letters* 11, no. 12 (2004): 749–753.

43. David Whitson and John Horne, "Understated Costs and Overstated Benefits? Comparing the Outcomes of Sports Mega-events in Canada and Japan," *Sociological Review* 54 (2006): 75.

44. See, for instance, Christopher Rhoads, "Post Olympics, Facilities Left to Rot in Athens," *Wall Street Journal,* June 19, 2010.

45. Giles Atkinson et al., "Are We Willing to Pay Enough to 'Back the Bid'? Valuing the Intangible Impacts of London's Bid to Host the 2012 Summer Olympic Games," *Urban Studies* 45, no. 2 (2008): 419–444.

Chapter 8

1. Steroid users place themselves at risk for psychological issues, cardiovascular and liver damage, alterations to their reproductive systems, and musculoskeletal injury, inter alia. HGH users risk cancer, harm to their reproductive health, thyroid and cardiac problems, and disproportionate growth of bone and connective tissue. When HGH is used by adolescents, these difficulties potentially multiply. It is estimated today that between 3 and 6 percent of high school students in the United States use steroids. National Institute on Drug Abuse, *Monitoring the Future: National Survey Results on Drug Use, 1975–2006,* vol. 1 (Washington, DC: Department of Health and Human Services, 2006), 44.

2. Sometimes the origin of professional baseball is cited as 1869, the year of the first professional team, the Cincinnati Red Stockings. There was also a professional baseball league between 1871 and 1875, but it was so discombobulated and corrupt that few see any positive legacy from its existence.

3. There was scarcely a whimper in the media as the New England Patriots prepared to meet the New York Giants in the 2008 Super Bowl that the Patriots' star defensive back Rodney Harrison was suspended for four games earlier in the season for violating the league's PED policy. Similarly, rather than calling hearings, Congress mostly yawned in 2005 when it was revealed that a Dr. James Shortt was facilitating steroid use for nine or more players on the Carolina Panthers. See a nice discussion of this disparate

treatment of baseball by George Vecsey, "Same Chemicals, Different Reactions," *New York Times,* January 27, 2008.

4. The sanctioning body in North American stock car racing.

5. Gary Wadler, WADA board member, medical professor at NYU, and acknowledged expert in PEDs, has stated that research indicates that amphetamines can be possibly more performance enhancing than anabolic steroids. Will Carroll, *The Juice: The Real Story of Baseball's Drug Problems* (Chicago: Ivan R. Dee, 2005), 78–79.

6. The survey was jointly sponsored by the commissioner's office and the Players Association. Eighty percent of players participated during spring training of 1991. Cited in George J. Mitchell, "Report to the Commissioner of Baseball of an Independent Investigation into the Illegal Use of Steroids and Other Performance Enhancing Substances by Players in Major League Baseball," December 13, 2007, available at http://files.mlb.com/mitchrpt .pdf, 67 (hereafter, Mitchell Report). Many individuals find that caffeine has a similar, though weaker, effect as amphetamines.

7. Michael Schmidt, "Baseball Is Challenged on Rise in Stimulant Use," *New York Times,* January 16, 2008. ADD is estimated to afflict between 2 and 6 percent of the U.S. adult population. A study commissioned by the National Institute of Mental Health in 2006 found that 4.4 percent of adults ages eighteen to forty-four in the United States experience symptoms of ADD and attention deficit hyperactivity disorder. With 108 therapeutic exemptions among major leaguers, the rate is 9.0 percent, based on the extended 40-man rosters.

8. *Sports Business News,* December 2, 2009.

9. Mitchell Report, 34.

10. Interestingly, in a February 24, 2008, interview, Yankee star shortstop Derek Jeter stated that he did not regard mandatory testing as an invasion of privacy. He said that he believed this for either urine or blood testing, indicating that players have their blood tested multiple times each year during health assessments in any event. Several other players subsequently stated that they agreed with Jeter. Soon thereafter, Don Fehr, the head of the baseball players' union, said that he would be willing to consider a mandatory blood test for HGH, if an effective test existed. According to Wadler and WADA officials, as of early 2008, an effective blood test does exist, and a European company has begun to produce the necessary antigens to make the test commercially available. The limitation of the test is that the tested individual must have ingested the HGH within forty-eight hours of the test. Many users, however, take HGH several times a week. It is also possible to

freeze plasma for subsequent testing, but this creates chain of custody and cost, as well as scientific, issues. Nonetheless, U.S. Anti-Doping Agency plans to freeze and store urine, and possibly blood, samples of 2008 Olympians for four years to deter PED use.

11. Rob Manfred, MLB's vice president of player relations, states that nevertheless there was sufficient discussion of random drug testing at the time to make it clear that the union wanted no part of it.

12. The number of positives on the minor league tests continued to fall: to 4 percent in 2003, to 1.7 percent in 2004, to 1.8 percent in 2005, and to 0.4 percent in 2006. The upward blip in 2005 may have resulted from improved and tighter testing procedures. Mitchell Report, 46.

13. The results of some tests were disputed, hence the range between 5 and 7 percent.

14. First-time offenders would be suspended for ten days, second-time offenders for thirty days, third-time offenders for sixty days, and fourth-time offenders for one year.

15. The McKay and Armstrong estimates appear in the Mitchell Report, SR-2.

16. Mitchell Report, 67.

17. Peter Gammons, "They've Met Disappointment," *Boston Globe,* August 16, 1992.

18. Bob Nightengale, "Baseball Still Doesn't Get It," *Palm Beach Post,* July 2, 1995; Nightengale, "Steroids Become an Issue," *Los Angeles Times,* July 15, 1995; Nightengale, "Steroids in Baseball: Say It Ain't So, Bud," *Sporting News,* July 24, 1995.

19. Ross Newhan, "Pitchers Hit the Showers in April," *Los Angeles Times,* May 5, 1996.

20. Peter Gammons, "Birds Have Feathered Their Nest," *Boston Globe,* March 2, 1997.

21. Mitchell Report, 16.

22. Ibid., SR-15.

23. Mark Fainaru-Wada and Lance Williams, *Game of Shadows* (New York: Gotham Books, 2006). Also see their articles that preceded the book in the *San Francisco Chronicle.*

24. Tom Verducci, "Totally Juiced," *Sports Illustrated,* June 3, 2002. Ken Caminiti also stated that steroid use was widespread in baseball, suggesting that over half of major leaguers had used steroids.

25. Mel Antonen, "USA Today Poll: 79% of Players Want Drug Testing," *USA Today,* July 8, 2002.

26. Ibid. The survey included 556 of the active 750 major leaguers and was taken between June 12 and June 23. Of course, many details about how the tests should be taken, how often, and with what kind of discipline were left out of the survey. Although likely to be understated, the survey also found that 75 percent of polled players believed that fewer than 50 percent of players used steroids. The article also reported on a separate poll of fans. Eighty-six percent of fans thought baseball should test for steroids, and almost 80 percent felt that steroids accounted for the then-recent outburst of power.

27. Of course, the concept of complete independence is itself nebulous. For instance, many analysts point to WADA and USADA as completely independent; yet, these organizations are creatures of the Olympic Movement, and if the IOC withdrew its support, these bodies would likely fold.

28. Alan Schwarz, "A Voice of Skepticism on the Impact of Steroids," *New York Times,* January 27, 2008. Eric Walker's argument is also touted on BaseballProspectus.com and on the *Baseball Prospectus* radio show.

29. Available at http://steroids-and-baseball.com (accessed January 28, 2008).

30. In a separate section, Walker argues that a batter's power comes from his waist down, and, therefore, steroids are not likely to aid power. Even if this premise were accurate, it is still the case that steroids can help build lower body strength.

31. Walker makes a similar mistake when he asserts that expansions (increases in the number of teams) do not lead to record-setting performances. Again, Walker focuses on averages and not the distribution of performance. Why, until 1998, were almost all of baseball's personal achievement records set between 1910 and 1930? Hornsby batted .424 in 1924, Wilson knocked in 190 runs in 1930, Webb whacked 67 doubles in 1931, Ruth scored 177 runs in 1921, and Leonard had a 1.01 ERA in 1914. Many believe that players in the good old days were better than today's players— not so. Baseball stats are the product of competing forces and reveal little about the absolute quality of the players.

The reason has to do with relative degrees of talent compression. The distribution of baseball skills in the population follows a normal distribution (like a bell-shaped curve). For any given curve, the larger the number of people selected to play major league baseball, the greater the difference between the best and the worst players in the league. If the population grows and the number of baseball teams does not, then the proportion of the population playing falls, and the distribution of talent becomes more compressed. This is what happened in MLB between 1903 and 1960, with the population growing from 80 million to 181 million and the number of teams remaining constant at sixteen.

Moreover, in the late 1940s, baseball began to accept black players and to recruit Latin and other international players in greater numbers. This accentuated the compression, while better nurturance of baseball skills through the development of youth baseball leagues and of physical abilities in general offset the talent dispersion resulting from the growing appeal of football and basketball to American youth.

With talent increasingly compressed, the difference in skills between the best and worst players grew narrower, and it became more difficult for the best players to stand out. Hence, records ceased being broken or even approached (save the asterisked performance by Roger Maris in 1961, the first year of MLB expansion).

Thus, it makes little sense to argue that Babe Ruth hit more home runs per season than Harmon Killebrew did, because he was stronger or had superior baseball skills. It makes more sense to suspect that Ruth played during a time when talent was more dispersed, so he faced many superb pitchers, but he also faced a much larger number of weak pitchers than did Killebrew. Similarly, Dutch Leonard or Walter Johnson (ERA of 1.09 in 1913) faced some spectacular hitters, but they also faced a much larger number of weak hitters than did Sandy Koufax, Ron Guidry, Roger Clemens, or Curt Schilling.

The ratio of the U.S. population to the number of major league players rose from 250,000 to 1 in 1903 to 307,500 to 1 in 1930 and 452,500 to 1 in 1960; thereafter, it fell gradually to 385,000 to 1 in 1990 and 360,000 to 1 in 1998, after MLB's second expansion by two teams in the 1990s. Thus, talent decompression gradually set in after 1960, and by 1998 the ratio had almost fallen back to the level of 1930.

32. The data are for both the American and National Leagues together from 1901 through 2007. Time equals 1 in 1901, 2 in 1902, and so forth. WWI is a dummy variable equaling 1 during the U.S. involvement in the war and 0 in other years. WWII is the same. Rabbit is a dummy variable equaling 1 in 1920 (the end of the dead-ball era) and thereafter and 0 before. Rawlings is a dummy variable equaling 1 in 1977 (when Rawling took over the manufacturing contract for baseballs from Spalding) and thereafter and 0 before. MfgCh is a dummy variable equaling 1 in 1993 (when, according to Walker, Rawlings changed the manufacturing process to make the ball livelier) and thereafter and 0 before. Of course, 1993 also marks the year of baseball's first expansion since 1977. Exp98 is a dummy variable equal to 1

in 1998 and thereafter and 0 before. SteroidEra is a dummy variable equaling 1 from 1996 through 2001 and 0 in other years. The year 1996 was chosen, because it is when evidence suggests that steroid use became more widespread, and it is also the year when observers began to comment on an abrupt jump in power. The year 2001 was chosen as the last year for that era, because it is when MLB introduced mandatory, random steroid testing among its minor leaguers, and it is the last year before the Players Association and the commissioner's office agreed to introduce a protocol leading to the mandatory testing policy in the major leagues. That is, I choose to delineate the steroid era by identifying the years of most widespread and intense use. Other dummy variables, representing other years of expansion, the introduction of the lower pitcher's mound and new strike zone in 1965, and the introduction of the designated hitter in the American League in 1973 were attempted, but there was too much collinearity with the dummy variables and not enough variance for these variables to allow for a clean statistical test. *** indicates that the variable is significant at the .01 level, ** at the .05 level, and * at the .10 level.

33. Exp98 and SteroidEra had t values of 1.16 and 1.10, respectively, with P values of .247 and .275.

34. This quote appears on p. 4 of Walker's section on "Changes in the Baseball" on his site. On p. 8 of this section, he reiterates: "The Penn State study showed a marked increase in zip from 1977 on."

35. Rawlings's records do not show any modification in the ball-manufacturing specifications in the 1992–1994 period. I have reviewed Rawlings's tests on the COR (coefficient of restitution—a measure of the balls' liveliness) of their baseballs. The evidence shows no upward ratchet in that time frame.

36. A separate analysis that considers the home runs per hit of the leading home-run hitter from 1959 through 2007 reveals an average 0.3312. The only years this average jumped above 0.40 were during the period 1995–2001, when it exceeded 0.40 four times.

37. The regressions using HTH and top ten PF and top ten HTH and entering "Time" quadratically showed similar modifications in the results.

38. Howard Bryant, *Juicing the Game: Drugs, Power, and the Fight for the Soul of Major League Baseball* (New York: Viking Press, 2005).

39. Because the Fourth Amendment provides protection from state actors and not private employers, it is questionable whether the MLBPA's privacy claim would hold up in court. The union could claim that the private employer—MLB, in this instance—was doing the government's bidding.

40. In this context, it is interesting that in late February 2008, several players, including Derek Jeter, began to express the opinion that neither urine nor blood testing was an invasion of privacy. Accordingly, Fehr has modified his opposition to blood testing, now asserting that if an effective blood test can be developed, the Players Association would be willing to consider it.

41. Antonen, "USA Today Poll."

42. According to figures from MLB, the minor league testing program has been remarkably successful. Positive test rates have declined steadily, and by 2009 they were under 1 percent.

43. See, for instance, a scathing critique of the NCAA testing program in Michael Lewis and Nate Carlisle, "Broken College System Lets Drug Cheats Slip through the Cracks," *Salt Lake Tribune*, November 18, 2007.

44. Under plausible assumptions in a prisoner's dilemma framework, indulging can be shown to be a dominant strategy for players when decisions are taken independently. Yet joint player welfare can be maximized when a strong deterrent program is introduced.

45. Although disputed, it does appear that a commercially available and reliable blood test for HGH is now available. The test, used for the 2008 Summer Olympic Games in Beijing, is said to only work if the athlete ingests the HGH within forty-eight hours of the test. In any event, none of the team sports in the United States currently admits blood testing in its antidoping programs.

46. Mitchell Report, 9. The report cites four medical papers in this connection.

47. The Mitchell Report contains another fascinating assertion on p. SR-30: "Dr. [Jay] Hoffman [a former professional athlete and an expert in the field] proposes that education about the dangers of performance enhancing substances be combined with education on how to achieve *the same results* through proper training, nutrition, and supplements that are legal and safe" [italics mine]. One presumes that the amount of effort to achieve such results naturally is out of reach for most individuals, but taken at its face this assertion informs us that the power heroics of the 1998 and 2001 may be repeated in a PEDs-free game.

48. Cited in Mitchell Report, 24.

49. See, for instance, Duff Wilson and Juliet Macur, "Antidoping Officials Give Baseball Leaders Failing Grade," *New York Times*, January 17, 2008.

50. For interesting discussions of gene doping, see Carroll, *Juice*, chap. 11; and Nathan Jendrick, *Dunks, Doubles, Doping: How Steroids Are Killing American Athletics* (Guilford, CT: Lyons Press, 2006), chap. 14.

51. Of course, the NFL has a much longer history of steroid use than baseball. Will Carroll traces PED's systematic use in the NFL back to 1968. Carroll, *Juice,* 39. The NBA began drug testing in 1983. The NFL began in 1987, and the NCAA began in 1986. Ibid., 40. The NFL suspends a player testing positive for the first time for four games, for the second time for six games, and for the third time indefinitely, with a one-year minimum. Carroll writes: "If the league's tests are to be believed, the NFL's performance-enhancing drug policy is working. According to published reports, the league on average has fewer than five positive tests a year. This doesn't match up with the increasing size of the players." Ibid., 109. Positive tests in the Olympics carry stiffer sanctions: The first positive brings a two-year suspension; the second positive brings a permanent suspension. Ibid., 112.

52. See, for instance, the summaries of the other programs in Antonen, "USA Today Poll"; and the Mitchell Report. The only program that has a nominally independent administrator is the Olympic Games. In response to a doping scandal in cycling, the IOC created WADA in November 1999 to implement its program.

53. An interesting wrinkle developed with the accusation of David Ortiz. Ortiz claimed that he only used supplements that might have given him the positive test. He was backed up strongly by the Players Association. Whatever the real facts are regarding Ortiz, his situation raises the question of whether some of the players on the list actually used illegal drugs.

Index

ABC television network, 4, 49, 51
admission applications, impact of college
    sports on, 33–34, 55, 175nn7–8
Alabama, University of, 39, 174–175n4,
    177n21, 184n20, 185n24
Albertville Olympic Games (1992), 120,
    202n14
amateur status: of college athletes, 21–26,
    29; of Olympic athletes, 118–119
American Needle v. NFL, 19–20, 21
amphetamines, as performance-enhancing
    drugs, 149–150, 169, 207nn5–7
Anabolic Steroid Control Act (1990), 148,
    150
Anabolic Steroid Control Act (2004), 148
anabolic steroids, as performance-enhanc-
    ing drugs, 147, 148, 150–169, 206–207n3;
    claims of Walker on effects of, 157–163;
    health effects of, 154, 206n1; legislation
    on, 148, 150; in NFL, 213n51; testing for,
    150–151
androstenedione, as performance-enhanc-
    ing drug, 148, 153, 154
antitrust laws, 19–21; in college sports, 38,
    44, 48, 65–71, 178n29; in MLB, 21, 27,
    173n15; in NFL, 19–20
Associated Press college football poll, 51,
    65, 188n41
Association for Intercollegiate Athletics for
    Women (AIAW), 77

Athens Olympic Games (2004): facility use
    after, 128, 143, 203–204n23; infrastruc-
    ture and facility costs in, 125; profes-
    sional status of athletes in, 119; public
    investment in, 121; security costs in, 124;
    stock market impact of, 141–142; tele-
    vision revenue in, 122–123; tourism
    impact of, 134, 136
Atlanta Olympic Games (1996), 132–133,
    134, 137–138, 143, 201n5, 203n21
Atlantic Coast Conference, 50, 56, 69,
    185n24
AT&T Stadium (San Francisco), 110,
    199n13
attendance rates, 2, 3; in multiplier-based
    estimates on Olympic Games, 132–135
attention deficit disorder, 149, 207n7
auction experiment, 9–11
automatic berths in Bowl Championship
    Series, 56, 183nn17–18

BALCO (Bay Area Laboratory Coopera-
    tive), 155, 168
Barcelona Olympic Games (1992), 119,
    120, 121, 126, 134, 204n24
basketball, college: coach compensation in,
    38, 83, 84, 177n20; gifts to players in, 23;
    National Invitational Tournament in, 44,
    69–70, 190n50; video games based on
    players in, 25

Basketball Related Income, 89–90, 92–93, 196n6
Beijing Olympic Games (2008), 121, 124, 125, 128, 134, 143, 203n16, 205n33
Bettman, Gary, 27
bidding process: in Olympic Games, 121, 122, 123–124, 125, 202n12; in professional sports, 10–12
Big East Conference, 50, 56, 69, 185n24
Big Ten Conference, 51, 56, 67, 68, 184n21, 185n24
Big 12 Conference, 56
Bloomberg, Michael, 116
Board of Trustees of the University of Oklahoma v. NCAA, 66
Boise State University, 57, 64, 69, 182n15, 186n27, 188n36
Bonds, Barry, 154, 155, 164
Bosh, Chris, 18
Boston Red Sox, 12, 154
Bouton, Jim, 149
Bowl Alliance, 190n49
Bowl Championship Series (BCS), 21, 41–43, 47–74, 179–180nn36–38; alternatives to, 70, 72–73, 191nn52–53; antitrust issues in, 48, 65–71, 188–192nn42–55; automatic berths in, 56, 183nn17–18; benefits of participation in, 54–55; charitable donations from, 181–182n7; conference revenue from, 42, 56–57, 62, 69, 179–180n37, 184–185nn21–24; exclusionary acts in, 68–70; gifts to players in, 186n30; guaranteed payouts in, 184nn20–21; history of, 49–53; home field games in, 57, 185n25; local economic benefits of, 49; net revenue in, 187n34; number of post-season games in, 53; price fixing in, 69; quality of teams in, 49–50; rationale for current system, 58–62; as recruitment incentive, 54–55; reimbursement for team expenses in, 53–54, 182n16; selection criteria in (*see* selection criteria in BCS); television revenue from, 67–68, 189n46; ticket sales for, 179–180n37, 184n22, 190n49
boxing, 67, 68, 119
Brand, Myles, 31, 72, 174n20
Brigham Young University, 52–53
Brown, Mike, 14, 15, 16
Brown, Paul, 16, 17, 172n11
Bryant, Bear, 39, 84
Buffalo Bills, 14, 15, 16, 17
Busch Stadium, 110, 199n13

Bush administration (G.H.W. Bush), 79
Bush administration (G.W. Bush), 80, 81

cable television companies, 3–7
Cablevision, 6, 89, 199n14
Calgary Olympic Games (1988), 138, 143
California, University of, at Berkeley, 31, 174n3
Calipari, John, 38
Camden Yards (Baltimore), 2
Caminiti, Ken, 154, 208n14
Canseco, Jose, 151, 155
Cap Adjustment Mechanism in NFL, 92
capital expenses: in college sports, 31–32; in facility finances, 101, 104, 105–110
Carroll, Pete, 177n21, 177n24
Carter, Hodding, III, 45
case studies on Olympic Games, 130, 131
casual attendees at Olympic Games, 133
CBS television network, 4
Centenary College, 39
Citi Field Stadium, 110, 199n13
Clemens, Roger, 156
Clinton administration, 79
Clotfelter, Charles, 177n20
coach compensation in college sports, 38–41, 83, 84–85, 177–178nn20–29, 195n11
cocaine, 149
collective bargaining agreements: in MLB, 95, 97, 114; in NBA, 88–89; in NFL, 8, 13, 14, 17, 88, 89, 196–197n12; in NHL, 93; on performance-enhancing drugs, 150, 155
College Football Association, 62, 186n33
college sports, 1, 21–26, 28–29, 30–85; and admission applications, 33–34, 55, 175nn7–8; antitrust laws on, 38, 44, 48, 65–71, 178n29; baseball in, 24, 73; basketball in (*see* basketball, college); capital expenses in, 31–32; coach compensation in, 38–41, 83, 84–85, 177–178nn20–29, 195n11; and donations to school, 34, 175–176nn9–10; football in (*see* football, college); gender equity in, 75–85; gifts to players in, 23, 173n17, 186n30; government intervention in, 44–45; grants-in-aid to players in, 32, 36; indirect costs in, 32; lawsuits concerning, 24–26; legal counsel obtained by players in, 24, 44; operating deficit in, 30–33; payments to players in, 22–24, 26, 173n16; performance-enhancing drugs in, 166, 212n43; publicity rights regulations on, 24–26, 36, 44, 173–174nn19–20; recruitment

of athletes in, 40, 54–55, 177–178n24; return on investment in, 34–35, 176n12; tax policies on, 72, 192n57; video games based on, 25

Collegiate Licensing Company, 25, 26

Comcast, 6, 171n4

compensation: of college athletes, 22–24, 26, 32, 36; of college coaches, 38–41, 83, 84–85, 177–178nn20–29, 195n11; of IOC members, 119–120; of Olympic athletes, 119; of professional athletes (*see* salary of players)

Contingent Valuation Method in assessment of Olympic Games, 144

contract length, league differences in, 87, 96

Controlled Substances Act (1970), 148

Cotton Bowl, 50, 181n7

creatine supplements, 148–149, 153, 167

Creative Artists Agency, 18

crowding out of tourists during Olympic Games, 133–134

Curt Flood Act, 21, 27, 173n15

de Coubertin, Pierre, 117

Deficit Reduction Act (1984), 112

Defined Gross Revenues, 91–92, 196n6

Delaney, Jim, 67, 180n38

Dempsey, Ced, 31

Designated Market Areas for televised sports, 3

DHEA, 148

displacement phenomenon during Olympic Games, 134

Dodds, DeLoss, 180n38, 189n46

Dorgan, Byron, 154

draft in NFL, 14

drugs, performance-enhancing, 28, 146–169. *See also* performance-enhancing drugs

Dykstra, Len, 152

econometric analysis of Olympic Games, 130–131, 138

educational expenses of college athletes, 23

Electronic Arts, 25, 26

employment measures on impact of Olympic Games, 138

entrapment game, 9–11

Equity in Athletics Disclosure Act, 30, 31

ESPN, 4, 5, 184n21

essential facility doctrine, 69, 190n48

facility finances, 2, 100–116; benefits to local economy, 27, 100; capital costs in, 101, 104, 105–110; data sources on, 107; in G3 program of NFL, 89, 113, 196nn7–10, 200n17; infrastructure costs in, 101, 107, 108; land costs in, 101, 107, 108; league definitions of, 89, 90; measurement issues in, 101–104; from naming rights, 16, 90, 106, 112; in NFL revenue-sharing program, 13–17; nonticket revenue in, 13; for Olympic Games, 120–121, 124–125, 127–128, 142–144, 202n12, 203n16, 203–204n23; operating costs in, 103, 104; opportunity costs in, 101; public subsidization of, 15, 100–116; recession affecting, 2; renovation costs in, 199n11; revenue sources in, 106, 112, 113; in stadiums and arenas, comparison of, 108–110, 115; tax policies on, 102, 112; trends in, 108–116

Federal Food, Drug, and Cosmetic Act (1938), 148

Fehr, Don, 86, 154, 164, 165, 166, 207n10

Fiesta Bowl, 50–51, 182n15, 190n49, 191n52

financial aid to college athletes, 22–24, 32, 36

Fleischer, Ari, 48–49, 181nn5–6

Flood Act, 21, 27, 173n15

Florida Marlins, 154

Flutie, Doug, 175n7, 181n6

football, college, 41–43, 47–74; antitrust issues in, 65–71, 188–192nn42–55; coach compensation in, 38–40, 41, 83, 84, 177nn20–23; home field games in, 57, 65, 185n25; margin of victory in, 64; number of regular season games in, 59, 67; playoff system and bowl games in, 21, 41–43, 47–74 (*see also* Bowl Championship Series); revenues and expenses in, 31–33, 35–36, 39–40, 176n16; roster size in, 41, 83, 178–179nn30–33; strength of schedule in, 64; tax policies on, 72, 192n57; televised games in, 49–50, 51, 65, 66, 67, 184n21, 188n40; video games based on players in, 25

football, professional. *See* National Football League

Football Bowl Subdivision (FBS), 41–43, 59, 181n4; coach compensation in, 39, 40, 41; revenues and expenses in, 31–33, 35–36, 176n16; roster size in, 41, 178–179n30

Football Championship Subdivision (FCS), 59, 181n4

FOX television network, 4, 5, 182n15, 184n21
franchise values, 7, 17
Fraser v. MLS, 20
free agents: in NBA, 87, 195n4; in NFL, 17, 172–173n12

G3 program for NFL stadium financing, 89, 113, 196nn7–10, 200n17
Game of Shadows (Fainaru-Wada and Williams), 154, 208n23
Gammons, Peter, 152, 153
Genachowski, Julius, 6
gender equity in college sports, 75–85; three-pronged test on, 79, 194n3
Gender Equity Report of NCAA, 80
gene doping, 168, 212n50
Giambi, Jason, 155
gifts: to college athletes, 23, 173n17, 186n30; to IOC members, 119–120
Gillette Stadium, 16, 110, 199n13
Giuliani, Rudy, 116
golf, 2–3, 76
grants-in-aid to college athletes, 32, 36
Grove City College case, 79
growth hormone, as performance-enhancing drug, 167; health effects of, 206n1; legislation on, 148; testing for, 151, 207n10
gymnastics, 82

Hatch, Orrin, 71, 148, 181n3
Hawaii, University of, 57
Health, Education, and Welfare Department: Office of Civil Rights, 78, 80–81; Title IX regulations of, 78
high school sports, performance-enhancing drugs in, 166
hockey, professional. *See* National Hockey League
Hockey Related Revenue, 90, 93, 197n13
home field games in college football, 57, 65, 185n25
home runs, trends in rate of, 157–163, 211n36; baseball manufacturing changes affecting, 158, 160–163, 210n32, 211n35; homers-to-hits ratio in, 160, 161, 162
housing for student athletes, 37

Idaho, University of, 183n19
Igawa, Kei, 96
income measures on impact of Olympic Games, 138, 139, 140

Indianapolis Colts, 14, 15, 16, 17
infrastructure costs for sports facilities, 101, 107, 108; for Olympic Games, 124–125, 126, 127–129, 143–144, 203n16
Innsbruck Olympic Games (1976), 140
intercollegiate athletics. *See* college sports
International Boxing v. United States, 67, 68
International Olympic Committee, 117, 118, 119–120
Internet streaming of sporting events, 6, 28
Iowa, University of, 182n15
Irsay, Jim, 14, 15
Isch, Jim, 31

James, LeBron, 18
Jeter, Derek, 207n10, 212n40
Johnson, Ben, 152
Johnson, Walter, 210n31
Jordan, Michael, 18
Juiced (Canseco), 155
Juicing the Game (Bryant), 164

Keillor, Garrison, 11
Keller, Sam, 24–25, 44
Kentucky, University of, 38
Kiffin, Lane, 177–178n24
Kiffin, Monte, 38–39, 177n24
Knight Commission, 35, 44, 46, 180n39
Kraft family ownership of Patriots, 16
Kuhn, Bowie, 149

labor relations, 7–17
Lake Placid Olympic Games (1980), 138, 140
Lake Wobegon Effect, 11
land costs for sports facilities, 101, 107, 108; for Olympic Games, 124–125, 142, 144
Law v. NCAA, 24, 84
legal issues: in antitrust laws, 19–21 (*see also* antitrust laws); in gender equity in college sports, 75–85; legal counsel for college athletes in, 24, 44; in performance-enhancing drug use, 148–149; in publicity rights of college athletes, 24–26, 36, 44, 173–174nn19–20
Leonard, Dutch, 209–210n31
Lewis, Michael, 157
licensing: of NFL apparel, 19–20; and publicity rights in college sports, 24–26, 173–174nn19–20
Lillehammer Olympic Games (1994), 139, 140

location of sports teams: and market size of NFL teams, 15–16; and relocation, 26–27
lockouts and strikes, 7–8
London Olympic Games (2012), 125, 143, 144, 203n19
Los Angeles Lakers, 89
Los Angeles Olympic Games (1984), 118, 120, 127, 138, 143, 201n5

Machen, Bernie, 45, 73–74, 180n40, 192n58
Madison Square Garden, 199n14
Major League Baseball: antitrust laws in, 21, 27, 173n15; attendance rates in, 3; baseball manufacturing changes in, 158, 160–163, 210n32, 211n35; collective bargaining agreements in, 95, 97, 114; contract length in, 87, 96; facility finances in, 104, 113–114, 116, 200nn18–20; franchise values in, 7; labor relations in, 7, 8; marginal revenue product in, 98, 197n17; performance-enhancing drugs in, 149–169; player development and minor league costs in, 88, 95–96; posting system in, 96, 197n16; relocation of teams in, 27; revenue in, 90, 95–96, 97–99, 114; roster size in, 87, 95, 197n15; salary of players in, 86, 94–99; talent compression in, 209–210n31; work stoppages in, 97, 150
Major League Baseball Advanced Media (MLBAM), 3, 95
Major League Baseball Players Association, 86, 97, 98, 150, 156, 164, 165
Major League Soccer, single-entity status of, 20, 173n14
Manfred, Rob, 154
marginal revenue product, 12, 172n9; in college sports, 40; in MLB, 98, 197n17
Matsuzaka, Daisuke, 96
McConnell, Mitch, 52, 182n12
McGwire, Mark, 153–154, 164
Metrodome (Minneapolis), 103
Miami, University of, 63, 187n36
Miami Heat, 18
MIBA v. NCAA, 69–70, 190n50
Michigan, University of, 187–188n36
Minnesota Twins, 24, 103
Minnesota Vikings, 27, 103
minor league teams, 88, 95–96; drug testing in, 150, 166, 208n12, 212n42
Mitchell Report, 149, 151, 155–156, 157, 167, 207n6, 212n47

MLB. See Major League Baseball
Moag & Company, 2, 171n1
Moneyball (Lewis), 157
Montreal Olympic Games (1976), 118, 143, 201n1
Moscow Olympic Games (1980), 118, 136–137
Mountain West Conference, 69, 70, 183–184n19, 184n21, 191n53
MSG network, 89
multiplier-based estimates on Olympic Games, 130, 131–135
Munich Olympic Games (1972), 205n36
Munson, Lester, 20, 173n13

Nagano Olympic Games (1998), 120, 121, 123, 126, 142–143, 204n23
naming rights in sports facilities, 16, 90, 106, 112
NASCAR, 2, 148
National Basketball Association: attendance rates in, 3; collective bargaining agreements in, 88–89; contract length in, 87; development league of, 88; drug testing program in, 168, 213n51; facility finances in, 104, 115; franchise values in, 7; free agents in, 87, 195n4; labor relations in, 7, 8; relocation of teams in, 27; represented in Olympic Games, 119; revenue in, 88, 89–90, 92–93, 96, 195–196n6; salary of players in, 18–19, 86, 88, 92–93, 96
National Collegiate Athletic Association, 21–26; athletic scholarship rules of, 22–24; drug testing in, 166, 212n43; and football playoff system, 41–43, 72–73; Gender Equity Report, 80; housing regulations of, 37; legal counsel rule of, 24; number of colleges in, 82; publicity rights regulations of, 24–26, 173–174nn19–20; representation on committees of, 45; response to Title IX, 78; on revenues and expenses in college sports, 31, 174n2; television appearance regulations of, 66
National Football League: antitrust issues in, 19–20; apparel licensing in, 19–20; attendance rates in, 3; Cap Adjustment Mechanism in, 92; collective bargaining agreements in, 8, 13, 14, 17, 88, 89, 196–197n12; contract length in, 87; facility finances in, 89, 104, 113, 196nn7–10, 200n17; franchise values in, 7, 17;

National Football League (*continued*)
free agents in, 17, 172–173n12; G3 program for stadium financing in, 89, 113, 196nn7–10, 200n17; labor relations in, 7–8, 13; minor league players in, 88; performance-enhancing drugs in, 147, 168, 206–207n3, 213n51; post-season games in, 16, 60; relocation of teams in, 26–27; revenue in, 13–17, 90, 91–92, 97, 196n6, 196–197n12; roster size in, 41, 83, 178n30; salary of players in, 13, 14, 15, 17, 86, 88, 91–92, 97, 172n12; signing bonuses in, 87; single-entity status, 19–21; team performance and revenue in, 15–16
National Football League Players Association, 89
National Hockey League, 1; collective bargaining agreement in, 93; drug testing in, 168; facility finances in, 104, 115; franchise values in, 7; minor league teams in, 88; revenue in, 90, 93, 96, 197n13; salary of players in, 86, 88, 93, 96, 197n13; work stoppage in, 7
National Invitational Tournament, 44, 69–70, 190n50
National Sports Commission proposal, 73
Nationals Park, 102, 116, 197n2
NBA. *See* National Basketball Association
NBC television network, 4, 122, 171n4
NCAA. *See* National Collegiate Athletic Association
Nebraska, University of, 24, 52, 63–64, 187n36
NESN, 12
New England Patriots, 15, 16, 206n3
New Jersey Nets, 102, 116
New Orleans Saints, 16
New York Giants, 15, 206n3
New York Knicks, 89
New York Mets, 101–102, 116
New York Yankees stadium, 101–102, 110, 114, 116, 199n13
NFL. *See* National Football League
NHL. *See* National Hockey League
Notre Dame, University of, 50, 56, 184n20

Obama, Barack, 6, 44, 47–48, 71
O'Bannon et al. v. NCAA, 25–26, 44
Office of Civil Rights of HEW Department, 78, 80–81
Ohio State University, 69, 180n1, 188n36
Oklahoma, University of, 39, 47, 63, 66, 180n1, 185n24, 187–188n36

Oliver, Andrew, 24, 44
Olympic Games, 117–145; bidding process in, 121, 122, 123–124, 125, 202n12; case studies of, 130, 131; compensation of athletes in, 119; computable general equilibrium models on, 130, 131, 138–139; Contingent Valuation Method in assessment of, 144; crowding out of tourists during, 133–134; displacement phenomenon in, 134; econometric analysis of, 130–131, 138; economic impact of, 126–145; facility costs in, 120–121, 124–125, 127–128, 142–144, 202n12, 203n16, 203–204n23; multiplier-based estimates on, 130, 131–135; revenue in, 121–126; security costs in, 124; stock market impact of, 129, 141–142; television broadcasting of, 122–123; ticket sales for, 127, 132–133; time switcher and casual attendees at, 133
Olympic Stadium (Montreal), 143, 199n14
operating cost of sports facilities, 103, 104
opportunity costs in sports facilities, 101
Orange Bowl, 50–51, 181n7, 182n15, 190n49, 191n52
Oregon, University of, 63, 187n36
Orszag, Jonathan, 32
Orszag, Peter, 32
Ortiz, David, 168, 213n53
Orza, Gene, 165, 166

Pac-10 Conference, 51, 56, 68, 69, 71, 185n24
Paige, Rodney, 80
Papa Johns.com Bowl, 54
Pell Grants, 45
Pennsylvania State University, 52
performance of college teams, 40–41; and admission applications, 33–34, 175nn7–8; and coach compensation, 40, 83; and donations to college funds, 34, 175–176nn9–10; and selection for bowl games, 59–60, 63–65
performance-enhancing drugs, 28, 146–169; collective bargaining agreements on, 150, 155; in college sports, 166, 212n43; congressional hearings on, 155; health effects of, 146, 164, 206n1; in high school sports, 166; mandatory testing for, 150, 154–155, 164, 207n10; in minor league teams, 150, 166, 208n12, 212n42; Mitchell Report on, 149, 151, 155–156, 157, 207n6; in MLB, 149–169; national legislation on, 148–

149; in NBA, 168, 213n51; in NFL, 147, 168, 206–207n3, 213n51; privacy rights concerns in testing for, 150, 165, 207n10, 211n39, 212n40; Walker on, 157–163, 209–210nn30–31
Pettitte, Andy, 156
Pitino, Rick, 38
playoff system and post-season games: in college baseball, 73; in college basketball, 44, 69–70, 190n50; in college football, 41–43, 47–74 (see also Bowl Championship Series); in NFL, 16, 60
posting system in MLB, 96, 197n16
Power Factor of Walker, 158–163
privacy rights concerns in drug testing, 150, 165, 207n10, 211n39, 212n40
profit maximizers, 12, 172n9
public subsidization of sports facilities, 15, 100–116; measurement issues in, 101–104; for Olympic Games, 120–121, 143–144; trends in, 108–116
publicity rights regulations on college athletes, 24–26, 36, 44, 173–174nn19–20

Radovich v. NFL, 19
Rawlings baseballs, 158, 160–163, 210n32, 211n35
Reagan administration, 79, 113
recession period (2007-2009), 1–3, 37
recruitment of college athletes, 40, 54–55, 177–178n24
Reebok, 19, 20
regional sports networks: revenue from, 90; team ownership of, 3, 6, 7, 12
Reinsdorf, Jerry, 18
related-party transactions, 88–89, 90, 99
renovation expenditures on sports facilities, 199n11
retransmission consent, 4–5
return on investments in college sports, 34–35, 176n12
revenue in college sports, 39–40; compared to expenses, 31–33, 35–36, 176n16; conference revenue in BCS, 42, 56–57, 62, 69, 179–180n37, 184–185nn21–24; guaranteed payouts in BCS, 184nn20–21; net revenue in BCS, 187n34; television revenue in BCS, 67–68, 189n46
revenue in Olympic Games, 121–126
revenue in professional sports: Defined Gross Revenues in, 91–92, 196n6; in facility finances, 106, 112, 113; league differences in definition of, 87–91; in

MLB, 90, 95–96, 97–99, 114; in NBA, 88, 89–90, 92–93, 96, 195–196n6; in NFL, 13–17, 90, 91–92, 97, 196n6, 196–197n12; in NHL, 90, 93, 96, 197n13; in related-party transactions, 88–89, 90, 99
Rodriguez, Alex, 96, 168
Rogers Centre (Toronto), 199–200n14
Romney, Mitt, 121
Rose Bowl, 49, 51, 180n38, 181n7, 187n34, 189n46, 191n52
Rosenbloom, Carroll, 14
roster size: in college football, 41, 83, 178–179nn30–33; in MLB, 87, 95, 197n15; in NFL, 41, 83, 178n30
Rozelle, Pete, 14
Rutgers University, 54
Ruth, Babe, 209–210n31

Saban, Nick, 177n21
salary of coaches in college sports, 38–41, 83, 84–85, 177–178nn20–29, 195n11
salary of players, 86–99; bidding strategy on, 10–12; league differences in definition of, 87–91; on minor league teams, 88; in MLB, 86, 94–99; in NBA, 18–19, 86, 88, 92–93, 96; in NFL, 13, 14, 15, 17, 86, 88, 91–92, 97, 172n12; in NHL, 86, 88, 93, 96, 197n13; restraints on, 8–13; strikes and lockouts concerning, 7–8; and team performance, 15
Salt Lake City Olympic Games (2002), 121, 123, 134, 201n5, 204n24
Samaranch, Juan Antonio, 119–120
San Diego Chargers, 16
San Francisco Giants, 27
Sanity Code, 22–23
scholarships, athletic, 22–24, 41, 83, 173n16
Schultz, Richard, 31, 189n46
seating contracts, 2, 90
Seattle Seahawks, 15, 16
Seattle SuperSonics, 27
security costs in Olympic Games, 124
selection criteria in BCS, 51, 55–57, 58–60, 69, 179n36, 187–188nn35–41; Associated Press poll in, 51, 65, 188n41; coaches poll in, 42, 47, 51, 65; computer rankings in, 42, 47, 51, 62–63, 187n35; criticism of, 41–42, 47, 62–65; margin of victory in, 64; strength of schedule in, 51, 64; voter bias in, 65, 188n41
Selig, Bud, 150, 151, 153, 154, 156, 164–165
Seoul Olympic Games (1988), 121
Sheffield, Gary, 155

Shubik, Martin, 9, 10, 172n7
signing bonuses in NFL, 87
single-entity status: of MLS, 20, 173n14;
of NFL, 19–21
SkyDome (Toronto), 199–200n14
soccer leagues, 1, 3, 28; single-entity status
in, 20, 173n14; women in, 3
Sochi Olympic Games (2014), 125
Sosa, Sammy, 153
Southeastern Conference, 50, 56, 184n21,
185n24
Southern California, University of, 47, 177–
178n24, 187–188n36
Southwest Conference, 50
Spalding baseballs, 158, 160, 210n32
sponsorship revenue, 2–3, 90
stadium finances, 108–110, 115. See also
facility finances
steroids, anabolic. See anabolic steroids, as
performance-enhancing drugs
stock market impact of Olympic Games,
129, 141–142
Stoops, Bob, 39
strikes and lockouts, 7–8
subscription fees for television programs,
4, 5
Sugar Bowl, 50–51, 181n7, 190n49, 191n52
Super Bowl, 16, 60
Superdome (New Orleans), 199n14
Sydney Olympic Games (2000), 121, 126,
138–139, 141, 203n22

Takacs, Artur, 120
talent compression in MLB, 209–210n31
Tampa Bay Rays, 27
tax policies: on college sports, 72, 192n57;
on facility construction, 102, 112; on
Olympic Games, 124, 202–203n15
Tax Reform Act (1986), 112
televised sports, 3–7; college football games
in, 49–50, 51, 65, 66, 67–68, 184n21,
188n40, 189n46; in Designated Market
Areas, 3; Internet streaming affecting, 6;
in NFL revenue-sharing program, 13; in
Olympic Games, 122–123; on regional
sports networks, 3, 6, 7, 12, 90; retransmission consent in, 4–5; value of player
contributions in, 12
Tennessee, University of, 38–39, 177–178n24
tennis, 2
Texas, University of, 47, 52, 177n21, 185n24
ticket sales: for college football bowl games,
179–180n37, 184n22, 190n49; and league

definition of revenue, 90; for Olympic
Games, 127, 132–133
time switcher attendees at Olympic Games,
133
Time Warner, 4, 5, 6
Title IX, 21, 37, 45, 46; and gender equity
in college sports, 75–85; impact on male
sports, 82; three-pronged test on, 79, 194n3
Tokyo Olympic Games (1964), 136–137,
205n34
TOP Program, 122
Torino Olympic Games (2006), 204n23
Total Revenue in NFL, 90, 91–92
tourism, Olympic Games affecting, 127, 129,
136, 139, 140; in crowding out, 133–134
Tower, John, 78
transportation infrastructure improvements for Olympic Games, 128–129
Tulane University, 57, 74, 185n22, 185n25

Ueberroth, Peter, 120, 150
United Football League, 3
Utah, University of, 47, 57, 69, 71, 73–74,
183–184n19, 184n20

Vancouver Olympic Games (2010), 201n5
Versus sports channel, 5, 171n4
video games based on college sports, 25
Vincent, Fay, 150
Virginia Tech, 52, 69, 184n22

Wade, Dwayne, 18
wages, regional, impact of hosting Olympic
Games on, 138, 139, 140
Walker, Eric, 157–163, 209–210nn30–31
Washington, University of, 63
Washington Nationals stadium, 102, 116,
197n2
Western Athletic Conference, 52, 182n13
White, Jason, 44
Wilson, Ralph, 14, 15, 16, 17
win maximizers, 12
Wisconsin, University of, 188n36
Women's Professional Soccer, 3
women's sports, 28; benefits of participa-
tion in, 77–78, 192–193n1; in college,
36, 75–85; professional, 3
work stoppages, 1, 7–8; in MLB, 97, 150
World Anti-Doping Agency (WADA), 156
wrestling, 81–82
Wyoming, University of, 182n13

Young, Michael, 183n19